MICROSOFT® OFFICE

FrontPage® 2003

Introductory Concepts and Techniques

Gary B. Shelly
Thomas J. Cashman
Jeffrey J. Quasney

THOMSON
COURSE TECHNOLOGY

COURSE TECHNOLOGY
25 THOMSON PLACE
BOSTON MA 02210

SHELLY
CASHMAN
SERIES®

Australia • Canada • Denmark • Japan • Mexico • New Zealand • Philippines • Puerto Rico • Singapore
South Africa • Spain • United Kingdom • United States

Microsoft Office FrontPage 2003
Introductory Concepts and Techniques

Gary B. Shelly
Thomas J. Cashman
Jeffrey J. Quasney

Executive Editor:
Cheryl Costantini

Senior Acquisitions Editor:
Dana Merk

Senior Product Manager:
Alexandra Arnold

Associate Product Manager:
Reed Cotter

Editorial Assistant:
Selena Coppock

Print Buyer:
Laura Burns

Signing Representative:
Cheryl Costantini

Series Consulting Editor:
Jim Quasney

Director of Production:
Becky Herrington

Production Editor:
Deb Masi

Production Assistant:
Jennifer Quiambao

Development Editor:
Ginny Harvey

Copy Editor:
Mark Goodin

Proofreader:
Lori Silfen

Interior Designer:
Becky Herrington

Cover Designer:
Richard Herrera

Illustrators:
Richard Herrera
Andrew Bartel
Ken Russo

Compositors:
Jeanne Black
Andrew Bartel
Kellee LaVars

Indexer:
Cristina Haley

Printer:
Banta Menasha

MICROSOFT® OFFICE

FrontPage 2003

Introductory Concepts and Techniques

Contents

Preface

The Shelly Cashman Series® offers the finest textbooks in computer education. We are proud of the fact that our series of Microsoft Office 4.3, Microsoft Office 95, Microsoft Office 97, Microsoft Office 2000, and Microsoft Office XP textbooks have been the most widely used books in education. With each new edition of our Office books, we have made significant improvements based on the software and comments made by the instructors and students. The *Microsoft Office FrontPage 2003* books continue with the innovation, quality, and reliability that you have come to expect from the Shelly Cashman Series.

In this *Microsoft Office FrontPage 2003* book, you will find an educationally sound, highly visual, and easy-to-follow pedagogy that combines a vastly improved step-by-step approach with corresponding screens. All projects and exercises in this book are designed to take full advantage of the FrontPage 2003 enhancements. The project material is developed to ensure that students will see the importance of learning FrontPage for future coursework. The popular Other Ways and More About features offer in-depth knowledge of FrontPage 2003, and the new Q&A feature offers students a way to solidify important Web page authoring and site management concepts. The Learn It Online page presents a wealth of additional exercises to ensure your students have all the reinforcement they need.

Objectives of This Textbook

Microsoft Office FrontPage 2003: Introductory Concepts and Techniques is intended for a one-unit course or a portion of a three-unit Web-related course that presents an introduction of Microsoft Office FrontPage 2003. No experience with a computer is assumed, and no mathematics beyond the high school freshman level is required. The objectives of this book are:

- To teach the fundamentals of FrontPage 2003
- To acquaint students with the proper procedures to design and create Web pages
- To expose students to practical examples of the computer as a useful tool
- To develop an exercise-oriented approach that allows learning by doing
- To introduce students to new input technologies
- To encourage independent study and help those who are working alone

The Shelly Cashman Approach

Features of the Shelly Cashman Series *Microsoft Office FrontPage 2003* books include:

- **Project Orientation:**   Each project in the book presents a practical problem and complete solution using an easy-to-understand methodology.
- **Step-by-Step, Screen-by-Screen Instructions:**   Each of the tasks required to complete a project is identified throughout the project. Full-color screens accompany the steps.
- **Thoroughly Tested Projects:**   Unparalleled quality is ensured because every screen in the book is produced by the author only after performing a step, and then each project must pass Course Technology's award-winning Quality Assurance program.
- **Other Ways Boxes and Quick Reference Summary:**   The Other Ways boxes displayed at the end of many of the step-by-step sequences specify the other ways to perform the task completed in the steps. Thus, the steps and the Other Ways box make a comprehensive reference unit.
- **More About and Q&A Features:**   These marginal annotations provide background information, tips, and answers to common questions that complement the topics covered, adding depth and perspective to the learning process.

- Web Design Tips: Web Design Tips boxed throughout the book emphasize important Web design concepts to help students as they design a Web site.
- Integration of the World Wide Web: The World Wide Web is integrated into the FrontPage 2003 learning experience by (1) More About annotations that send students to Web sites for up-to-date information and alternative approaches to tasks; (2) a FrontPage 2003 Quick Reference Summary Web page that summarizes the ways to complete tasks (mouse, menu, shortcut menu, and keyboard); and (3) the Learn It Online page at the end of each project, which has project reinforcement exercises, learning games, and other types of student activities.

Organization of This Textbook

Microsoft Office FrontPage 2003: Introductory Concepts and Techniques provides basic instruction on how to use FrontPage 2003. The material is divided into three projects, a Table feature, five appendices, and a Quick Reference Summary.

Project 1 – Creating a FrontPage Web Site Using a Template In Project 1, students are introduced to the basic components of the World Wide Web and of HTML, the FrontPage environment, and they lean how to use FrontPage templates. Students create a simple three-page Web site consisting of a Home page, a Professional Interests page, and a Favorite Links page. Topics include basic Web page editing and customization techniques; applying a theme using FrontPage commands and features; and saving, printing, and publishing the three pages to an available Web server. Students then can use a browser to view their own personal Web pages.

Project 2 – Adding a New Web Page to a Web Site In Project 2, students learn how to add a new page to an existing Web site and then how to customize that page. Topics include basic Web page design criteria; setting up the page background; inserting tables, images, and a Photo Gallery component; adding, replacing, and applying special formatting to text; and adding linked targets to the page. Students also learn how to preview the printout of a page.

Project 3 – Customizing and Managing Web Pages and Images In Project 3, students are introduced to techniques for using graphics and images in Web pages. Topics include opening an existing FrontPage Web site; displaying and using the Pictures toolbar to apply formatting to images; creating and applying a customized theme to a page; assigning a hyperlink to an image; creating an image map and assigning a URL to the image map hotspot; highlighting hotspots on an image map; copying and pasting from a Word document; inserting a hit counter, a shared border, and an AutoShapes drawing; using FrontPage reporting features; displaying and verifying the hyperlinks in a FrontPage Web site in a browser; and modifying the navigation structure of a Web site.

Table Feature – Creating a Stand-Alone Web Page Using a Layout Table In the Table feature, students are introduced to creating a stand-alone Web page and using layout tables to construct the layout of a Web page. Topics include creating a new stand-alone Web page; using a layout table to design a Web page; formatting layout cells in a layout table with rounded corners, shadows, and borders; and modifying the structure of a layout table.

Appendices The book includes five appendices. Appendix A presents an introduction to the Microsoft FrontPage 2003 Help system. Appendix B describes how to use the speech and handwriting recognition capabilities of FrontPage 2003. Appendix C explains how to publish Web sites to a folder on a hard drive. Appendix D shows how to reset menus and toolbars. Appendix E summarizes the design tips that are introduced throughout the book.

Quick Reference Summary In Microsoft FrontPage 2003, you can accomplish a task in a number of ways, such as using the mouse, menu, shortcut menus, and keyboard. The Quick Reference Summary at the back of the book provides a quick reference to each task presented.

End-of-Project Student Activities

A notable strength of the Shelly Cashman Series *Microsoft Office FrontPage 2003* books is the extensive student activities at the end of each project. Well-structured student activities can make the difference between students merely participating in a class and students retaining the information they learn. The activities in the Shelly Cashman Series *Microsoft Office FrontPage 2003* books include the following.

- **What You Should Know** A listing of the tasks completed within a project together with the pages on which the step-by-step, screen-by-screen explanations appear.
- **Learn It Online** Every project features a Learn It Online page that contains 12 exercises. These exercises include True/False, Multiple Choice, Short Answer, Flash Cards, Practice Test, Learning Games, Tips and Tricks, Newsgroup usage, Expanding Your Horizons, Search Sleuth, Office Online Training, and Office Marketplace.
- **Apply Your Knowledge** This exercise usually requires students to open and manipulate a file on the Data Disk that parallels the activities learned in the project. To obtain a copy of the Data Disk, follow the instructions on the inside back cover of this textbook.
- **In the Lab** Three in-depth assignments per project require students to utilize the project concepts and techniques to solve problems on a computer.
- **Cases and Places** Five unique real-world case-study situations, including one small-group activity.

Instructor Resources CD-ROM

The Shelly Cashman Series is dedicated to providing you with all of the tools you need to make your class a success. Information on all supplementary materials is available through your Course Technology representative or by calling one of the following telephone numbers: Colleges and Universities, 1-800-648-7450; High Schools, 1-800-824-5179; Private Career Colleges, 1-800-347-7707; Canada, 1-800-268-2222; Corporations with IT Training Centers, 1-800-648-7450; and Government Agencies, Health-Care Organizations, and Correctional Facilities, 1-800-477-3692.

The Instructor Resources for this textbook include both teaching and testing aids. The contents of each item on the Instructor Resources CD-ROM (ISBN 0-619-20053-7) are described below.

INSTRUCTOR'S MANUAL The Instructor's Manual is made up of Microsoft Word files, which include detailed lesson plans with page number references, lecture notes, teaching tips, classroom activities, discussion topics, projects to assign, and transparency references. The transparencies are available through the Figure Files described below.

LECTURE SUCCESS SYSTEM The Lecture Success System consists of intermediate files that correspond to certain figures in the book, allowing you to step through the creation of an application in a project during a lecture without entering large amounts of data.

SYLLABUS Sample syllabi, which can be customized easily to a course, are included. The syllabi cover policies, class and lab assignments and exams, and procedural information.

FIGURE FILES Illustrations for every figure in the textbook are available in electronic form. Use this ancillary to present a slide show in lecture or to print transparencies for use in lecture with an overhead projector. If you have a personal computer and LCD device, this ancillary can be an effective tool for presenting lectures.

POWERPOINT PRESENTATIONS PowerPoint Presentations is a multimedia lecture presentation system that provides slides for each project. Presentations are based on project objectives. Use this presentation system to present well-organized lectures that are both interesting and knowledge based. PowerPoint Presentations provides consistent coverage at schools that use multiple lecturers.

SOLUTIONS TO EXERCISES Solutions are included for the end-of-project exercises, as well as the Project Reinforcement exercises.

TEST BANK & TEST ENGINE The ExamView test bank includes 110 questions for every project (25 multiple choice, 50 true/false, and 35 completion) with page number references and, when appropriate, figure references. A version of the test bank you can print also is included. The test bank comes with a copy of the test engine, ExamView, the ultimate tool for your objective-based testing needs. ExamView is a state-of-the-art test builder that is easy to use. ExamView enables you to create paper-, LAN-, or Web-based tests from test banks designed specifically for your Course Technology textbook. Utilize the ultra-efficient QuickTest Wizard to create tests in less than five minutes by taking advantage of Course Technology's question banks, or customize your own exams from scratch.

DATA FILES FOR STUDENTS All the files that are required by students to complete the exercises are included. You can distribute the files on the Instructor Resources CD-ROM to your students over a network, or you can have them follow the instructions on the inside back cover of this book to obtain a copy of the Data Disk.

ADDITIONAL ACTIVITIES FOR STUDENTS These additional activities consist of Project Reinforcement Exercises, which are true/false, multiple choice, and short answer questions that help students gain confidence in the material learned.

Online Content

Course Technology offers textbook-based content for Blackboard, WebCT, and MyCourse 2.1.

BLACKBOARD AND WEBCT As the leading provider of IT content for the Blackboard and WebCT platforms, Course Technology delivers rich content that enhances your textbook to give your students a unique learning experience.

MYCOURSE 2.1 MyCourse 2.1 is Course Technology's powerful online course management and content delivery system. MyCourse 2.1 allows nontechnical users to create, customize, and deliver Web-based courses; post content and assignments; manage student enrollment; administer exams; track results in the online grade book; and more.

Acknowledgments

The Shelly Cashman Series would not be the leading computer education series without the contributions of outstanding publishing professionals. First, and foremost, among them is Becky Herrington, director of production and book designer. She is the heart and soul of the Shelly Cashman Series, and it is only through her leadership, dedication, and tireless efforts that superior products are made possible.

Under Becky's direction, the following individuals made significant contributions to these books: Deb Masi, production editor; Jennifer Quiambao, production assistant; Ken Russo, senior Web and graphic designer; Richard Herrera, cover designer and illustrator; Kellee LaVars, Andrew Bartel, Phillip Hajjar, and Kenny Tran, graphic artists; Jeanne Black, Andrew Bartel, and Kellee LaVars, QuarkXPress compositors; Mark Goodin, copy editor; Lori Silfen, proofreader; and Cristina Haley, indexer.

We also would like to thank Kristen Duerr, executive vice president and publisher; Cheryl Costantini, executive editor; Dana Merk, senior acquisitions editor; Jim Quasney, series consulting editor; Alexandra Arnold, senior product manager; Reed Cotter, associate product manager; Marc Ouellette and Heather McKinstry, online product managers; and Selena Coppock, editorial assistant.

Gary B. Shelly
Thomas J. Cashman
Jeffrey J. Quasney

MICROSOFT

Office FrontPage 2003

MICROSOFT OFFICE

FRONTPAGE

Creating a FrontPage Web Site Using a Template

CASE PERSPECTIVE

As a Business and Technology major at Trelane College, you benefited from taking classes that included Web page authoring and other communications courses. After you developed the Trelane College Alumni Web site, the Alumni club president, Shirley Blair, was very impressed. She wanted to know if she might pass along your name to others who had an interest in Web site development. You wholeheartedly agreed, and she indicated that she already had a potential client for you. James Keeler, a close friend of hers, was looking for help in developing a personal Web site that he plans to use to promote his skills and knowledge as he approaches graduation. You told Shirley to have James contact you so you could set up a meeting to discuss his needs for the site.

At your first meeting, you explained to James that making a simple Web site was very easy to do with Microsoft FrontPage. Because he demonstrated a desire both to learn about Web page creation and eventually to maintain his own Web site, you thought it appropriate that he learn some basics about Web page construction and maintenance in an incremental fashion. By learning about the components of a Web page, then building an initial Web site, and later making modifications to the Web site, he would accomplish his goal of learning how to create and maintain his Web site. You explain to him that templates and themes included with FrontPage allow novices and those without artistic experience to create compelling Web sites quickly and with relative ease.

As you read through this project, you will learn about the fundamentals of how a Web page is constructed. You also will learn how to use FrontPage to create, save, print, and publish a Web site that includes several pages, text, and links.

MICROSOFT
Office FrontPage 2003

Creating a FrontPage Web Site Using a Template

PROJECT

1

Objectives

You will have mastered the material in this project when you can:

- Discuss the basic components of the World Wide Web
- Identify common elements of a Web page
- Define and describe a FrontPage Web site
- Start and quit FrontPage
- Describe FrontPage window elements
- Create a FrontPage Web site using a template
- Apply a theme to a FrontPage Web site
- Add and modify text elements on a Web page
- Save and preview a Web page
- Delete a Web page from a FrontPage Web site
- Add and modify hyperlinks on a Web page
- Print a Web page
- Publish and test a FrontPage Web site
- Use the FrontPage Help system

What Is Microsoft Office FrontPage?

Microsoft Office FrontPage is a Web page authoring and site management program that allows you to create and manage professional-quality Web sites without programming. Microsoft Office FrontPage offers two key types of functionality:

Web page creation   Microsoft FrontPage allows you to create and edit Web pages without needing to know HTML or other programming languages. FrontPage includes many features that make Web page creation easy, such as templates, graphics, and more.

Web site management   Microsoft Office FrontPage allows you to view Web pages, publish them to the World Wide Web, and manage existing Web sites. Using FrontPage, you can test and repair hyperlinks on a Web page, view all of the files and folders on a site, import image files, and more.

Project One — Personal Web Pages

The following needs, formatting requirements, and content requirements are determined to be the basis for creating the personal Web pages for this project. The easiest way to develop a personal Web site is to use the Personal Web Site template, and then make appropriate modifications to the generated pages.

Needs: A group of related Web pages is referred to as a **Web site** in Microsoft Office FrontPage. For this site, the Web site will include three Web pages: a Home page, a Professional Interests page, and a Favorite Links page. The Home page introduces James Keeler to site visitors (Figure 1-1a); the Professional Interests page outlines his interests relating to his major and career goals (Figure 1-1b); and the Favorite Links page includes links to three Web sites, including his favorite site about music (Figure 1-1c). The Home page includes links to the other two pages in the FrontPage Web site. Once complete, you will publish the Web site to make it available for viewing on the World Wide Web.

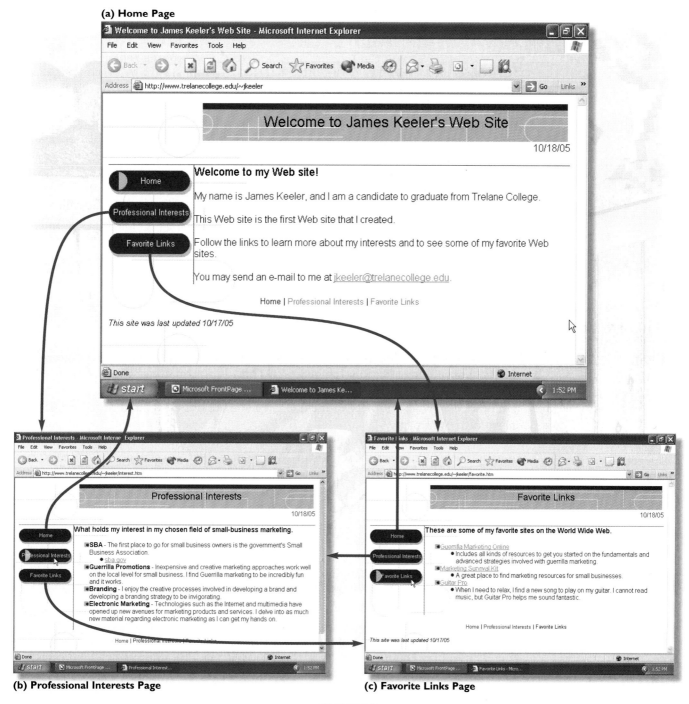

(a) Home Page

(b) Professional Interests Page

(c) Favorite Links Page

FIGURE 1-1

Formatting Requirements: To create the Web pages, you will use the Personal Web Site template included with Microsoft Office FrontPage. The Web pages then are formatted using the Microsoft Office FrontPage Capsules theme, which is just one of many complete themes that are available for immediate use. The Home page includes graphical hyperlinks to the other pages in this Web site.

Content Requirements: The Home page lists James Keeler's name, specifies his position as a student at Trelane College, and provides an e-mail address so visitors can contact him. The Professional Interests page includes a minimum of four topics that are associated directly with his major. The Favorite Links page includes links to at least three Web sites, one of which is a music-related site.

World Wide Web Basics

The **World Wide Web** (**WWW**), often referred to simply as the **Web**, consists of a worldwide collection of electronic documents that have built-in links to other related documents. Each of these electronic documents on the Web is called a **Web page**; a Web page can contain text, graphics, sound, and video, as well as connections to other documents. These connections to other documents, called hyperlinks or links, allow you to move quickly from one document to another, regardless of whether the documents are located on the same computer or on different computers in different countries.

A collection of related Web pages that you can access electronically is called a Web site. Most Web sites have a starting point, called a **home page**, which is similar to a book cover or table of contents for the site and provides information about the site's purpose and content. In a personal Web site, for example, the home page probably will list your name, your e-mail address, some personal information, and links to other information on your Web site.

Hypertext Markup Language (HTML)

A Web page is a file that contains both text and Hypertext Markup Language (HTML). **Hypertext Markup Language** (**HTML**) is a formatting language that tells the browser how to display text and images; how to set up list boxes, hyperlinks, and other elements; and how to include graphics, sound, video, and other multimedia on a Web page.

HTML uses a set of special instructions called **tags** to define the characteristics of items such as formatted text, images, hyperlinks, lists, and forms. HTML tags are used throughout the text document to indicate (or mark) how these items should display and function when viewed as a Web page in a **browser**, which is a software program used to access and view Web pages. HTML thus is considered a **markup language**, because the HTML tags mark elements in the text file.

Although HTML includes hundreds of tags, most Web developers use only a small subset of these tags when building a Web page. Table 1-1 lists some of the more commonly used HTML tags and an explanation of their functions.

Defining the type and layout of an element on a Web page requires one or more HTML tags. As shown in Table 1-1, HTML tags begin with the less than sign (<) and end with the greater than sign (>). Tags may be entered as either uppercase or lowercase. Tags often are used in pairs to indicate the start and end of an element or format. The end tag contains a forward slash (/). The tag, <B>, for example, indicates the beginning of a section of bold text, and </B> indicates the end of a section of bold text. To display the text, World Wide Web, as bold text, you type the tags as follows:

```
<B>World Wide Web</B>
```

Table 1-1 Common HTML Tags	
HTML TAG	**FUNCTION**
<HTML> </HTML>	Indicates the beginning and end of a Web document.
<HEAD> </HEAD>	Indicates the beginning and end of the header section of a Web document (used for the title and other document header information).
<TITLE> </TITLE>	Indicates the beginning and end of the Web page title. The title appears in the title bar of the browser, not in the body of the Web page itself.
<BODY> </BODY>	Indicates the beginning and end of the main section (body) of the Web page.
<Hn> </Hn>	Indicates the beginning and end of a section of text called a heading, which uses a larger font than normal text. In the tag, <Hn>, n indicates the size of the heading font; sizes range from <H1> through <H6>.
<P> </P>	Indicates the beginning of a new paragraph; inserts a blank line above the new paragraph. The end tag of </P> is optional. It will insert a blank line below the new paragraph, unless followed by a new paragraph.
<B> </B>	Indicates the beginning and end of a section of bold text.
<I> </I>	Indicates the beginning and end of a section of italic text.
<U> </U>	Indicates the beginning and end of a section of underlined text.
<UL> </UL>	Indicates the beginning and end of an unordered (bulleted) list
<OL> </OL>	Indicates the beginning and end of an ordered (numbered) list.
<LI> </LI>	Indicates that the item in the tag is an item within a list.
<HR>	Inserts a horizontal rule.
<A> </A>	Indicates the beginning and end of a hyperlink.
HREF="URL"	Indicates a hyperlink to a file in the location specified by the URL in quotation marks.
<IMG SRC="URL">	Inserts an inline image in the page. The URL in quotation marks specifies the location of the image.
<CENTER> </CENTER>	Indicates that the text, graphic, or other elements between the tags should display centered on the Web page.
<LEFT> </LEFT>	Indicates that the text, graphic, or other elements between the tags should display left-aligned on the Web page.
<RIGHT> </RIGHT>	Indicates that the text, graphic, or other elements between the tags should display right-aligned on the Web page.

You also can use tags in combination to apply multiple formatting features to text or other Web page elements. The tag

```
<CENTER><B>World Wide Web</B></CENTER>
```

for example, bolds and centers the words on the page. If you use HTML tags in combination, as in the example above, be sure to place the end tags in an order opposite that of the start tags.

Keywords included in HTML tags further define the appearance of the element created by the tag. Keywords take the form

```
keyword=value
```

where keyword is an HTML tag describing a characteristic of a Web page element and value is one of a range of numbers or words describing that characteristic. Instead of using the <CENTER> tag to center text on the page, for instance, you can use the keyword, <ALIGN>, and the value, <CENTER>. The tag, which you can use within another tag, might display as

```
<B ALIGN=CENTER>My Favorite Web Sites</B>
```

The tag tells the browser to display the text in bold and center the text on the page.

All of these elements are defined using HTML tags. The HTML used to create a Web page is called the **HTML source**, or **source code**. Figure 1-2 shows the HTML source for the Web page displayed in Figure 1-1c on page FP 5.

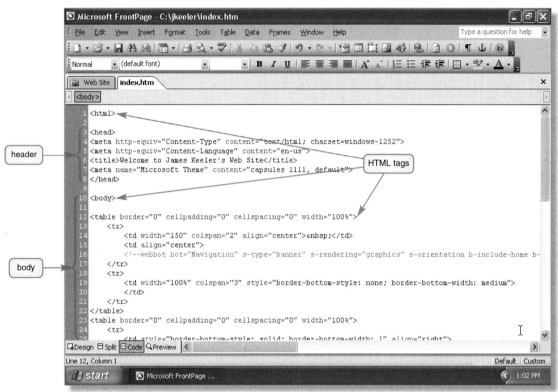

FIGURE 1-2

More About

Viewing HTML Source Code

To see the HTML tags that FrontPage creates as you build a Web page, you can use the Show Code View button or the Show Split View button. These two views of the code allow you to display HTML tags and then edit them just as you would edit text using a word-processing program, utilizing standard editing commands such as cut, paste, find, and replace.

Most Web browsers allow you to view the HTML source for the Web page currently displayed in the browser window. If you are using Internet Explorer, for example, you can click the Source command on the View menu to display the HTML source.

Many HTML tags exist to help you design a Web page exactly as you want. Although a more detailed discussion of HTML is beyond the scope of this book, when using FrontPage to develop Web pages, you do not need to know every HTML tag. Instead, you simply determine the best way to convey the information and then make those changes on the Web page using FrontPage commands. FrontPage inserts the appropriate HTML code for you.

Web Browsers

You access and view Web pages using a software program called a Web browser. A **Web browser**, also called simply a browser, is a software program that requests a Web page, interprets the HTML codes and text used to create the page, and then displays the Web page on your computer screen. Today, the two more popular browsers are **Microsoft Internet Explorer** and **Netscape Navigator** (Figure 1-3a and 1-3b). Browsers have special buttons and other features to help you navigate Web sites.

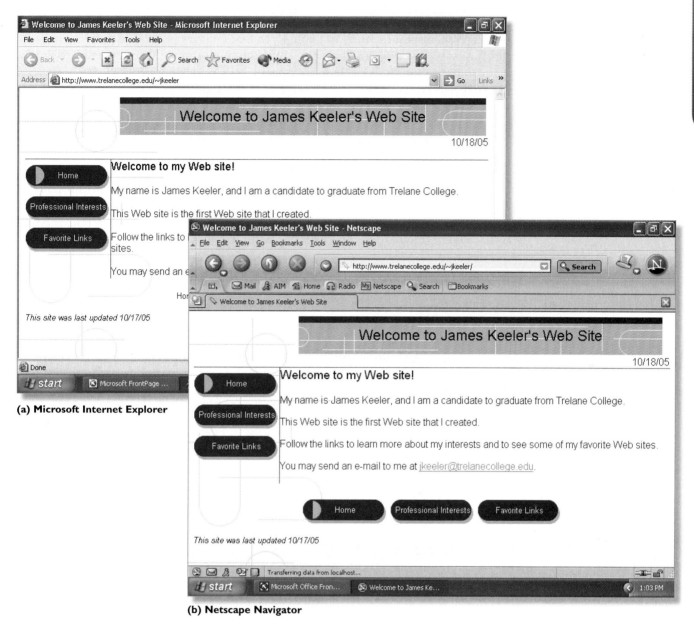

(a) Microsoft Internet Explorer

(b) Netscape Navigator

FIGURE 1-3

Different browsers will display the same Web page with slight variations. Netscape Navigator, for example, may display fonts, hyperlinks, tables, and other Web page elements in a manner different from Microsoft Internet Explorer. Some special features in a Web page may be available when using one browser, but may not work at all with a different browser. When developing a Web site, you should test the Web pages using Netscape Navigator, Microsoft Internet Explorer, and any other browsers your audience might use to ensure that the Web pages will be displayed correctly in the various browsers. FrontPage includes the capability of testing Web pages in a variety of browsers and screen resolutions.

Design Tip

As you develop a Web site, test the Web pages in as many browsers as your audience might use.

More About

Testing Web Pages in Browsers

When testing Web pages in various browsers, you may want to test the pages in several versions of the same browser (usually the two most recent versions). Consider whether you need to test the pages on both PC and Macintosh platforms.

The Web pages that comprise a Web site are stored on a server, called a Web server. A **Web server**, or **host**, is a computer that delivers (serves) requested Web pages. Every Web site is stored on and run from one or more Web servers; a Web server can have thousands of Web pages available for viewing. Multiple Web sites also can be stored on the same Web server. For example, many Internet service providers (ISPs) grant their subscribers storage space on a Web server for their personal or company Web sites. Each Web page on the Web site consists of one or more files that are stored on the hard disk of the Web server or other computer. ISPs are discussed later in this project.

A Web server runs **Web server software** that allows it to receive the requests for Web pages and sends the pages over the Internet to your browser, so you can view them on your computer. For example, when you enter a Web page address in your browser, your browser sends a request to the server; the server then uses the Web server software to fetch the Web page and send it to your browser.

Uniform Resource Locators (URLs)

Each Web page on a Web site has a unique address called a **Uniform Resource Locator** (**URL**). As shown in Figure 1-4, a URL consists of a protocol, a domain name, the path to a specific document, and the file name of the document. Most Web page URLs begin with http://. The **http** stands for **Hypertext Transfer Protocol**, which is the communications protocol used to transfer pages on the Web. The **domain name** identifies the Web server or computer on the Internet where the Web document is located. The **path** and **file name** indicate where the Web document is stored on the computer. In the URL shown in Figure 1-4, for example, the domain name is www.nationalgeographic.com, the path to the file is /ngm/, and the file name is index.htm.

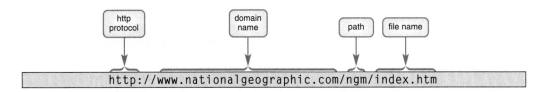

FIGURE 1-4

Each hyperlink on a Web page is associated with a URL, thus making it possible for you to navigate the Web using hyperlinks. When you click a hyperlink on a Web page, you are issuing a request to display the Web document specified by the URL. If, for example, you click a hyperlink associated with the URL, http://www.scsite.com/index.htm, your browser sends a request to the server whose domain name is www.scsite.com. The server then fetches the page named index.htm and sends it to your computer, where the browser displays it on your screen.

Elements of a Web Page

Although Web pages can be as distinctive and unique as the individuals who create them, almost every Web page has several basic features, or **elements**. Web page elements include basic features such as the background, text, hyperlinks, and images; and more advanced features such as forms, frames, and layers. As you begin to view Web pages through the eyes of a Web page developer, you will notice that most Web pages use variations on one or more of the elements identified in Figure 1-5.

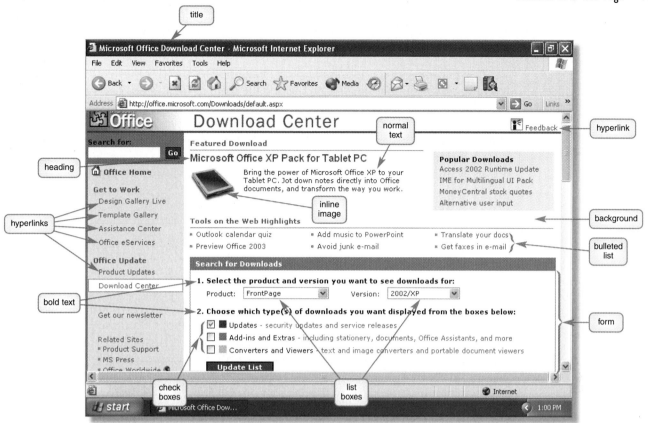

FIGURE 1-5

> *Design Tip*
>
> Many Web pages use common elements to which users are accustomed. When designing your page, consider using standard design elements such as a title, page banners, and link bars.

Window Elements

The **title** of a Web page is the text that appears on the title bar of the browser window when the Web page appears. The **background** of a Web page is either a solid color or a small graphic image that provides a backdrop against which the other elements display. Like the wallpaper in Windows, a background color or graphic can be **tiled**, or repeated, across the entire page.

Text Elements

On a Web page, the **body** contains the text that makes up the main content of a Web page, as opposed to the **header**, which contains the page title and other information about the page. The body of the Web page usually uses the default font format, known as **Normal text**. You also can format Normal text to display in color or in bold, italic, or underlined styles. **Headings** are used to separate different paragraphs of text or different sections of a Web page. Headings generally appear as a larger font size than normal text and usually are formatted with bold or italic styles.

Many Web pages present a series of text items as a **list**. Typically, lists are numbered or bulleted. A **numbered list** (also called an **ordered list**) presents an ordered list of items, such as the steps in this project. Numbers precede the items in a numbered list. A **bulleted list** (also called an **unordered list**) presents an unordered (unnumbered) list of items. Bulleted lists often use a small image called a **bullet** to mark each item in the list.

Hyperlink Elements

A **hyperlink**, or **link**, is an area of the page that you click to instruct the browser to go to a location in a file or to request a file from a Web server. On the World Wide Web, hyperlinks are the primary way to navigate between pages and among Web sites. Links point not only to Web pages, but also to graphics, sound, multimedia, e-mail addresses, program files, and even other parts of the same Web page. Text hyperlinks are the most commonly used hyperlinks. When text identifies a hyperlink, it usually appears as underlined text, in a color different from the regular text.

Image Elements

Web pages typically use several different types of graphics, or images. An **image** is a graphic file that can be inserted on a Web page and displayed in a Web browser. An **inline image** is an image or graphic file that is not part of the page's HTML file itself. Rather, an inline image is a separate graphic file that is merged into the page as it is displayed. The HTML file contains an <IMG SRC> tag that tells the browser which graphic file to request from the server, where to insert it on the page, and how to display it. Some inline images are **animated**, meaning they include motion and change in appearance. Inline images often identify hyperlinks.

An **image map** is a special type of inline image that is divided into sections, often with a hyperlink associated with each section. Clicking one of the hyperlinked sections, called a **hotspot**, instructs the browser to link to a Web page, graphic, sound, e-mail address, or other file.

As just described, the background of a Web page is the solid color, image, or pattern that serves as the backdrop on which text, images, hyperlinks, and other elements appear on the Web page. If you use an image for the background, the image repeats across and down the page.

Horizontal rules are lines that display across the page to separate different sections of the page. Although the appearance of a horizontal rule varies, many Web pages use an inline image as a horizontal rule.

Form, Table, Frame, and Layer Elements

A **form** is an area of a Web page that allows the viewer to enter data and information to be sent back to the Web server. Input elements within the form, such as **option buttons**, which allow for a single choice among several choices, or **text boxes**, which provide an area for the user to enter text, instruct the individual what items to enter and how to send them to the server.

A **table** is used to present text and graphics in rows or columns. The intersection of a row and a column is called a **cell**. The text or graphic within a cell often acts as a hyperlink. The border width of the table determines the width of the gridlines surrounding the cells. When the border width is greater than 0, gridlines surround the cells. When the border width is set to 0, gridlines are not displayed.

A **frame** allows Web page developers to divide the display area of the browser into sections, so the browser can display a different Web page in each frame. Web pages with frames have many possible applications. A table of contents for your Web site can be displayed in a smaller frame, for example, while different content pages appear in a separate main frame. Users can click hyperlinks in the smaller table of contents frame and display the linked page in the main frame.

A **layer** is a container you create on your Web page to hold text, graphics, or other content. Layers provide another dimension to Web pages beyond the horizontal and vertical. You can overlap layers, nest layers, and hide layers. You animate layers by assigning behaviors to layers.

FrontPage Web Sites

As previously defined, a collection of related Web pages that you can access electronically is called a Web site. A typical Web site contains one to several thousand Web pages, often with links to other pages in the same Web site and pages on separate Web sites.

In FrontPage, a group of related pages also is called a Web site. A **FrontPage Web site** consists of the Web pages, images, and other files, folders, and programs that make up the related content that will comprise the Web site. The Web pages in a FrontPage Web site usually are related by topic or purpose; most Web sites use a series of hyperlinks to connect the related pages. A Web site may consist of one or more FrontPage Web sites.

When working with a Web site in FrontPage, the Web site that currently is open is called the **current Web site**. Once created, a FrontPage Web site can be stored on the computer on which FrontPage is installed or on a Web server anywhere on the World Wide Web. Using FrontPage, you can upload and download a complete Web site to and from your computer and a Web server, or just upload the portions of the Web site that you have modified. Publishing involves sending, or uploading, copies of Web pages, image files, and other files, folders, and programs to a server where they then are made available on the World Wide Web. To publish a FrontPage Web site, you must have access to a Web server or other shared location to which you are allowed to upload files. As you complete this project, you will use FrontPage to develop and publish a personal Web site to the World Wide Web.

 Design Tip Plan to publish your Web site on a regular basis to keep content up-to-date after your Web site is up and running. Do not allow your content to become stale, or out-of-date.

Starting and Customizing FrontPage

To learn how to develop a Web site, this project starts FrontPage and then uses a template to create a personal Web site that introduces an individual, describes the person's professional interests, and lists links to several favorite Web sites. If you are stepping through this project on a computer and you want your screen to match the figures in this book, then you should change your computer's resolution to 800 × 600. For more information about how to change the resolution on your computer, see Appendix D. The steps on the next page start FrontPage.

To Start and Customize FrontPage

1

• **Click the Start button on the Windows taskbar, point to All Programs on the Start menu, point to Microsoft Office on the All Programs submenu, and then point to Microsoft Office FrontPage 2003 on the Microsoft Office submenu.**

Windows displays the Start menu, the All Programs submenu, and the Microsoft Office submenu (Figure 1-6).

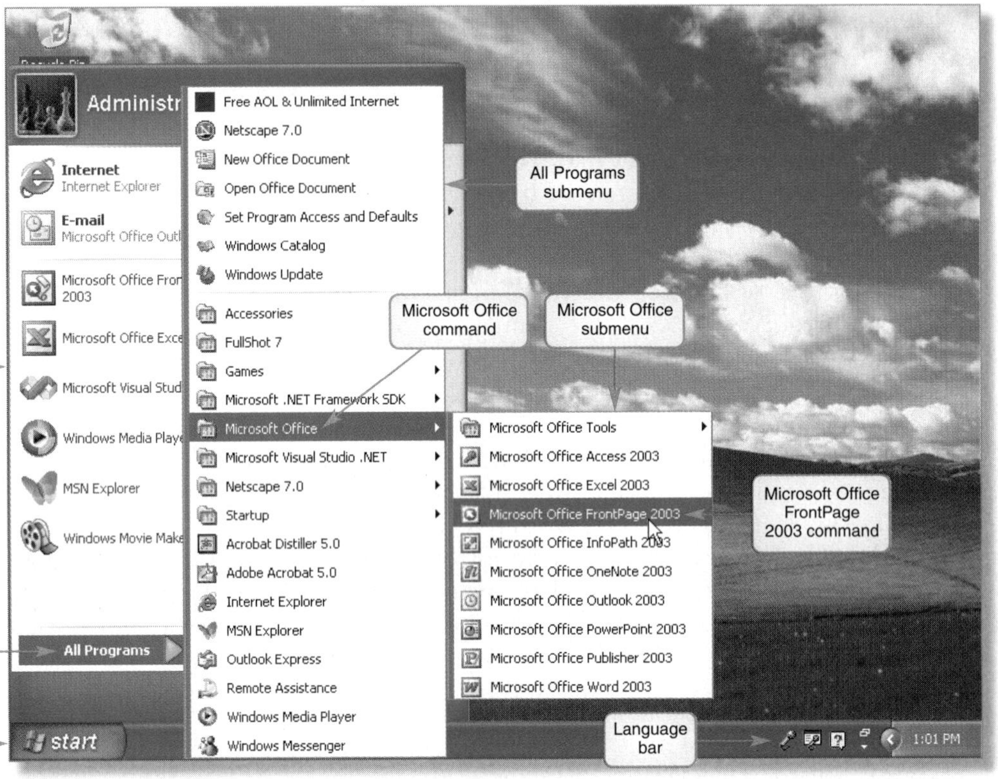

FIGURE 1-6

2

• **Click Microsoft Office FrontPage 2003.**

Microsoft FrontPage 2003 is started. The document window is displayed in the default Page view of Design view (Figure 1-7). When you first start FrontPage, a blank page is displayed.

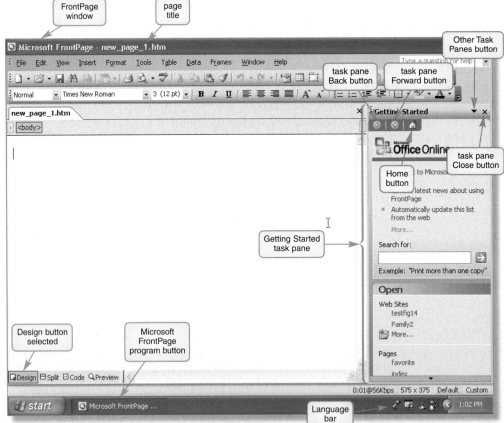

FIGURE 1-7

3

• **Click the Close button in the Getting Started task pane.**

• **If the Language bar shows and it indicates that the microphone is on, click the Microphone button to turn it off.**

• **To close the Language bar, right-click it to display a list of commands and then click Close the Language bar on the shortcut menu.**

The Getting Started task pane is closed, resulting in the maximum width for the new page. The Language bar disappears (Figure 1-8).

4

• **If the FrontPage window is not maximized, double-click its title bar to maximize it.**

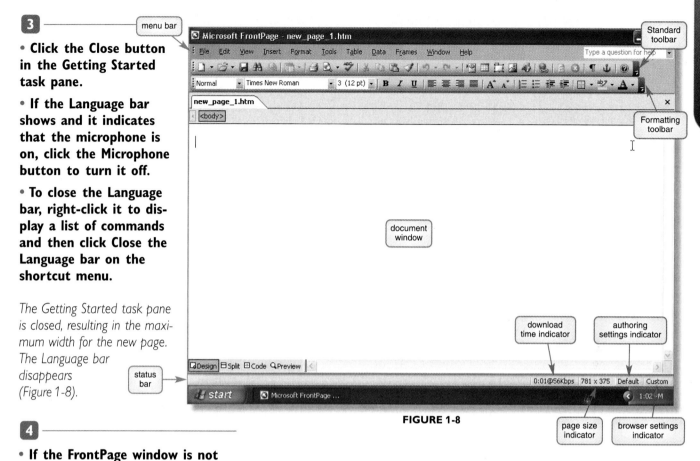

FIGURE 1-8

Other Ways

1. Double-click Microsoft Office FrontPage icon on desktop
2. Click Start button on Windows taskbar, click Microsoft Office FrontPage 2003 on Start menu

The screen shown in Figure 1-8 illustrates how the FrontPage window looks the first time you start FrontPage after installation on most computers. If the Office Speech Recognition software is installed and active on your computer, then, when you start FrontPage, the Language bar is displayed on the screen. The **Language bar** allows you to speak commands and dictate text. It usually is located on the right side of the Windows taskbar next to the notification area and changes to include the speech recognition functions available in FrontPage. In this book, the Language bar is closed because it takes up computer resources and with the Language bar active, the microphone can be turned on accidentally, causing your computer to act in an unstable manner. For additional information about the Language bar, see page FP 19 and Appendix B.

As shown in Figure 1-7, FrontPage displays a task pane on the right side of the screen. A **task pane** is a separate window that enables users to carry out some FrontPage tasks more efficiently. When you start FrontPage, it displays the Getting Started task pane, which is a small window that provides commonly used links and commands that allow you to open files, create new files, or search Office-related topics on the Microsoft Web site. In this book, the Getting Started task pane is hidden to allow the maximum window space in the FrontPage window. When you start FrontPage, the FrontPage window is displayed the same way it displayed the last time you quit FrontPage. Thus, if the Getting Started task pane previously displayed on the right side of the window, then the task pane will be displayed when you start FrontPage.

Microsoft Office
FrontPage 2003

Q: Can I change the position of the task pane?

A: Yes. When you first start FrontPage, a small window called a task pane may be docked on the right side of the screen. You can drag a task pane title bar to float the pane in your work area or dock it on either the left or right side of a screen, depending on your preference.

As you work through creating a Web site, you will find that certain FrontPage operations cause FrontPage to display a task pane. FrontPage provides 15 additional task panes, in addition to the Getting Started task pane shown in Figure 1-7 on page FP 14. Some of the more important ones are the Clipboard task pane, the Help task pane, and the Clip Art task pane. Throughout the book, these task panes are discussed when they are used.

At any point while working with a FrontPage Web site, you can open or close a task pane by clicking the Task Pane command on the View menu. You can activate additional task panes by clicking the Other Task Panes button to the left of the Close button on the task pane title bar (Figure 1-7) and then selecting a task pane on the Other Task Panes menu. The Back and Forward buttons below the task pane title bar allow you to switch between task panes that you opened during a session. The Home button causes FrontPage to display the Getting Started task pane.

The FrontPage Window

The FrontPage window consists of a variety of features to help you work efficiently. It contains a title bar, a status bar, a menu bar, toolbars, and a pane in the document window that displays different content, depending on the current view.

Title Bar

The **title bar** (Figure 1-8 on the previous page) displays the application name, Microsoft FrontPage, and the location of the current FrontPage Web site. If you open a Web site saved in the webpages folder on drive C, for example, the title bar will display the title, Microsoft FrontPage - C:\webpages, on the title bar.

Status Bar

The **status bar**, which is located at the bottom of the FrontPage window, consists of a message area, a download time indicator, an authoring settings indicator, and a browser settings indicator (Figure 1-8). As you are developing a page or Web site, the message area on the left side of the status bar displays information about file location, file name, hyperlinks, and more. The right side of the status bar includes indicators related to download times, page size, browser settings, and authoring features. The download time indicator displays the number of seconds it will take the page to download on the Web, based on a certain connection speed. The browser setting indicator displays the browser for which you are building the Web page. Double-clicking the browser settings indicator displays a dialog box that allows you to change the target browser and the target browser's capabilities. The authoring settings indicator displays information about which set of features you are allowed to use on Web sites created in FrontPage. You disable or enable more features by double-clicking the authoring settings indicator and changing the options in the Page Options dialog box.

Menu Bar

The **menu bar** displays the FrontPage menu names (Figure 1-8). Each name represents a menu of commands that allows you to create, retrieve, edit, save, print, and publish a FrontPage Web site. To display a menu, such as the Format menu, click the Format menu name on the menu bar. If you point to a command with an arrow on the right, a submenu appears, from which you can choose a command.

When you click a menu name on the menu bar, a **short menu** appears listing only basic or the most recently used commands (Figure 1-9a). If you wait a few seconds or click the arrows at the bottom of the short menu, the full menu appears. The **full menu** lists all the commands associated with a menu (Figure 1-9b). You also can display a full menu immediately by double-clicking the menu name on the menu bar. In this book, when you display a menu, you should always display the full menu using one of the following techniques:

1. Click the menu name on the menu bar and then wait a few seconds.
2. Click the menu name and then click the arrows at the bottom of the short menu.
3. Click the menu name and then point to the arrows at the bottom of the short menu.
4. Double-click the menu name on the menu bar.

Both short and full menus display some dimmed commands. A **dimmed command** appears gray, or dimmed, instead of black, which indicates it is not available for the current selection. A command with medium blue shading to the left of it on a full menu is called a **hidden command** because it does not appear on a short menu. As you use FrontPage, it automatically personalizes the short menus for you based on how often you use commands. That is, as you use hidden commands on the full menu, FrontPage unhides them and places them on the short menu.

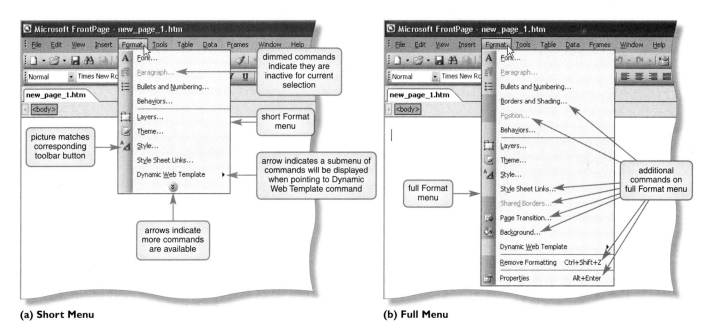

(a) Short Menu　　　　　　　　　(b) Full Menu

FIGURE 1-9

Toolbars

A **toolbar** consists of buttons that allow you to perform tasks more quickly than when using the menu bar. To save a Web page, for example, you can click the Save button on a toolbar, instead of clicking File on the menu bar and then clicking Save on the File menu. Each button uses a graphical representation to help identify the button's function.

More About

Sizing Toolbar Buttons

If you have difficulty seeing the small buttons on the toolbars, you can increase their size by clicking View on the menu bar, pointing to Toolbars, clicking Customize on the Toolbars submenu, clicking the Options tab, clicking the Large icons check box, and then clicking the Close button.

More About

Toolbars

You can move a toolbar to any location on the screen. Drag the move handle (Figure 1-10a) to the desired location. Once the toolbar is in the window area, drag the title bar to move it. Each side of the screen is called a dock. You can drag a toolbar to a dock so it does not clutter the window.

More About

Resetting Toolbars

If your toolbars have a different set of buttons than shown in Figures 1-10a and 10b, it probably means that a previous user added or deleted buttons. To reset the toolbars to their default, see Appendix D.

When you first start FrontPage, some of the buttons on the toolbars are dimmed (or grayed) to indicate that the toolbar buttons are inactive. When a button or command is **inactive**, the function performed by that button or command is not available. Once you have opened a Web page or a Web site, the buttons on the FrontPage toolbars are **active**, meaning you can use them to perform tasks in FrontPage. Figure 1-10a and Figure 1-10b show the buttons on each of the two toolbars that display when you open a Web page or Web site using FrontPage: the Standard toolbar and the Formatting toolbar. The book explains each button in detail when it is used.

STANDARD TOOLBAR The Standard toolbar (Figure 1-10a) contains buttons that execute commonly used commands such as Open, Print, Save, Cut, Copy, Paste, and many more. The Standard toolbar also contains a Microsoft Office FrontPage Help button that you can click to start **FrontPage Help**, which is a collection of reference materials, tips, and other assistance you can access at any time while using FrontPage.

FORMATTING TOOLBAR The Formatting toolbar (Figure 1-10b) contains buttons used to execute commonly used formatting commands that allow you quickly to change font, font size, and alignment. It also contains buttons, such as Bold, Italic, and Underline, which allow you to change text styles, and others that create lists and so on.

FrontPage has several other toolbars to help you perform your work. You can display a toolbar by right-clicking any toolbar to display a shortcut menu that lists the available toolbars and then clicking the name of the toolbar you want to display. A **shortcut menu** contains a list of commands that are related to the items to which you are pointing when you right-click.

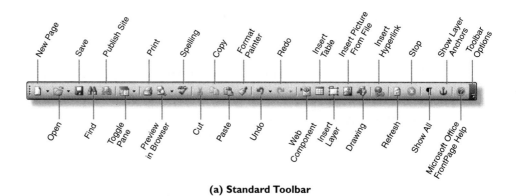

(a) Standard Toolbar

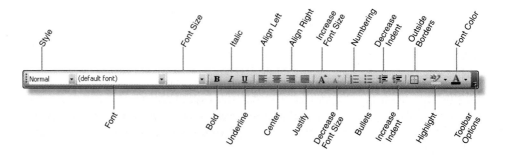

(b) Formatting Toolbar

FIGURE 1-10

Speech Recognition

With the **Office Speech Recognition software** installed and a microphone, you can speak the names of toolbar buttons, menus, menu commands, list items, alerts, and dialog box controls, such as OK and Cancel. You also can dictate cell entries, such as text and numbers. To indicate whether you want to speak commands or dictate cell entries, you use the Language bar. The Language bar can be in one of four states: (1) **restored**, which means it is displayed somewhere in the FrontPage window (Figure 1-11a); (2) **minimized**, which means it is displayed on the Windows taskbar (Figure 1-11b); (3) **hidden**, which means you do not see it on the screen but it will be displayed the next time you start your computer; or (4) **closed**, which means it is hidden permanently until you enable it. If the Language bar is hidden or closed and you want it to display, then do the following:

1. Right-click an open area on the Windows taskbar at the bottom of the screen.
2. Point to Toolbars and then click Language bar on the Toolbars submenu.

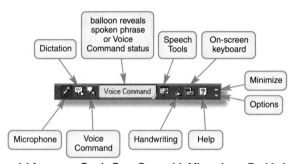

(a) Language Bar in FrontPage with Microphone Enabled   **(b) Language Bar Minimized on Windows Taskbar**

FIGURE 1-11

If the Language bar command is dimmed on the Toolbars submenu or if the Speech command is dimmed on the Tools menu, the Office Speech Recognition software is not installed.

In this book, the Language bar does not appear in the figures. If you want to close the Language bar so that your screen is identical to what you see in the book, right-click the Language bar, click Close the Language bar on the shortcut menu, and then click OK in the Language Bar dialog box.

Using a Template to Create a FrontPage Web Site

Designing a Web site is a complex process that requires you to make decisions concerning the structure of the Web site and the appearance and content of each Web page within the site. When developing a Web site composed of several pages, for example, you should use a consistent layout and design on each page. In addition, you should be sure to link appropriate pages using a navigation scheme that is easy to understand. To help simplify this process, FrontPage includes several wizards and preformatted Web sites that will help you create a set of pages for a Web site. These preformatted Web sites are called templates.

Design Tip

Before creating a Web site from scratch, lay out the navigation structure of your Web site and consider a template to alleviate a great deal of manual work when creating the Web site.

A FrontPage **template** is a series of files and Web pages that are organized and formatted with a basic framework of content upon which you can base new pages and new FrontPage Web sites. You also can apply the formatting in a template to existing pages and Web sites. Each template consists of linked Web pages that already include basic elements such as headings, formatted text, images, and hyperlinks.

When you create a new Web site, you can choose to:

- Create an empty Web site or a Web site with one page
- Import a Web site from a Web server or your personal computer
- Create a Web site using a template or wizard

Table 1-2 outlines the options from which you can choose when creating a FrontPage Web site using a template.

Table 1-2 FrontPage Web Site Options		
OPTION	TYPE	DESCRIPTION
One Page Web Site	Template	Creates a FrontPage Web site with a single page (a home page). Used to create a FrontPage Web site from scratch with no suggested content.
Corporate Presence Wizard	Wizard	Creates a FrontPage Web site with pages tailored to an organization's Web site.
Customer Support Web Site	Template	Creates a FrontPage Web site to help organizations improve a company's online customer support, particularly for software companies.
Database Interface Wizard	Wizard	Creates a FrontPage Web site that allows you to connect to a database, and then view, update, delete, or add records.
Discussion Web Wizard	Wizard	Helps the developer create a discussion group with threads, a table of contents, and full-text searching.
Empty Web Site	Template	Creates a FrontPage Web site with nothing in it. Used to create a FrontPage Web site from scratch with no suggested content.
Import Web Site Wizard	Wizard	Imports an existing Web site into a new FrontPage Web site. Starts the Import Web Site Wizard, which guides you through the process of importing an existing Web site.
Personal Web Site	Template	Creates a FrontPage Web site with Web pages about an individual's interests, photos, and favorite Web sites.
Project Web Site	Template	Creates a FrontPage Web site designed to support a project. The Web site includes pages for a list of members, a schedule, status, an archive, and discussions.
SharePoint Team Site	Template	Creates a Web site for team collaboration with a team events calendar, library for shared documents, task list, and contact list. Must be created on a Web server.

After you create a page or Web site using a template, you can customize the page or Web site. To reduce the editing work required to finish your Web site, you should choose the template closest to your desired site design and structure. Because FrontPage creates many files for a Web site, it is advisable to create the project using the computer's hard disk (typically drive C) rather than the floppy drive (A:). The following steps show how to use a template to create a FrontPage Web site on a hard disk.

To Use a Template to Create a FrontPage Web Site

1

• **Click File on the menu bar and then click Close.**

FrontPage closes the new_page_1.htm page.

2

• **Click the New Page button arrow on the Standard toolbar.**

FrontPage displays the New Page menu (Figure 1-12).

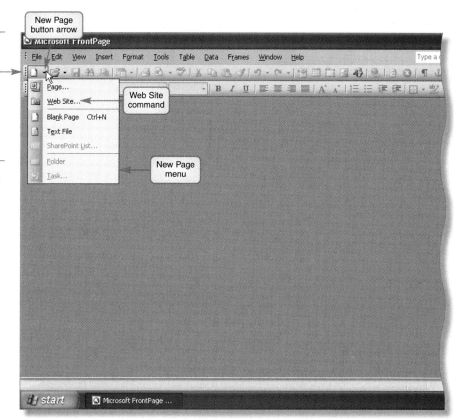

FIGURE 1-12

3

• **Click Web Site.**

• **When the Web Site Templates dialog box appears, click the Personal Web Site icon.**

The Web Site Templates dialog box is displayed, prompting you for information needed to create a new FrontPage Web site. The Personal Web Site icon is selected; the Description area describes the Web site the Personal Web Site template creates. The Specify the location of the new Web site text box indicates the location where FrontPage will store the new Web site (Figure 1-13).

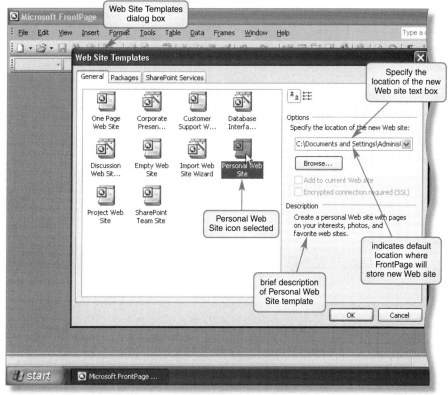

FIGURE 1-13

4

• **Click the Specify the location of the new Web site text box and select the default location text.**

• **Type** c:\jkeeler **or a location specified by your instructor in the text box.**

FrontPage displays the new location in the text box. FrontPage will save the new Web site in the jkeeler folder on drive C (Figure 1-14).

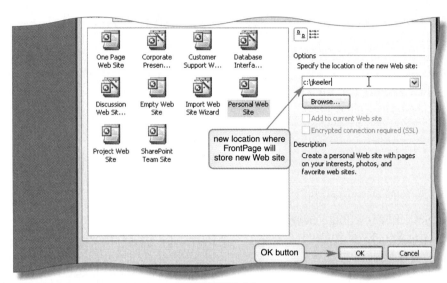

FIGURE 1-14

5

• **Click the OK button.**

FrontPage begins creating a set of folders and making copies of the Web pages in the Personal Web Site template for you to customize. When finished, the FrontPage window is displayed in Folders view with the Folder List pane open on the left side (Figure 1-15).

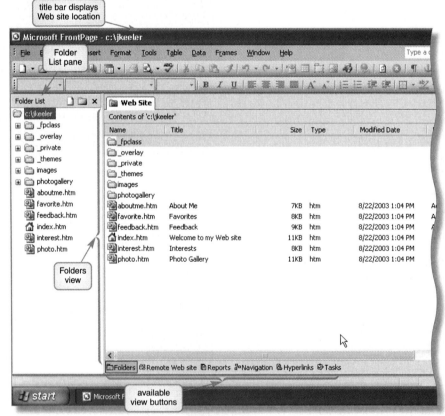

FIGURE 1-15

While FrontPage is copying the Personal Web Site template pages, FrontPage briefly displays a Create New Web Site dialog box indicating that FrontPage is creating the new Web site in the folder, jkeeler, on drive C and the status of the copying process. As shown in Figure 1-15, when FrontPage creates a new Web site, the Folder List pane opens on the left side of the FrontPage window. The Folder List pane lists the name of all of the files and folders in the current FrontPage Web site. If it is not displayed, display the Folder List pane by using the Folder List command on the View menu or pressing ALT+F1.

Views

The document window shown in Figure 1-15 displays the Web Site tab in Folders view. The Web Site tab always is available when you are working on a Web site. FrontPage includes several types of views that display in the main FrontPage window. When you first create a new Web site, FrontPage is displayed in Folders view. A **view** provides a different way of looking at the information in your Web site, so you can manage your Web site effectively. The View menu contains commands that allow you to switch to different views of your Web site. You also can click the buttons at the bottom of the document window to switch to several different views. The selected view determines how the FrontPage window appears. For example, **Navigation view** displays a graphical representation of the Web site's **structure**, which is the set of relationships among the pages in a FrontPage Web site.

A Web site's structure defines the overall site organization and navigation, determining the pages that are linked, how many levels of pages exist, and so on. The structure of one Web site, for example, might be linear, with few levels; another site might use a hierarchical structure, with several levels of pages.

Design Tip

If your Web site's navigation structure is both well-designed and focused on your users, your visitors will be able to move to different locations on a page or to other pages in your Web site to find usable information quickly and easily.

Table 1-3 identifies the views available on the View menu and buttons at the bottom of the document window on the Web Site tab and provides a description of each view. All of the views appear on buttons at the bottom of the Web Site tab except for the Page view. Individual Page views for each page that is open appear in separate tabs to the right of the Web Site tab.

Q&A

Q: Can I stop FrontPage from automatically opening the last Web site?

A: Yes. When FrontPage starts, it opens the last Web site you edited. To stop this behavior, click Options on the Tools menu. When the Options dialog box is displayed, click the General tab. Make certain that the Open last Web site automatically when FrontPage starts check box is cleared.

Table 1-3	Views on the View Menu	
BUTTON	**VIEW**	**DESCRIPTION**
	Page	Used for creating, editing, and previewing Web pages. Page view displays Web pages in a manner similar to how they will be displayed in a Web browser.
	Folders	Displays a view of a Web site that shows how the content of the Web site is organized. Similar to Windows Explorer, Folders view allows you to create, delete, copy, and move folders.
	Remote Web Site	Allows you to view and publish the current Web site or portions of the current Web site to a Web server.
	Reports	Allows you to analyze a Web site's contents. You can calculate the total size of the files in your Web site, show which files are not linked to any other files, identify slow or outdated pages, group files by the task or person to whom the files are assigned, and so on.
	Navigation	Used to create, display, print, and change a Web site's structure and navigation. Navigation view also allows you to drag and drop pages into the Web site structure.
	Hyperlinks	Displays a list showing the status of the hyperlinks in the Web site. The list includes both internal and external hyperlinks, and graphically indicates whether the hyperlinks have been verified or whether they are broken.
	Tasks	Displays a list of the tasks required to complete or maintain a Web site.

Opening and Modifying a Web Page in Page View

When a Web site is opened, the path and name of the Web site appear on the title bar. When you create a new Web site, FrontPage automatically creates certain files and folders, such as Web pages, images, and other files in the Web site. The **Page view** displays a page currently being edited. FrontPage allows you to edit several pages at once by opening a tab for each page to the right of the Web Site tab.

Opening a Web Page in Page View

FrontPage allows you to open and modify text, images, tables, and other elements on each individual page in the current Web site. If the page is in the current Web site in any view or the Folder List pane, you can open the page by double-clicking the page's icon or file name. To open a Web page in Page view, for example, you simply double-click the file name of the page in the Folder List pane. After FrontPage displays the page in the document window, you can edit the page by selecting text, images, and other elements. The page being edited in Page view is referred to as the **active page** or **current page**. After you open a page, the document window displays the active page as a tabbed page. The file name of the active page, such as index.htm, appears in the tab at the top of the document window. The following step shows how to open a Web page in Page view.

To Open a Web Page in Page View

1

• **Double-click the file name, index.htm, in the Folder List pane.**

The Home page is displayed in the document window (Figure 1-16). The page contains placeholder text that you can edit to display your own message. A small pencil icon in the Folder List pane indicates that the Home page file, named index.htm, is open. The Design button is selected at the bottom of the document window, which indicates that the page is displayed in Design view. In Design view, you can edit the page. The tab at the top of the document window shows the name of the file opened for editing.

Other Ways

1. Click page name in Folder List pane, press ENTER key
2. On File menu click Open
3. Right-click page name in Folder List pane, click Open on shortcut menu
4. Press ALT+F, O
5. Press CTRL+O
6. In Voice Command mode, say "File, Open"

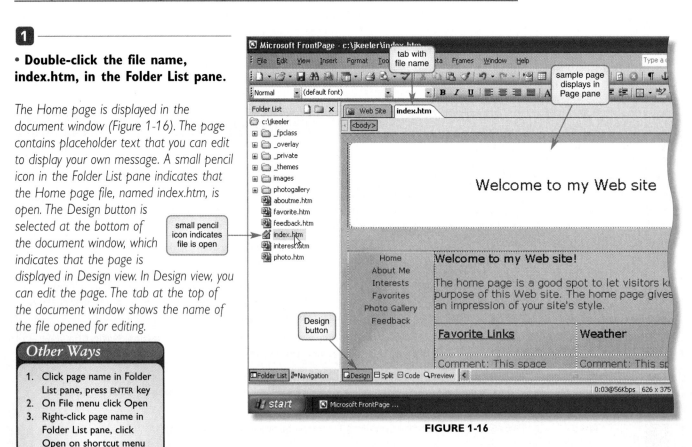

FIGURE 1-16

When a page is opened in the default Page view, the page appears in Design view. Design view is indicated by a button at the bottom of the Page view tab. There are four views in which to view a page while in Page view, including Design, Split, Code, and Preview. The Design view, which is the default button selected in Page view, is a **WYSIWYG** (**What You See Is What You Get**) design tool that displays a page as it will appear in a Web browser. As you create or modify a Web page in Design view, FrontPage displays the page as it will display on the Web, while generating the needed HTML code for you. If you insert an image on a page, for example, FrontPage automatically enters the proper HTML code (in this case, the <IMG> tag). Using FrontPage, you can insert text, images, hyperlinks, and other elements without having to type any HTML code.

As shown in Figure 1-16, the Folder List pane displays the pages and folders in the current Web site. When you first create a new Personal Web site, it contains six folders: _fpclass, _overlay, _private, _themes, images, and photogallery — included in the Personal Web Site template. The _fpclass, _overlay, and _themes folders include files used internally by FrontPage for special functionality. For example, the _themes folder contains files used for FrontPage themes, which are discussed in the next section. The **images folder** is a convenient place to store image files used in the FrontPage Web site. The _private folder holds files that you can use on the Web pages in the current Web site, but do not want people who are browsing your Web site to access individually. If you store a logo image in the _private folder, for example, you can use this on your Web pages, but others browsing your Web site cannot access the logo image. The **photogallery folder** is where FrontPage stores thumbnail images when a particular component, which is discussed later, is used. FrontPage also automatically creates a file named **index.htm**, which serves as the home page for your Web site.

Applying a Theme to a FrontPage Web Site

When developing a Web site that consists of many pages, you should maintain a consistent, professional layout and design throughout all of the pages. The pages in a Web site, for example, should use similar features such as background color, margins, buttons, and headings. To help you create pages with a cohesive and professional appearance, FrontPage includes a gallery of more than 75 preset themes. A **theme** is a unified set of design elements and color schemes for bullets, fonts, graphics, navigation bars, and other page elements.

 Design Tip Generate a sense of unity or familiarity within your Web site by utilizing a common graphic theme and a common color theme.

When applied to a Web site, a theme formats the Web page elements (images, backgrounds, text, and so on) so they share a consistent layout and design. You also have the option of applying themes to individual pages. The theme affects all aspects of a page's appearance, including text, color, and images, as follows:

- **Text:** A theme uses a unique set of fonts for the body text and headings.
- **Colors:** A theme uses a color scheme to set the color of body text, headings, hyperlinks, table borders, page background, and more.
- **Images:** A theme uses images (graphics) for several page elements, such as the background, bullets, horizontal rules, and more.

When you insert new elements on a page that uses a theme, FrontPage automatically formats those elements to match the theme. FrontPage also applies the theme automatically to any new pages you create in the Web site.

Each FrontPage template uses a default theme. When the Personal Web Site template was selected in the previous set of steps, FrontPage automatically applied a theme to the Web site. The following steps show how to preview the default theme used for the Web site and apply a new theme to the Web site.

To Apply a Theme to a FrontPage Web Site

1

• **Click Format on the menu bar (Figure 1-17).**

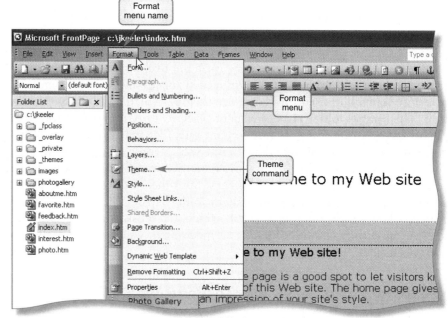

FIGURE 1-17

2

• **Click Theme.**

• **When the Theme task pane is displayed, click the Vivid colors check box to select it.**

• **Scroll to Capsules in the Select a theme list.**

The Theme task pane is displayed and the Vivid colors check box is selected (Figure 1-18). The Select a theme list allows you to preview a sample page of each theme in the list. The Select a theme list shows all of the themes provided with FrontPage.

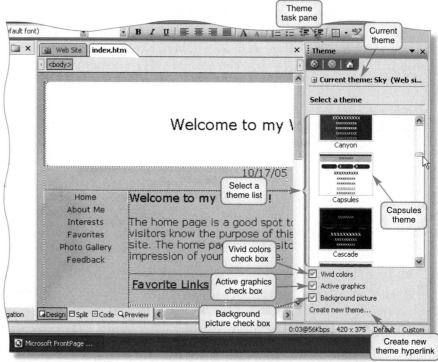

FIGURE 1-18

3

• **Click the c:\jkeeler folder in the Folder List pane.**

• **Double-click Capsules in the Select a theme list.**

FrontPage displays the Microsoft FrontPage 2003 dialog box. The dialog box warns that the theme will be applied to all pages in the Web site (Figure 1-19). Selecting the c:\jkeeler folder ensures that all pages in the Web site receive the theme.

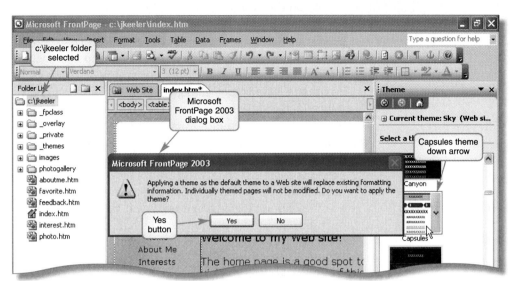

FIGURE 1-19

4

• **Click the Yes button.**

FrontPage displays a message on the status bar, indicating that FrontPage is applying the new theme to all pages in the Web site. When finished, FrontPage is displayed in Page view. The active page, index.htm, is displayed in the document window with the Capsules theme applied (Figure 1-20).

5

• **Click the Close button on the Theme task pane.**

FrontPage displays the index.htm page in Page view in the document window.

FIGURE 1-20

Other Ways

1. Press ALT+O, H
2. In Voice Command mode, say "Format, Theme"

The Theme task pane (Figure 1-18) contains options you can select to control how the current Web site uses themes. Selecting the Vivid colors check box changes the theme's normal set of colors to a brighter color scheme. Selecting the Active graphics check box animates certain graphic elements. Selecting the Background picture check box applies a textured background image to the pages in the current Web site.

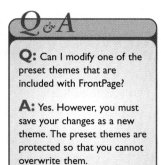

Q: Can I modify one of the preset themes that are included with FrontPage?

A: Yes. However, you must save your changes as a new theme. The preset themes are protected so that you cannot overwrite them.

When the mouse is moved over a theme in the Select a theme list, a down arrow appears next to the theme (Figure 1-19 on the previous page). Clicking the arrow displays a menu that allows you to change features of the theme or apply the theme to one or more pages in the Web site. The menu also includes a Customize command and a Delete command. The Customize command displays the Customize Theme dialog box that allows you to change colors, graphics, and text in the theme. You can change a theme's background picture or heading font, for example, to create a new theme that displays a company logo on every page. The Delete command allows you to delete themes that you have created. You create new themes by clicking the Create new theme hyperlink at the bottom of the Theme task pane. As you saw in Step 3 on the previous page, selecting the main folder in the Folder List pane before applying the theme instructs FrontPage to apply the theme to every page in the current Web site.

While applying a theme to a Web site, FrontPage displays information about the operation in progress on the status bar. Depending on the number of pages in the Web site, this process can take anywhere from a few seconds to a few minutes. When FrontPage has applied the theme to every page in the current Web site, FrontPage is displayed in Page view. Once the theme is applied, FrontPage changes the background, fonts, and graphics used in the Web site. Applying the Capsules theme, for example, adds an oval pattern and colors to the white background (Figure 1-20 on the previous page).

Editing Text on a Web Page

As you have learned, a FrontPage template is a series of linked Web pages that are organized and formatted with a basic framework of content upon which you can base new pages and new FrontPage Web sites. To help you design your own Web page, the template Web pages include placeholders for basic page elements such as headings, formatted text, images, and hyperlinks.

Adding your own content to the page involves editing one or more placeholders to convey the desired information — or deleting them altogether. On the Home page of the personal Web site, for example, you will want to edit the text to introduce yourself, delete any unneeded text, and add new text to complete the page. The following steps edit text on a Web page.

To Edit Text on a Web Page

1

• **Position the insertion point at the beginning of the second paragraph, which begins with the text, The home page is a good spot... (Figure 1-21).**

FIGURE 1-21

2

• **Drag through the text to select it.**

The selected text is highlighted (Figure 1-22).

FIGURE 1-22

3

• **Type** My name is James Keeler, and I am a candidate to graduate from Trelane College. **(You may substitute your personal information here.)**

The new text replaces the selected text (Figure 1-23). The asterisk in the tab indicates changes made to the page are not yet saved.

FIGURE 1-23

The previous steps edited a section of the placeholder text on the template page, which now displays the desired information. The other text sections remain unchanged.

Using FrontPage, you can edit and add text just as you would with word processing software. To begin editing, you position the insertion point where you want to make a change and then perform the desired action. You even can move around the text using your mouse or the arrow keys. If you make a mistake typing, you can use the BACKSPACE key or the DELETE key to correct the mistake. Use the Show All button on the Standard toolbar to toggle showing and hiding of hidden document formatting codes.

Adding New Text to a Web Page

If you want to include additional text beyond that contained in the template, you can add new text to the Web page. Just as you add new text to a word processing document, you add new text to a Web page by positioning the insertion point where you want the text to display and then typing the text. The following steps add text to a Web page.

To Add New Text to a Web Page

1

• **Press the ENTER key to start a new paragraph below the second paragraph.**

FrontPage displays the insertion point at the beginning of the new paragraph (Figure 1-24).

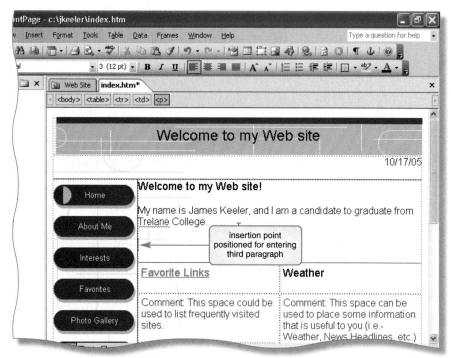

FIGURE 1-24

2

• **Type** This Web site is the first Web site that I created.

FrontPage displays the new text as the third paragraph on the Web page (Figure 1-25).

FIGURE 1-25

3

• **Press the ENTER key to start a new paragraph.**

• **Type** Follow the links to learn more about my interests and to see some of my favorite Web sites.

The inserted text automatically wraps to the next line as you type (Figure 1-26).

FIGURE 1-26

Editing and adding text on a Web page using FrontPage is similar to editing a word processing document. In the Design view of Page view, you can insert, delete, cut, copy, and paste text, just as you would with word processing software.

> **Design Tip**
>
> If the main content for your Web page is not already in a word processing document, consider first placing all of your content in one. You and other contributors can manage the content much easier in a common file format. When the content is ready to be made available on the Web, simply copy and paste the content from the document into the Web page in FrontPage.

As with many word processing applications, FrontPage automatically checks your spelling as you type and flags misspelled words with a red wavy underline. In the Home page, for example, the spell checker does not recognize the word, Trelane, and thus flags it with a red wavy underline. To add an unrecognized word to the spell checker dictionary, right-click the underlined word and then click Add to Dictionary on the shortcut menu. To correct a misspelled word, right-click the underlined word and then click the correct spelling on the shortcut menu.

Deleting Text Positioned with Tables

Often, cells in a table are used in a Web page to position textual elements. A table may contain only a single cell with text, may contain multiple cells containing text, or may contain another nested table. A table contained within another table is called a **nested** table. Although tables are discussed in a later project, the template used for this page incorporates tables to position some sections of text and also contains some nested tables. Because some of these tables and cells are not used in the Web site you are developing, they should be deleted. The steps on the next page select the tables and cells to be deleted.

To Select Tables and Cells

1

• **Click in the cell that contains the text, Favorite Links.**

FrontPage displays the insertion point at the end of the text (Figure 1-27).

FIGURE 1-27

2

• **Click Table on the menu bar and then point to Select.**

FrontPage displays the Table menu and the Select submenu (Figure 1-28).

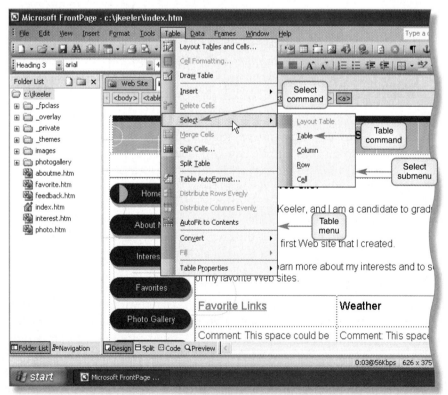

FIGURE 1-28

3

• **Click Table on the Select submenu.**

The selected cells are highlighted (Figure 1-29). The **Quick Tag Selector** *is displayed. It is a tool that makes it easier to select and edit tags.*

FIGURE 1-29

You should exercise care in selecting the table cells you want to delete. Because tables often are nested, you inadvertently may select material that you want to keep. Figure 1-29 shows that the <table> tag selector in the Quick Tag Selector becomes highlighted when you select the table. The Quick Tag Selector shows the hierarchy of HTML tags that leads to the currently selected item in the Page view. Moving the mouse over a tag selector in the Quick Tag Selector displays a down arrow next to the tag selector. Clicking the arrow displays a menu that allows you to perform various actions on the tag, such as selecting the tag. Once it is verified that the selected cells and/or tables are correct, the following steps delete the selected table and cells in the table.

To Delete a Selected Table

1

• **Right-click one of the selected cells.**

FrontPage displays the shortcut menu (Figure 1-30).

FIGURE 1-30

2

• **Click Delete Cells on the shortcut menu.**

The selected cells are deleted (Figure 1-31).

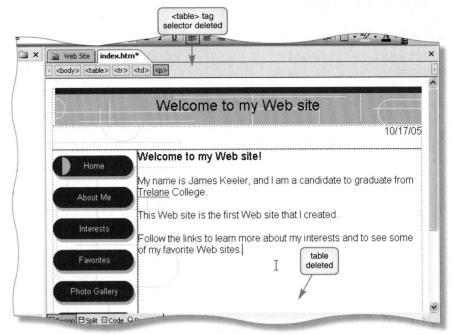

FIGURE 1-31

3

• **Use the scroll bar in Page view to scroll to the bottom of the Web page.**

The bottom of the Web page becomes visible (Figure 1-32).

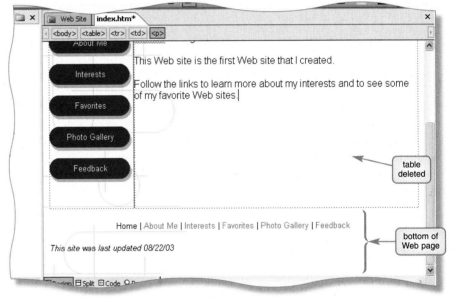

FIGURE 1-32

Other Ways

1. Select table, on Table menu click Delete Cells
2. Select table, press ALT+A, press D
3. Select table, press DELETE key
4. In Voice Command mode, say "Table, Delete Cells"

Editing a Bulleted List

In the previous steps, you edited the file, index.htm, which FrontPage created as the default Home page. To complete the Web site, you need to edit the other pages in the Web site. The template for the Interests page, for example, includes a bulleted list of interests for customization.

Recall that a bulleted list is an unordered list of items, which usually uses small icons called bullets to indicate each item in the list. In Design view, you can edit the bulleted list on the Interests page, changing, adding, and deleting items as needed to customize it to your interests. The following steps edit the bulleted list.

To Edit a Bulleted List

1

• **Double-click the file name, interest.htm, in the Folder List pane.**

The Interests page is displayed in Design view in the document window (Figure 1-33). The template for the Interests page includes a bulleted list of items; a bullet image precedes each item in the list. In the Folder List, a small pencil is displayed on the icon next to the file name, interest.htm, to indicate that the file is open. Also, tabs at the top of the page indicate the pages currently opened for editing.

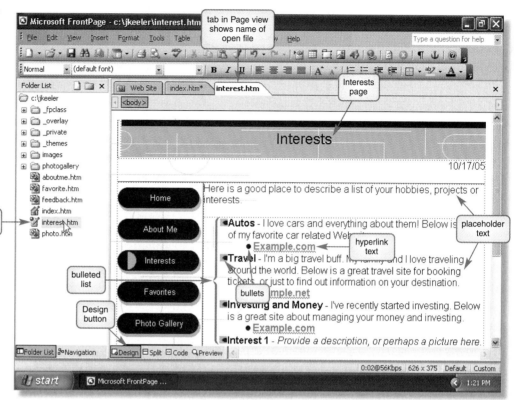

FIGURE 1-33

2

• **Drag through the first sentence of text that begins, Here is a good place, to select it.**

• **Type** What holds my interest in my chosen field of small-business marketing. **as the new text.**

The new text replaces the selected text (Figure 1-34).

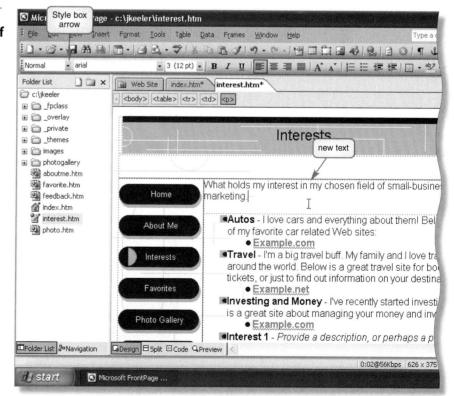

FIGURE 1-34

3

• **Drag through the text just entered to select it.**

• **Click the Style box arrow.**

• **If necessary, scroll down to Heading 3 in the Style list.**

FrontPage displays the Style list (Figure 1-35). It contains a list of styles for text, such as lists, headings, and normal text.

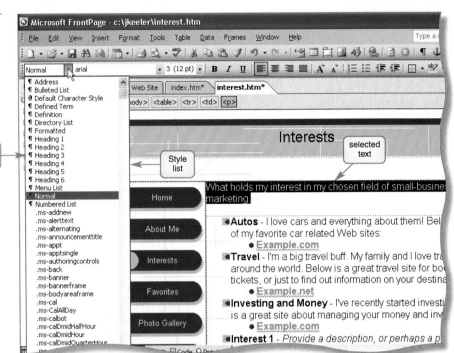

FIGURE 1-35

4

• **Click Heading 3 in the Style list.**

FrontPage displays the selected text with a style of Heading 3 (Figure 1-36).

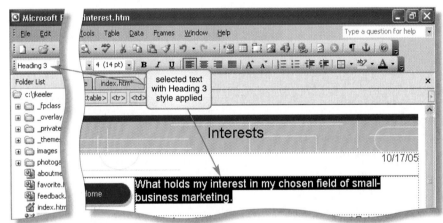

FIGURE 1-36

• **Drag through the text of the first line in the bulleted list to select it.**

• **Type** SBA - The first place to go for small business owners is the government's Small Business Association.

The new text replaces the placeholder text in the bulleted list (Figure 1-37).

FIGURE 1-37

6

• **Drag through the first hyperlink to select it and then type** sba.gov **as the new link.**

The new text replaces the hyperlink text in the bulleted list (Figure 1-38). The actual hyperlink has not changed, but will be modified later in this project.

FIGURE 1-38

7

• **Drag through the remaining lines of text in the bulleted list and their respective hyperlinks.**

FrontPage scrolls the Web page as you drag through the text. The remaining bullets become visible (Figure 1-39).

FIGURE 1-39

8

• **Type** Guerrilla Promotions - Inexpensive and creative marketing approaches work well on the local level for small business. I find Guerrilla marketing to be incredibly fun and it works.

• **Press the ENTER key.**

The new text replaces the placeholder text in the bulleted list (Figure 1-40). A third bullet is displayed below the last item in the list.

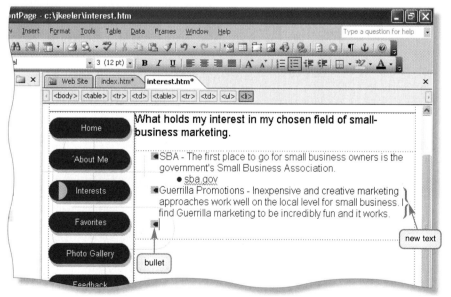

FIGURE 1-40

9

• **Type** Branding - I enjoy the creative processes involved in developing a brand and developing a branding strategy to be invigorating. **as the next item in the bulleted list.**

FrontPage displays the new text next to the bullet as the next item in the bulleted list (Figure 1-41).

FIGURE 1-41

10

• **Press the ENTER key.**

• **Type** Electronic Marketing - Technologies such as the Internet and multimedia have opened up new avenues for marketing products and services. I delve into as much new material regarding electronic marketing as I can get my hands on.

FrontPage displays the new text next to the bullet as the last item in the bulleted list (Figure 1-42).

FIGURE 1-42

11

• **Select the acronym, SBA, just after the first bullet (Figure 1-43).**

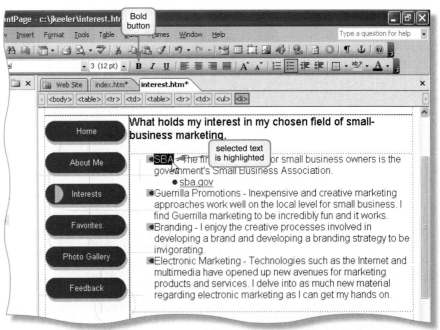

FIGURE 1-43

12

• **Click the Bold button on the Formatting toolbar.**

• **Select the phrase, Guerrilla Promotions, just after the second bullet.**

FrontPage displays the acronym SBA in bold text in the bulleted list (Figure 1-44). Guerilla Promotions is highlighted.

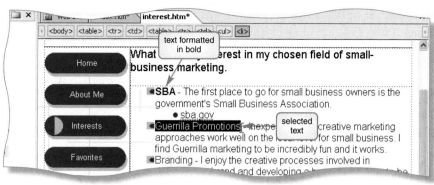

FIGURE 1-44

13

• **Repeat Step 12 to bold the words, Guerrilla Promotions, just after the second bullet; the word, Branding, just after the third bullet; and the words, Electronic Marketing, just after the fourth bullet.**

FrontPage displays the modified words in bold next to their respective bullets in the bulleted list (Figure 1-45).

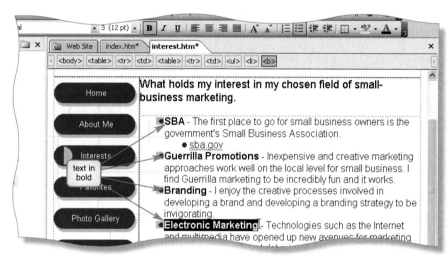

FIGURE 1-45

The previous steps edited the items in a bulleted list, deleted some items, added two items to the list, and modified some text properties. As you add text and make edits to a Web page, FrontPage automatically generates HTML source code that defines how the Web page will display on the Web.

The heading of a Web page is used to set apart document or section titles. Web browsers recognize six levels of headings, Heading 1 through Heading 6. Heading 1 (H1) produces the largest text and Heading 6 (H6) the smallest. The Style list shown in Figure 1-35 on page FP 36 shows the six levels of headings among the styles that you can apply to text on a Web page. The first several styles listed in the style list include standard styles recognized by most browsers. The styles lower in the list represent special styles associated with the theme applied to the current Web page.

To see how your changes will be displayed on the Web, you can click the Preview button at the bottom of the document window to preview the Web page. Before previewing the page, however, you should save your work to retain any changes.

Saving a Web Page

FrontPage allows you to save a Web page to many different locations, including the current Web site, a different Web site, or a location on your computer or a network. The steps on the next page save the Web page to the current Web site.

To Save a Web Page

1

• **If necessary, scroll up and then click anywhere in the first paragraph of the Web page to unselect the last bold term.**

The asterisk in the interest.htm tab indicates that the page needs to be saved (Figure 1-46).

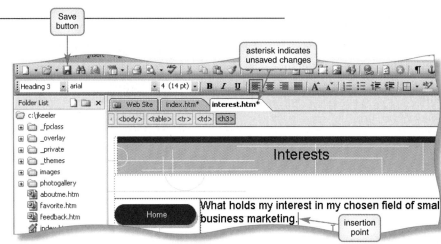

FIGURE 1-46

2

• **Click the Save button on the Standard toolbar.**

The Web page is saved in the jkeeler folder on drive C. Notice that the asterisk following the file name interest.htm in the tab has disappeared (Figure 1-47). The file name index.htm still has an asterisk, indicating that the page has changes that have not been saved yet.

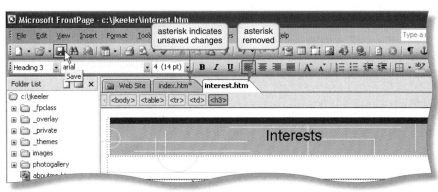

FIGURE 1-47

3

• **Click the index.htm tab at the top of the document window.**

• **Click the Save button on the Standard toolbar.**

Changes to the Home page are saved in the jkeeler folder on drive C (Figure 1-48).

FIGURE 1-48

Other Ways

1. On File menu click Save
2. Press CTRL+S
3. In Voice Command mode, say "File, Save"
4. Press ALT+F, S

Clicking the Save button on the Standard toolbar saves the active page in HTML format, using the default file name, interest.htm. Because the Web page was opened from the current Web site, FrontPage saves the page without prompting you for a file name or file location. If you save a new Web page, clicking the Save button will cause FrontPage to display a Save As dialog box that prompts you to enter a file name. When you save a Web page, FrontPage also will prompt you to save any new images, sound files, or other objects to the same location as the page.

Once you have saved a Web page, you can preview how the page will display when viewed on the World Wide Web.

Previewing a Web Page in Preview View

Clicking the Preview button allows you to preview your page as it will display when viewed by a site visitor. Using Preview view is a useful method of quickly checking changes you make to a Web page. Preview view does not require you to save changes to the page before previewing, so if a change does not work as expected, you do not need to undo your change. Rather, you simply can close the page without saving it. You also can preview the page in Page view. The following steps show how to preview the page in Preview view.

To Preview a Web Page in Preview View

1

• **In Page view, click the Preview button at the bottom of the document window.**

FrontPage displays the Web page in Preview view in Page view (Figure 1-49). In Preview view, you can see how the page will display on the Web when viewed with a Web browser.

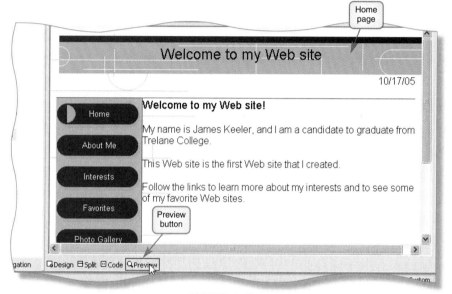

FIGURE 1-49

2

• **When you have finished viewing the Web page, click the interest.htm tab.**

• **When the interest.htm page appears, click the Preview button at the bottom of the document window.**

FrontPage displays the interest.htm Web page in Preview view (Figure 1-50).

3

• **When you have finished viewing the Web page, click the index.htm tab.**

• **Click the Design button.**

The Web page appears in Design view in Page view. With FrontPage, most Web page development and design takes place in Design view of Page view.

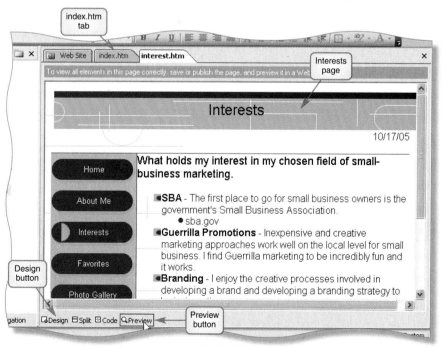

FIGURE 1-50

Other Ways

1. In Design view of Page view press CTRL+PAGE UP
2. In Code view of Page view press CTRL+PAGE DOWN

When you display a page in Preview view, a comment at the top of the document window may indicate that the page contains some elements that may need to be saved or published to preview correctly. Some elements, such as link bars, may not display properly until viewed on the Web. While it does not offer perfect viewing, using the Preview tab does eliminate the need to save a partially completed Web page continuously, preview it in your Web browser to test it, return to FrontPage to make changes, and so on.

Before you publish your Web site, you may want to add other elements to the page, such as a link bar or a graphical page banner. In FrontPage, you can add elements such as these using built-in FrontPage objects, called components.

Modifying Web Components

An active element, called a **Web component,** or just **component,** is a dynamic, built-in FrontPage object that is evaluated and executed when you save the page or, in some cases, when you display the page in a Web browser. Most Web components generate HTML automatically using the text, image files, and other items you supply. Examples of FrontPage Web components include a **Hit counter component** that keeps track of the number of visitors to a Web site and a **Photo Gallery component** that arranges a group of thumbnail images of photos on a page.

When working on a Web site, you easily can identify a component. Position the mouse pointer on the component and the shape of the pointer changes to look like a hand holding a written list.

A commonly used Web component is a link bar. In FrontPage, a **link bar** is a collection of graphical or textual buttons each containing a link to related Web pages in the current FrontPage Web site. The Capsules theme you applied to the Web site includes a link bar on the left side of the page. The link bar may be used for **parent-child navigation,** which allows you to move between the Home page (the parent) and the Interests page or Favorites page (the children), or for **same-level navigation,** which allows you to move back and forth between the Interests and Favorites pages. Another commonly used component is a **page banner,** which allows developers to add titles quickly to Web pages. The following steps modify the page banners in the index.htm and interest.htm pages. The page banner of the favorite.htm page will be updated later in this project.

To Modify a Page Banner

1

• **If necessary, scroll to the top of the Home page.**

• **Position the mouse pointer over the page banner component on the Home page.**

The mouse pointer changes shape to indicate that the designated item is a component (Figure 1-51).

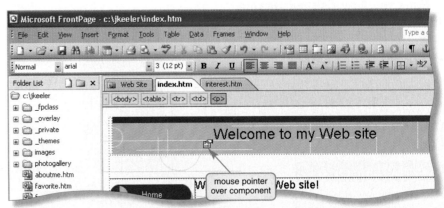

FIGURE 1-51

2

• **Right-click the page banner.**

FrontPage displays the shortcut menu (Figure 1-52).

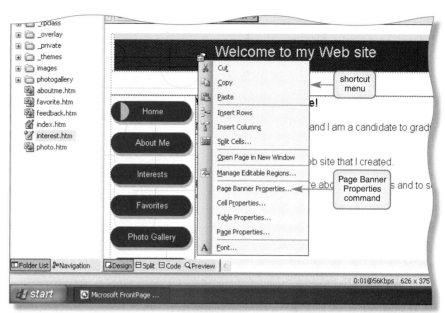

FIGURE 1-52

3

• **Click Page Banner Properties on the shortcut menu.**

• **When FrontPage displays the Page Banner Properties dialog box, select the text in the Page banner text box.**

• **Type** Welcome to James Keeler's Web Site **as the new text.**

• **If necessary, click Picture in the Properties area to select it.**

The new page banner text is entered (Figure 1-53).

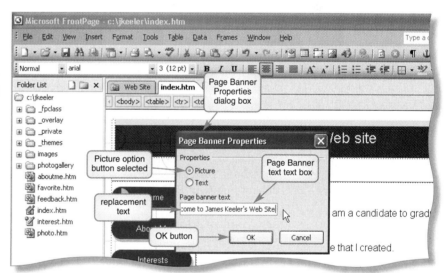

FIGURE 1-53

4

• **Click the OK button.**

FrontPage displays the modified page banner (Figure 1-54).

5

• **Click the interest.htm tab.**

• **Right-click the page banner.**

• **Click Page Banner Properties.**

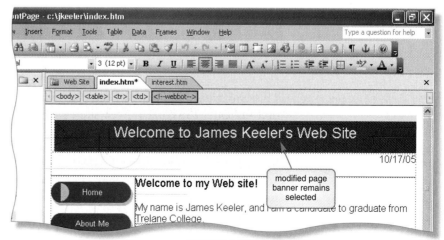

FIGURE 1-54

6

• **When FrontPage displays the Page Banner Properties dialog box, select the text in the Page banner text box, type** Professional Interests **as the new text, and then click the OK button.**

• **Click the first paragraph on the Web page.**

FrontPage displays the modified page banner and automatically modifies the text on the link button that links to the interest.htm page (Figure 1-55).

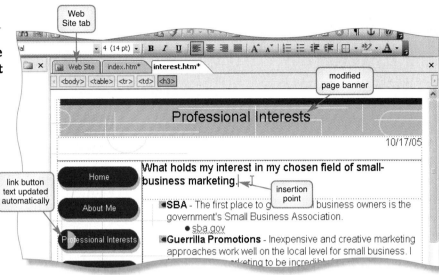

FIGURE 1-55

Different FrontPage components have different properties. The options that display in the component Properties dialog boxes vary, based on the properties of each specific component. Most FrontPage components change automatically in response to changes you make in the FrontPage Web site. The page banner just changed, for example, will display different text depending on the page title, on all pages where a page banner has been inserted and which have been included in your Web site navigation structure.

Deleting a Web Page from a Web Site

FrontPage provides several ways to delete pages from a current Web site. You can delete a page in Page view, for example, by selecting in the Folder List pane the file name of the page to delete and pressing the DELETE key. By holding down the CTRL key, you can select multiple files to delete at the same time. You also can delete individual pages in Navigation view by right-clicking the appropriate page icon and then clicking Delete on the shortcut menu. Finally, by selecting Navigation view in the Folder List pane, you can see a smaller Navigation pane in which you can select and delete individual pages. In this project, you will delete the Photo Gallery, Feedback, and About Me pages in Navigation view to create a Web site with three pages: a Home page, a Professional Interests page, and a Favorite Links page.

In FrontPage, **Navigation view** allows you to create, change, display, and print a Web site's structure and navigation. As previously discussed, a Web site's structure is the set of relationships among the pages in a FrontPage Web site; Navigation view includes a Navigation pane larger than the one displayed in the Folder List pane. This Navigation pane displays a graphical diagram similar to an organization chart that indicates the current Web site's structure. The Home page appears at the top (parent) level of the chart, and linked pages display at the lower (child) levels. You may choose to rotate the navigation structure to either a portrait or a landscape view by clicking the Portrait/Landscape button on the Navigation toolbar.

Making changes to the Web site's structure in Navigation view, such as deleting a page, allows you to see immediately how the change affects the structure. The following steps delete the Photo Gallery, Feedback, and About Me pages from the current Web site.

To Delete a Web Page from a Web Site

1

• **Click the Web Site tab.**
• **Click the Navigation button.**

FrontPage displays the current Web site in Navigation view, showing a graphical diagram of the Web site structure of the current Web site (Figure 1-56). A rectangular page icon represents each page in the Web site. The Folder List pane displays the file names for the pages in the Web site. The Navigation toolbar appears on the top-right of the Navigation pane. All buttons on the Formatting toolbar are dimmed, which indicates they currently are unavailable.

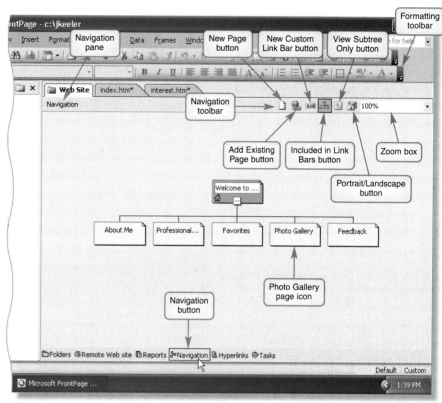

FIGURE 1-56

2

• **Right-click the Photo Gallery page icon.**

FrontPage displays a shortcut menu (Figure 1-57). The shortcut menu contains commands to manage individual pages within a FrontPage Web site.

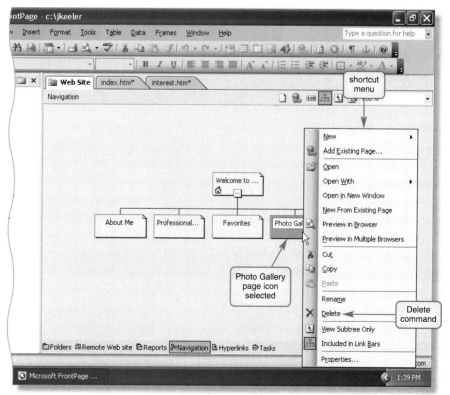

FIGURE 1-57

3

• **Click Delete on the shortcut menu.**

FrontPage displays the Delete Page dialog box, asking you what you want to do (Figure 1-58). The dialog box provides two options: you can remove this page from the navigation structure or delete the page from the Web site.

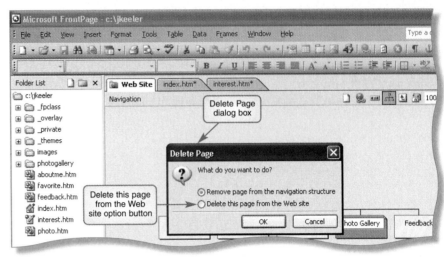

FIGURE 1-58

4

• **Click Delete this page from the Web site.**

FrontPage displays the Delete Page dialog box with the Delete this page from the Web site option button selected (Figure 1-59).

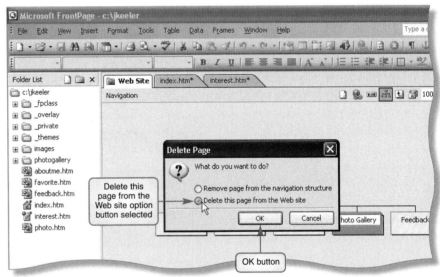

FIGURE 1-59

5

• **Click the OK button.**

After a few moments, FrontPage displays the Web site in Navigation view. The file name (photo.htm) is removed from the Folder List pane, and the Photo Gallery page icon is removed from the diagram of the Web site structure (Figure 1-60).

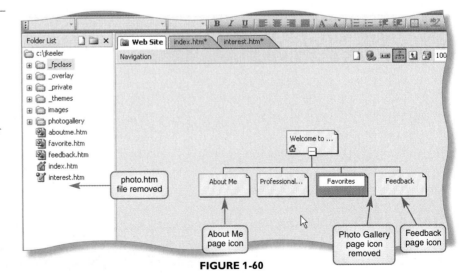

FIGURE 1-60

6

• **Repeat Steps 2 through 5 for the About Me page and the Feedback page.**

FrontPage displays the Web site in Navigation view with the About Me and the Feedback page icons removed. The file names aboutme.htm and feedback.htm are removed from the Folder List pane (Figure 1-61).

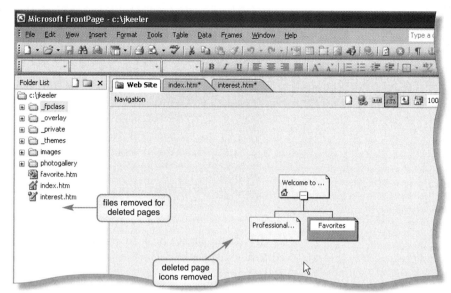

FIGURE 1-61

Other Ways

1. On Edit menu click Delete
2. Press ALT+E, O
3. Click file name in Folder List pane, press DELETE key
4. Right-click file name in Folder List pane, click Delete on shortcut menu
5. Click page icon in Navigation pane, press DELETE key
6. In Voice Command mode, say "Edit, Delete" or say "Delete"

If you choose to remove a Web page from the navigation structure, the Web page still exists on disk and can be linked to other pages. If you choose to delete a page from the Web site, as performed in the previous steps, the Web page is deleted from disk and removed from all link bars.

When you make changes to a Web site's navigation structure in Navigation view — for example, adding or deleting a page from the structure, or creating a new page — those changes are saved automatically when you switch to another view, such as Page view. You also can open files in Navigation view by double-clicking the page icon. Double-clicking the Favorites page icon, for example, will open the Favorites page so you can edit the final page in the current Web site.

Managing Hyperlinks on a Web Page

The final page to edit is the Favorites page, which contains hyperlinks to some of James Keeler's favorite Web sites. Because the Web site uses a template, the page already includes some placeholder hyperlinks. You can edit the links much like you edited the bulleted list on the Interests page.

Design Tip

Consider adding hyperlinks from key terms or phrases in the content on your page to other Web pages or external Web sites that include more information about the topic than you are willing to provide on your Web page.

Recall that a hyperlink, or link, is an area of the page that you click to instruct the browser to go to a location in a file or to request a file from a server. Often, a hyperlink consists of text or a picture that is associated with a URL that points to a page on the World Wide Web. Using FrontPage, you can create text or image links on your Web page. Adding a hyperlink to a Web page involves inserting text or an image on a Web page and then associating the text or image with a URL.

FrontPage provides several ways to associate a URL with the text or image on a Web page. You can type the URL, select a file within the current Web site or on your computer, or specify an e-mail link. You also can browse the Web to display the page to which you want to hyperlink; FrontPage automatically displays the URL in the appropriate text box.

> *Design Tip*
>
> If your Web page contains links to external Web sites, periodically check each link to be sure that the external Web site still exists or has not changed location. One of the more important elements of the World Wide Web is the ease of navigation to other sites through the use of hyperlinks.

To demonstrate how to manage hyperlinks on a Web page, the following steps edit the existing hyperlinks on the Favorites page and the Professional Interests page, and then add a new hyperlink. The page banner on the Favorites page also is changed to Favorite Links.

To Change a Hyperlink on a Web Page

1

• **Double-click the Favorites page icon in the Navigation pane.**

FrontPage displays the Favorites page in Page view (Figure 1-62). The vertical link bar consists of only three button links, because the Photo Gallery, About Me, and Feedback pages are deleted.

2

• **Right-click the page banner.**

• **Click Page Banner Properties.**

• **When FrontPage displays the Page Banner Properties dialog box, select the text in the Page banner text box, type** Favorite Links **as the new text, and then click the OK button.**

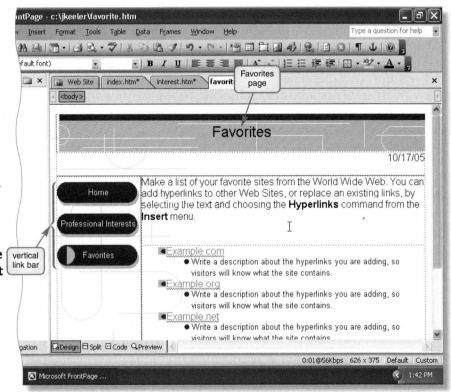

FIGURE 1-62

3

• **Select the first paragraph of text, which begins with, Make a list of your favorite sites.**

• **Click the Style box arrow on the Formatting toolbar and then click Heading 3.**

• **Type** These are some of my favorite sites on the World Wide Web.

• **Press the DELETE key once.**

The new text replaces the placeholder text and an extra blank line is deleted (Figure 1-63). The list entries are underlined, which identifies them as hyperlinks.

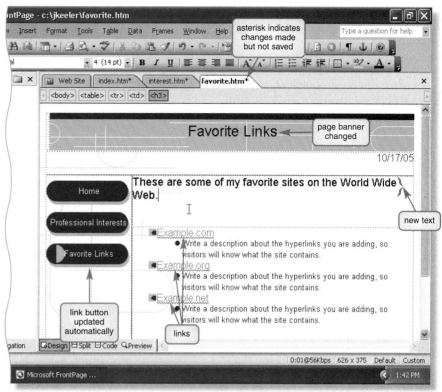

FIGURE 1-63

4

• **Right-click anywhere on the Example.com hyperlink.**

FrontPage displays a shortcut menu (Figure 1-64).

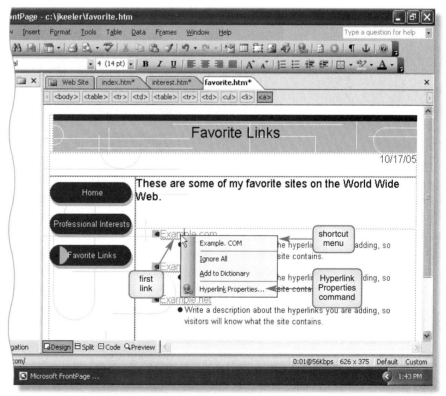

FIGURE 1-64

5

- **Click Hyperlink Properties on the shortcut menu.**

- **When FrontPage displays the Edit Hyperlink dialog box, select the text in the Text to display text box and then type** Guerrilla Marketing Online **as the new text.**

- **Select the text in the Address box and then type** http://www .gmarketing.com/main.html **as the new URL.**

FrontPage displays the Edit Hyperlink dialog box, with the new text to display for the hyperlink and the new URL, http://www .gmarketing.com/main.html, in the Address box (Figure 1-65). The Edit Hyperlink dialog box contains options that allow you to change the current URL and specify the URL of the Web resource to which you want to link.

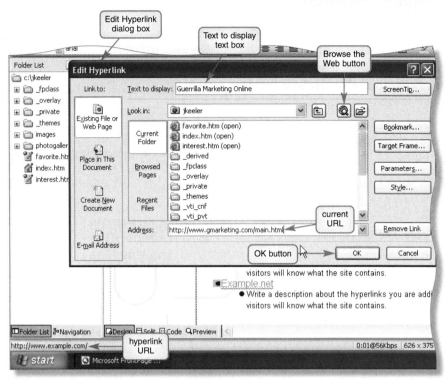
FIGURE 1-65

6

- **Click the OK button.**

FrontPage displays the new text for the hyperlink (Figure 1-66).

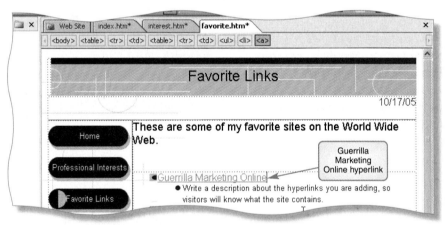
FIGURE 1-66

7

- **Below the first hyperlink, select the text that begins with, Write a description.**

- **Type** Includes all kinds of resources to get you started on the fundamentals and advanced strategies involved with guerrilla marketing.

The new text replaces the placeholder text (Figure 1-67).

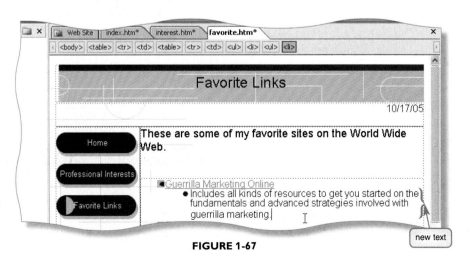
FIGURE 1-67

• **Repeat Steps 4 through 7 to replace the second hyperlink with the text** Marketing Survival Kit **that links to the URL** http://www .marketingsurvivalkit.com **and a description of** A great place to find marketing resources for small businesses.

• **Repeat Steps 4 through 7 to replace the third hyperlink with the text** Guitar Pro **that links to the URL** http://www.guitarpro .com **and a description of** When I need to relax, I find a new song to play on my guitar. I cannot read music, but Guitar Pro helps me sound fantastic.

The new text and hyperlinks replace the original placeholder text and hyperlinks (Figure 1-68).

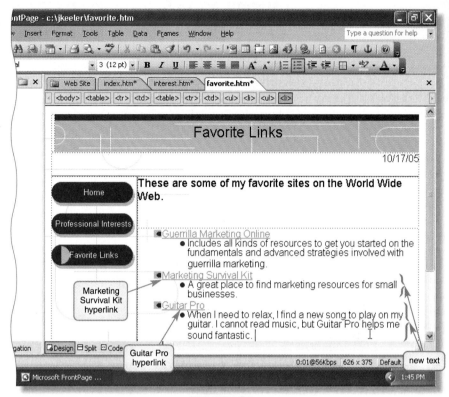

FIGURE 1-68

• **Click the Save button on the Standard toolbar to save changes.**

• **Click the interest.htm tab to view the Professional Interests page.**

• **Select the sba.gov link and then click the Insert Hyperlink button on the Standard toolbar.**

• **Type** http://www.sba.gov **as the address for the hyperlink.**

FrontPage displays the hyperlink (Figure 1-69).

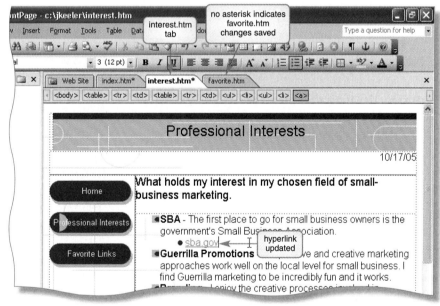

FIGURE 1-69

You also can edit a URL by clicking the Browse the Web button in the Edit Hyperlink dialog box and browsing the Web to locate the Web resource to which you want to link. Once the desired page is displayed in the browser window, return to FrontPage with the browser still open and the browser automatically will return the URL of the current page to the Address box.

Other Ways

1. Click Insert Hyperlink button on Standard toolbar
2. Click hyperlink to select it, press CTRL+K
3. In Voice Command mode, say "Insert, Hyperlink"

Adding an E-Mail Hyperlink to a Web Page

Using the Edit Hyperlink dialog box, you also can create e-mail hyperlinks on a Web page. When a user clicks an **e-mail hyperlink** on your Web page, the Web browser will start the designated e-mail program, such as Microsoft Outlook, and prompt the user to enter a message. The message automatically is addressed to the e-mail address specified in the e-mail hyperlink. Many Web pages include e-mail hyperlinks to allow visitors to send questions, comments, or requests via e-mail, simply by clicking the e-mail hyperlink.

> *Design Tip*
>
> Build into your Web pages simple and convenient ways for Web site visitors to interact with you or your organization.

E-mail hyperlinks use the **mailto protocol**, which is an Internet protocol used to send electronic mail. Because not all Web browsers and e-mail programs support the mailto protocol, you should specify the e-mail address somewhere on the Web page. The easiest way to do this is to use the e-mail address as the hyperlink text for the e-mail hyperlink. The following steps add an e-mail hyperlink to a Web page.

To Add an E-Mail Hyperlink to a Web Page

• **Click the Save button on the Standard toolbar to save the interest.htm Web page.**

• **Click the index.htm tab in Page view.**

• **Position the insertion point at the end of the fourth paragraph, which begins, Follow the links to learn more about.**

• **Press the ENTER key.**

• **Type** You may send an e-mail to me at jkeeler@ trelanecollege.edu.

FrontPage displays the Home page in Page view (Figure 1-70). Using the e-mail address as the e-mail hyperlink text provides a quick way for users to identify your e-mail address.

FIGURE 1-70

2

• **Drag through the text, jkeeler@trelanecollege.edu, to select it.**

• **Click the Insert Hyperlink button on the Standard toolbar.**

• **When FrontPage displays the Insert Hyperlink dialog box, click the E-mail Address button.**

• **Type** `jkeeler@trelanecollege.edu` **in the E-mail address text box.**

FrontPage displays the Insert Hyperlink dialog box and displays the complete e-mail hyperlink in the E-mail address text box (Figure 1-71). FrontPage automatically adds the mailto protocol before the e-mail address. It instructs the Web browser to start the designated e-mail program and address the message to the indicated e-mail address.

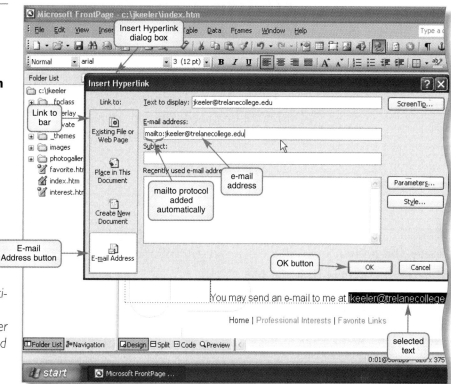

FIGURE 1-71

3

• **Click the OK button.**

• **Position the mouse pointer on the e-mail hyperlink.**

The e-mail hyperlink is displayed on the Home page. The URL for the e-mail hyperlink is displayed on the status bar, using the mailto protocol before the e-mail address, jkeeler@trelanecollege.edu (Figure 1-72).

4

• **Click the Save button on the Standard toolbar.**

The modified page is saved on disk as part of the current Web site. The asterisk in the tab of the modified page is removed.

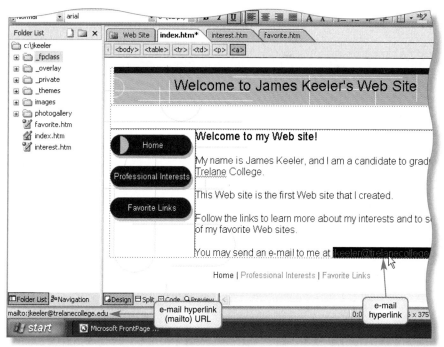

FIGURE 1-72

You now have included two new types of text hyperlinks — hyperlinks to other Web pages on the Favorite Links and Professional Interests pages, and an e-mail hyperlink on the Home page.

Printing a Web Page Using FrontPage

After you have created a Web page and saved it on disk, you may want to print the page. A printed version of a document — in this case, a Web page — is called a **hard copy** or **printout**.

To print a page in Page view, you open the Web page so it is displayed in the document window and then click the Print button on the Standard toolbar. After you print the first page, you can open additional pages to print the remaining pages in the Web site. The following steps print the Home page of the personal Web site.

To Print a Web Page

1

• **Ready the printer.**

• **If necessary, double-click the file name, index.htm, in the Folder List pane or click the index.htm tab at the top of the document window to display the Home page in Page view.**

• **Click File on the menu bar.**

FrontPage displays the File menu (Figure 1-73).

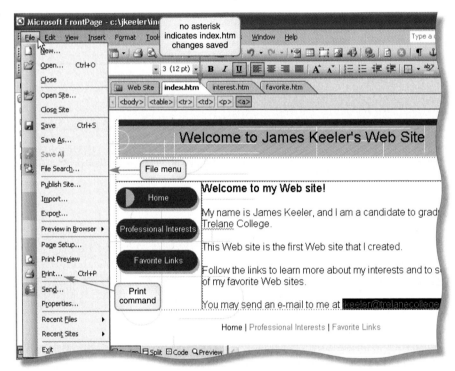

FIGURE 1-73

2

• **Click Print.**

FrontPage displays the Print dialog box (Figure 1-74). The All option button in the Print range area is selected, indicating that the entire document will print, regardless of its length.

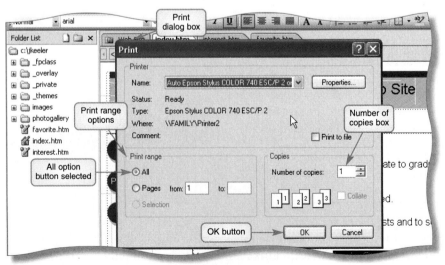

FIGURE 1-74

3

• **Click the OK button.**

The FrontPage message box is displayed momentarily, showing the status of the print process. The Home page is printed (Figure 1-75). FrontPage prints hyperlinks and images on the Web page as they are displayed in Design view of Page view.

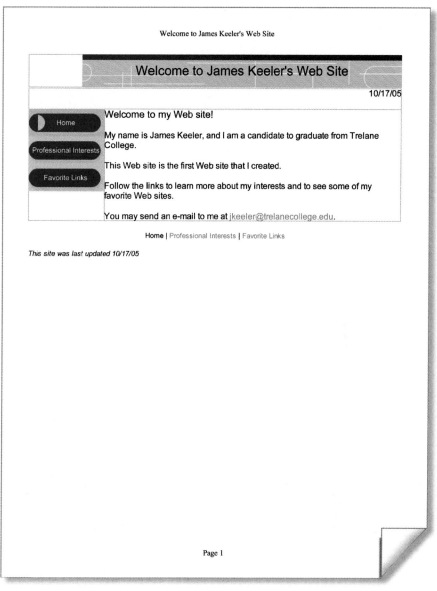

FIGURE 1-75

The Print dialog box in Figure 1-74 provides many printing options. In the Print range area, the All option button instructs FrontPage to print the entire document. The Pages option button lets you print selected pages of a multiple-page document. The Number of copies box allows you to specify the number of copies to print.

To print the Web page as shown in Figure 1-75, the Web page must display in Page view Design view. FrontPage also allows you to print the HTML source for a home page. To print the HTML source for a home page, click the Code button to display the Web page in Code view and then print the page. You cannot, however, print a Web page in Page view Preview view. When the page appears in Preview view, FrontPage disables the printing function.

Other Ways

1. Click Print button on Standard toolbar
2. Press CTRL+P, click OK button
3. Press ALT+F, P
4. In Voice Command mode, say "File, Print"

More About

Publishing a Web Page

FrontPage allows you to choose from options that allow you to publish only changed Web pages or publish all Web pages, which overwrites all previously published Web pages with the most recent versions. Click the Remote Web Site Properties button in Remote Web site view. When the Remote Web Site Properties dialog box is displayed, click the Publishing tab, and then select the desired options.

Publishing a FrontPage Web Site

If you have access to a Web server, FrontPage provides an easy way to publish your Web pages to the World Wide Web. As previously mentioned, **publishing a Web page** is the process of sending copies of Web pages, image files, multimedia files, and any folders to a Web server. Once saved on the Web server, the Web pages and files are available on the World Wide Web. With FrontPage, you use the Remote Web site view on the Web Site tab to manage the publishing process.

Many schools and companies provide a small amount of space on their Web servers for students and employees to publish personal Web pages and related files. For a modest fee, most Internet service providers (ISPs) also will provide space for publishing personal Web pages. An **Internet service provider** (**ISP**) is an organization that has a permanent connection to the Internet and provides temporary connections to individuals and companies for a fee. Some other Web-based services, such as Tripod, provide space on their Web servers for individuals to publish personal Web pages. To pay for the cost of maintaining these servers, these companies place advertisements at the top or bottom of your personal Web pages.

To publish your Web site to the World Wide Web, you will need access to an ISP or a Web server at your college, home, or office, preferably one with Microsoft FrontPage Server Extensions installed. Without FrontPage Server Extensions, some functionality in your Web site may not be available, such as most form handlers, hit counters, and other component features. With the server extensions, FrontPage will maintain your files and hyperlinks, comparing your local files with those on the server and updating any changes the next time you publish the Web site. Also, with the server extensions installed, FrontPage can publish your Web site using HTTP (Hypertext Transfer Protocol). Without the server extensions, your can publish your Web site using **FTP** (**File Transfer Protocol**), **WebDAV** (**Distributed Authoring and Versioning**), or a file system, such as the C: drive on your computer. Both HTTP and FTP are methods of transferring files over the Internet. Table 1-4 lists the types of servers to which FrontPage publishes Web sites and the situations in which you use each.

Table 1-4 Remote Web Server Types		
TYPE	DESCRIPTION	WHEN TO USE
FrontPage or SharePoint Services	Allows for the greatest flexibility and functionality when publishing FrontPage Web sites. The server must be running FrontPage 2000 Server Extensions or later, or SharePoint Team Services 1.0 or later.	Used when a server supports the FrontPage Extensions or the server is a SharePoint server. When synchronizing files to a SharePoint server, some elements may not be transferred because SharePoint Team Services handles the functionality in a different manner than the FrontPage Server Extensions.
WebDAV	WebDAV (Distributed Authoring and Versioning) is a protocol for publishing and managing files on a Web server. WebDAV can allow you to work with a folder on a Web server in much the same way you work with a folder on a local hard disk. You must know the server name, user name, and password for the WebDAV site.	Used when a server does not support the FrontPage Server Extensions but does support WebDAV.
FTP	FTP (File Transfer Protocol) is a standard protocol for transferring files over the Web. You must know the server name, user name, and password for the FTP site.	Used when a server does not support the FrontPage Server Extensions but does support FTP.
File System	A local or networked folder.	Used to make backup copies of a Web site while maintaining the site's structure and allowing components to be used.

The following steps show how to publish a FrontPage Web site to a Web server that uses FrontPage Server Extensions. These steps work only if you have an account that grants you publishing rights on a Web server. To ensure that you publish your personal Web site successfully, be sure to substitute the URL of your own Web server when you see the URL, http://www.trelanecollege.edu/~jkeeler, in the following steps. If you do not know which URL or account information to use, see your instructor for more information. If you do not have access to a server, choose the File System Web server type in the steps below and then select an appropriate folder on your hard disk in which to publish the files. For information regarding publishing a FrontPage Web site to a file system, see Appendix C on page APP 23.

More About

Quick Reference

For more information, see the Quick Reference Summary at the back of this book, or visit the FrontPage 2003 Quick Reference Web page (scsite.com/fp2003/qr).

To Publish a FrontPage Web Site

1

• **If necessary, save any unsaved pages.**

• **Click the Publish Site button on the Standard toolbar.**

• **If necessary, click the Remote Web server type as directed by your instructor.**

FrontPage displays the Remote Web Site Properties dialog box and changes the view to Remote Web site on the Web Site tab (Figure 1-76). The Remote Web site location box displays the URL of the location where FrontPage will publish the current Web site.

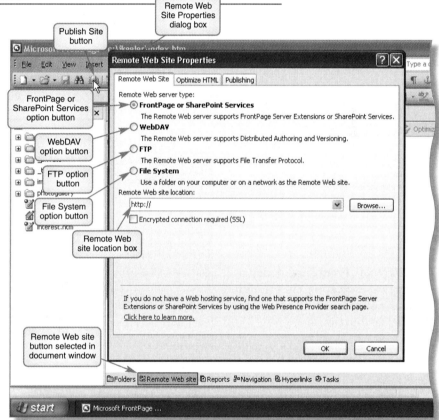

FIGURE 1-76

2

• **Click the Remote Web site location box and then type** http://www.trelanecollege.edu /~jkeeler **for the URL. Be sure to substitute your own URL when you see the URL, http://www .trelanecollege.edu/~jkeeler.**

FrontPage displays the destination URL in the Remote Web site location box (Figure 1-77).

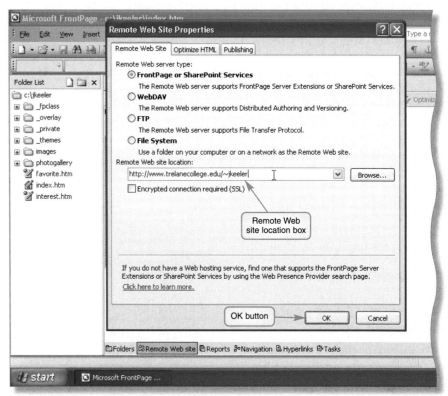

FIGURE 1-77

3

• **Click the OK button.**

• **If a Microsoft FrontPage dialog box appears indicating that a Web site does not exist at the location, click the Yes button.**

FrontPage displays the Connect to dialog box (Figure 1-78). This dialog box requests authorization information to allow you to publish your Web site to the server entered in the Remote Web site location box in Step 2.

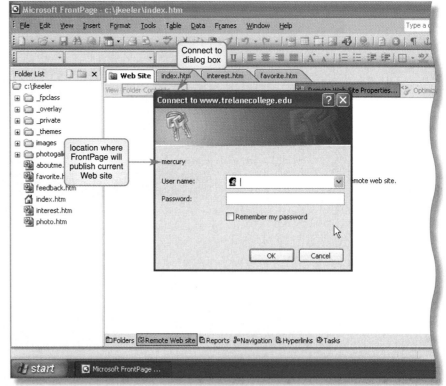

FIGURE 1-78

4

• **Type your name in the User name text box, and then type your password in the Password text box.**

FrontPage displays asterisks for the entered password for security purposes (Figure 1-79).

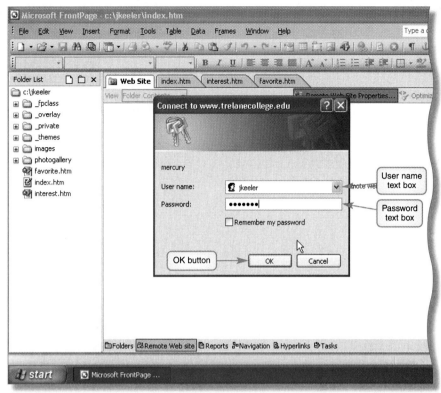

FIGURE 1-79

5

• **Click the OK button.**

The Web site appears in Remote Web site view and displays a list of files included in the current Web site and the Remote Web site (Figure 1-80). In Remote Web site view, FrontPage synchronizes files between this Web site and a remote site. Arrows indicate the files that are not yet on the remote Web site. The status area indicates the last time the Web site was published and includes hyperlinks and buttons that allow you to control the publishing process. If your Web server does not have the FrontPage Server Extensions installed, you will need to use another location to publish the Web site.

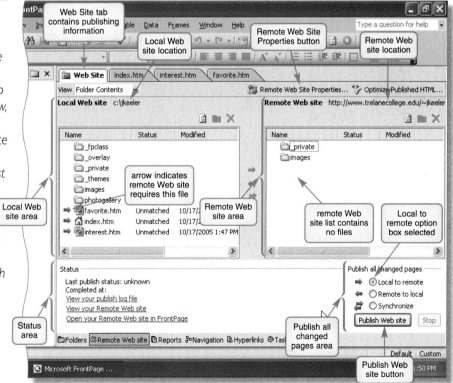

FIGURE 1-80

6

• **Click the Publish Web site button.**

A FrontPage dialog box displays a status bar indicating the progress of the file transfer. When FrontPage has finished publishing the Web site, the status area is updated and provides links you can click to view your published Web site and a log of files published. FrontPage updates the Remote Web site file list and removes the arrows next to the files in the Local Web site list (Figure 1-81).

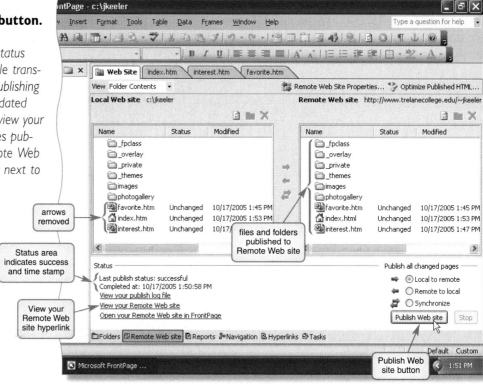

FIGURE 1-81

Other Ways

1. On File menu click Publish Site
2. Press ALT+F, U
3. Click Web Site tab at top of View pane, click Remote Web site button
4. In Voice Command mode, say "File, Publish Site"

Q: Can I change the header and footer that print when FrontPage prints a Web page?

A: Yes. When you print a Web page, a header and footer are included by default on each page. To change the header or the footer, or to change the print margins, click File on the menu bar, and then click Page Setup before printing or previewing. When the Print Page Setup dialog box is displayed, you may enter new values for these items.

Of the many files FrontPage will transfer, most of them contain elements in the Capsules theme selected for the Web site. The publishing process may take a few minutes, depending on the number of files in the Web site and the speed of your connection.

FrontPage remembers the location to which it published the current Web site, so the next time you click the Publish Site button on the Standard toolbar, FrontPage will publish to the previous location automatically. To publish to a new location or use a different method to publish, you can click the Remote Web Site Properties button in Remote Web site view. To manage the publishing process once the remote Web site is set up, display the Web site in Remote Web site view on the Web Site tab.

The three buttons between the Local Web site file list and the Remote Web site file list allow you to publish files selectively. You can publish files from the Local Web site to the Remote Web site or from the Remote Web site to the Local Web site. You may want to publish from the Remote Web site to the Local Web site if other FrontPage users are updating the Web site and you want to copy their changed files to your Local Web site.

Testing the FrontPage Web Site

With the Web site published, it is available to anyone on the World Wide Web. You should take the time to test the newly published Web site to ensure the pages look as you expected and the hyperlinks work. The following steps test the personal Web site.

To Test a FrontPage Web Site

1

• **Click the View your Remote Web site link (see Figure 1-81).**

The Internet Explorer window is opened and displays the Home page of the Web site in the browser window (Figure 1-82).

FIGURE 1-82

2

• **If necessary, click the Maximize button on the Internet Explorer title bar.**

• **Click the Favorite Links hyperlink on the link bar.**

The browser displays the Favorite Links page (Figure 1-83). The link bar displays the button hyperlink to the Favorite Links page in a different color than that of the button hyperlinks to the Home page and to the Professional Interests page. This is done to indicate that it links to the currently displayed page.

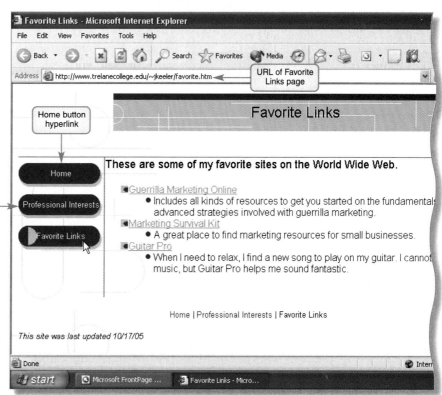

FIGURE 1-83

3

• **Click the Professional Interests button on the link bar.**

The browser displays the Professional Interests page (Figure 1-84). The link bar displays a button hyperlink to the Favorite Links page, which is located at the same level as the Professional Interests page. The link bar also includes a button hyperlink to the Home page, which is located at the parent level.

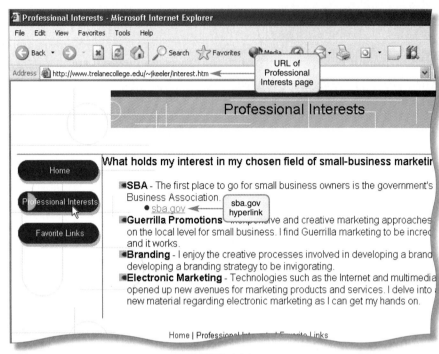

FIGURE 1-84

4

• **Click the sba.gov hyperlink.**

The Small Business Association home page is displayed in the Internet Explorer window (Figure 1-85).

5

• **Click the Back button to return to the Professional Interests page.**

• **After viewing all Web pages for accuracy and ensuring the hyperlinks function properly, click the Close button on the Internet Explorer title bar to close the browser.**

The Internet Explorer window is closed. The FrontPage window is displayed in Remote Web site view.

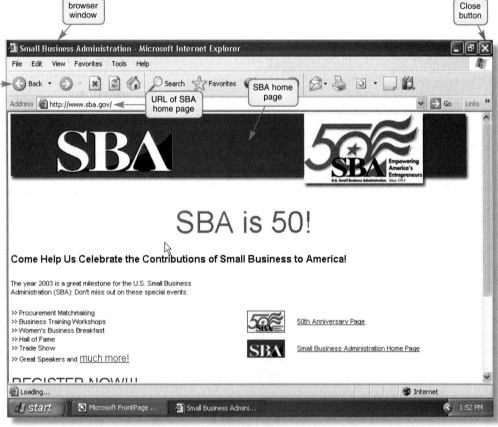

FIGURE 1-85

When you first link to your published Web site, the Web server displays a default Web page, called index.htm, in the URL in the Address bar. In your personal Web site, the Home page uses the file name, index.htm, and thus is displayed as the default page.

FrontPage Help System

At any time while you are using FrontPage, you can get answers to questions using the FrontPage Help system. You can activate the FrontPage Help system by using the Type a question for help box on the menu bar, by clicking the Microsoft Office FrontPage Help button on the Standard toolbar, or by clicking Help on the menu bar (Figure 1-86). Used properly, this form of online assistance can increase your productivity and reduce your frustrations by minimizing the time you spend learning how to use FrontPage.

The following section shows how to get answers to your questions using the Type a question for help box. Additional information on using the FrontPage Help system is available in Appendix A.

More About

The FrontPage Help System

The best way to become familiar with the FrontPage Help system is to use it. Appendix A includes detailed information on the FrontPage Help system and exercises that will help you gain confidence in using it.

Obtaining Help Using the Type a Question for Help Box on the Menu Bar

The Type a question for help box on the right side of the menu bar lets you type free-form questions such as, how do I save or how do I create a template, phrases such as, save a Web page or print a Web page, or key terms such as, copy, save, or formatting. FrontPage responds by displaying a list of topics related to the question or terms you entered in the Search Results task pane. The following steps show how to use the Type a question for help box to obtain information on saving a Web page.

To Obtain Help Using the Type a Question for Help Box

1

• **Type** save a Web page **in the Type a question for help box on the right side of the menu bar (Figure 1-86).**

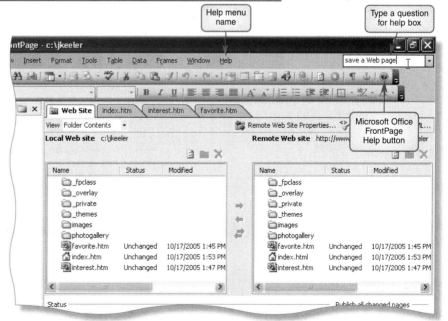

FIGURE 1-86

2

* **Press the ENTER key.**

* **If necessary, scroll the Search Results task pane, and then click the link Save a Web page.**

FrontPage displays the Search Results task pane with a list of topics related to the term, save. FrontPage found 30 search results (Figure 1-87). When the Save a Web page link is clicked, FrontPage opens the Microsoft Office FrontPage Help window on the right side of the screen.

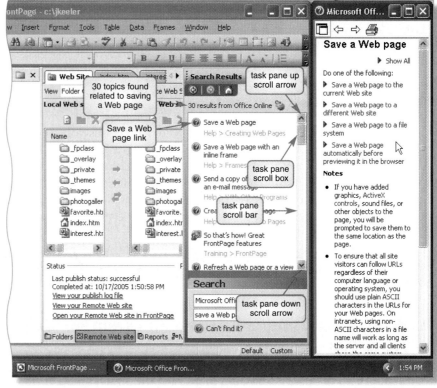

FIGURE 1-87

3

* **Double-click the Microsoft Office FrontPage Help title bar to maximize it.**

* **Click the Show All link on the right side of the Microsoft Office FrontPage Help window to expand the links in the window.**

FrontPage maximizes the Microsoft Office FrontPage Help window that provides Help information about saving Web pages to different locations (Figure 1-88). The links in the window are expanded.

4

* **Click the Close button on the Microsoft Office FrontPage Help window title bar.**

* **Click the Close button on the Search Results task pane.**

The Microsoft Office FrontPage Help window closes.

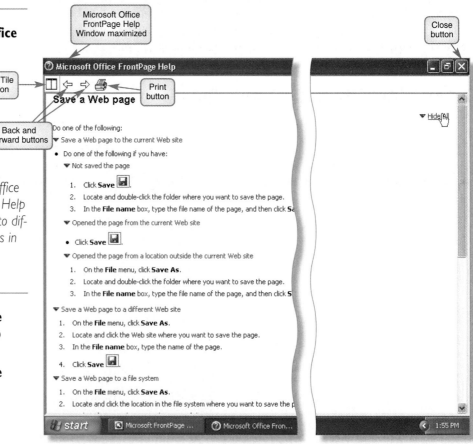

FIGURE 1-88

Use the buttons in the upper-left corner of the Microsoft Office FrontPage Help window (Figure 1-88) to navigate through the Help system, change the display, and print the contents of the window.

As you enter questions and terms in the Type a question for help box, FrontPage adds them to its list. Thus, if you click the Type a question for help box arrow (Figure 1-86 on page FP 63), FrontPage will display a list of previously entered questions and terms.

Closing a Web Site and Quitting FrontPage

After you have finished the steps in the project and developed and published the personal Web site, you can close the Web site and quit FrontPage. If you do not close a Web site in FrontPage, then FrontPage automatically opens the Web site the next time you start FrontPage. The following steps close the Web site and quit FrontPage.

More About

Quitting FrontPage 2003

Try to get into the habit of closing the last Web page or Web site that you work on before quitting FrontPage. FrontPage will open the last Web page or Web site that you worked on when it starts the next time.

To Close a Web Site and Quit FrontPage

1 Click File on the menu bar and then click Close Site.

2 Click the Close button on the right side of the FrontPage title bar (see Figure 1-86).

3 If necessary, click the Close button on the Internet Explorer title bar to quit Internet Explorer.

The FrontPage window closes.

Project Summary

With Project 1 complete, you developed a personal Web site and published the pages to a personal Web server. In this project, you learned the basic World Wide Web concepts, including HTML and the elements of a Web page. You learned how to create a FrontPage Web site using a template, to apply a theme, and to edit the place-holder text on a template page. You also learned how to modify a bulleted list, modify a FrontPage component, and edit and add hyperlinks on a Web page, including an e-mail hyperlink. You gained an understanding of how to use the view buttons in Page view to edit page layout and to preview a Web page. You learned how to use Navigation view to display and modify the structure of a Web site. Finally, you learned how to print Web pages, publish a Web site to the World Wide Web, and test the site in a browser.

What You Should Know

Having completed this project, you should be able to perform the tasks below. The tasks are listed in the same order they were presented in this project. For a list of the buttons, menus, toolbars, and commands introduced in this project, see the Quick Reference Summary at the back of this book and refer to the Page Number column.

1. Start and Customize FrontPage   (FP 14)
2. Use a Template to Create a FrontPage Web Site   (FP 21)
3. Open a Web Page in Page View   (FP 24)
4. Apply a Theme to a FrontPage Web Site   (FP 26)
5. Edit Text on a Web Page   (FP 28)
6. Add New Text to a Web Page   (FP 30)
7. Select Tables and Cells   (FP 32)
8. Delete a Selected Table   (FP 33)
9. Edit a Bulleted List   (FP 35)
10. Save a Web Page   (FP 40)
11. Preview a Web Page in Preview View   (FP 41)
12. Modify a Page Banner   (FP 42)
13. Delete a Web Page from a Web Site   (FP 45)
14. Change a Hyperlink on a Web Page   (FP 48)
15. Add an E-Mail Hyperlink to a Web Page   (FP 52)
16. Print a Web Page   (FP 54)
17. Publish a FrontPage Web Site   (FP 57)
18. Test a FrontPage Web Site   (FP 61)
19. Obtain Help Using the Type a Question for Help Box   (FP 63)
20. Close a Web Site and Quit FrontPage   (FP 65)

Learn It Online

Instructions: To complete the Learn It Online exercises, start your browser, click the Address bar, and then enter the Web address scsite.com/fp2003/learn. When the FrontPage 2003 Learn It Online page is displayed, follow the instructions in the exercises below. Each exercise has instructions for printing your results, either for your own records or for submission to your instructor.

1 Project Reinforcement TF, MC, and SA

Below FrontPage Project 1, click the Project Reinforcement link. Print the quiz by clicking Print on the File menu for each page. Answer each question.

2 Flash Cards

Below FrontPage Project 1, click the Flash Cards link and read the instructions. Type 20 (or a number specified by your instructor) in the Number of playing cards text box, type your name in the Enter your Name text box, and then click the Flip Card button. When the flash card is displayed, read the question and then click the ANSWER box arrow to select an answer. Flip through Flash Cards. If your score is 15 (75%) correct or greater, click Print on the File menu to print your results. If your score is less than 15 (75%) correct, then redo this exercise by clicking the Replay button.

3 Practice Test

Below FrontPage Project 1, click the Practice Test link. Answer each question, enter your first and last name at the bottom of the page, and then click the Grade Test button. When the graded practice test is displayed on your screen, click Print on the File menu to print a hard copy. Continue to take practice tests until you score 80% or better.

4 Who Wants To Be a Computer Genius?

Below FrontPage Project 1, click the Computer Genius link. Read the instructions, enter your first and last name at the bottom of the page, and then click the PLAY button. When your score is displayed, click the PRINT RESULTS link to print a hard copy.

5 Wheel of Terms

Below FrontPage Project 1, click the Wheel of Terms link. Read the instructions, and then enter your first and last name and your school name. Click the PLAY button. When your score is displayed, right-click the score and then click Print on the shortcut menu to print a hard copy.

6 Crossword Puzzle Challenge

Below FrontPage Project 1, click the Crossword Puzzle Challenge link. Read the instructions, and then enter your first and last name. Click the SUBMIT button. Work the crossword puzzle. When you are finished, click the Submit button. When the crossword puzzle is redisplayed, click the Print Puzzle button to print a hard copy.

7 Tips and Tricks

Below FrontPage Project 1, click the Tips and Tricks link. Click a topic that pertains to Project 1. Right-click the information and then click Print on the shortcut menu. Construct a brief example of what the information relates to in FrontPage to confirm you understand how to use the tip or trick.

8 Newsgroups

Below FrontPage Project 1, click the Newsgroups link. Click a topic that pertains to Project 1. Print three comments.

9 Expanding Your Horizons

Below FrontPage Project 1, click the Articles for Microsoft FrontPage link. Click a topic that pertains to Project 1. Print the information. Construct a brief example of what the information relates to in FrontPage to confirm you understand the contents of the article.

10 Search Sleuth

Below FrontPage Project 1, click the Search Sleuth link. To search for a term that pertains to this project, select a term below the Project 1 title and then use the Google search engine at google.com (or any major search engine) to display and print two Web pages that present information on the term.

11 FrontPage Online Training

Below FrontPage Project 1, click the FrontPage Online Training link. When your browser displays the Microsoft Office Online Web page, click the FrontPage link. Click one of the FrontPage courses that covers one or more of the objectives listed at the beginning of the project on page FP 4. Print the first page of the course before stepping through it.

12 Office Marketplace

Below FrontPage Project 1, click the Office Marketplace link. When your browser displays the Microsoft Office Online Web page, click the Office Marketplace link. Click a topic that relates to FrontPage. Print the first page.

Apply Your Knowledge

1 Modifying a Corporate Presence Web Site

Instructions: Start FrontPage. Open the file, index.htm, from the Project1/Apply1-1Ship-It-Here folder on the Data Disk. See the inside back cover of this book for instructions for downloading the Data Disk or see your instructor for information on accessing the files required in this book.

1. If necessary, close the new_page_1.htm page. If necessary, double-click the file index.htm in the Folder List pane to display the Ship-It-Here Home page in Page view.
2. Click the link bar component in the top-left of the page just below the image and above the Home banner to select it. Press the DELETE key three times to delete the link bar component and to move the graphic to the top of the page.
3. Click the fourth item in the bulleted list to select it and then type The widest range of shipping materials at the lowest cost as the new text.
4. Press the ENTER key to add a fifth item in the bulleted list and then type Expert advice on protecting and insuring your goods as the new text.
5. Select the heading, Our Mission, and then type Our Destination as the new text.
6. Scroll down. Position the insertion point after the word, Sales: in the Electronic mail section, and then type manager@shipithereinc.com as the e-mail hyperlink text. Create an e-mail hyperlink that sends e-mail to manager@shipithereinc.com.
7. Click the Preview button to preview the Web page. After you have previewed the page, click the Design button.
8. Print and then save the Web page.
9. Double-click the file products.htm in the Folder List pane to display the Products Web page in Page view.
10. Double-click the link bar component on the left side of the page. If necessary, edit the properties to include hyperlinks at the child level. Select the Home page check box and the Parent page check box.
11. Double-click the Products page banner component. To edit the page banner text, type Shipping Supplies as the new text.
12. If you have access to a Web server, publish the Web site and preview the Web site in your browser. Figure 1-89 shows the Web site as it should appear in the Web browser. Print and save the Web page, close the Web site, and then close FrontPage. Hand in the printouts to your instructor.

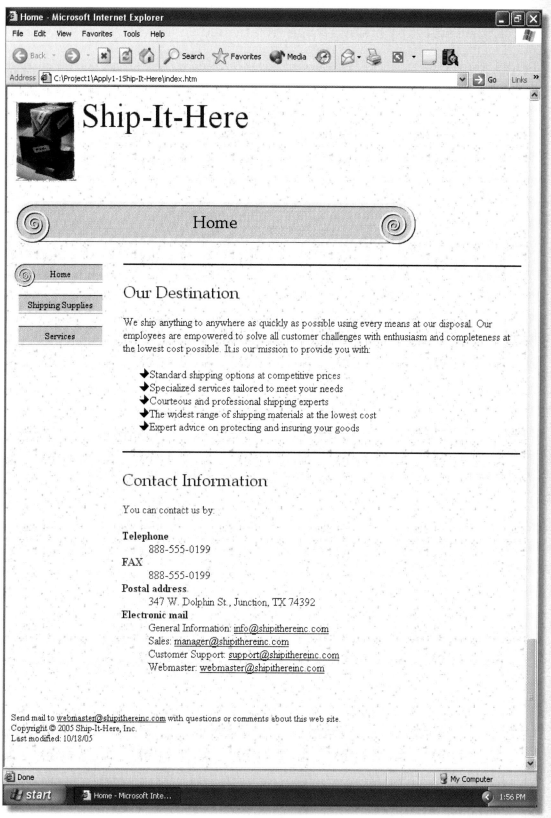

FIGURE 1-89

In the Lab

1 Creating and Modifying a One-Page Web Site

Problem: To help customers find support information for your company's products, you decide to develop a one-page Web site with commonly needed support information. The page should include a description of the company's quality philosophy, support options available through the company, one or more links to Web sites related to the products, and your contact information.

Instructions: Perform the following tasks.

1. Create a new Web site using the One Page Web Site template. In the Web Site Templates dialog box, click One Page Web Site and then type C:\Project1\Lab1-1Whalen, or a location specified by your instructor, in the Specify the location of the new Web site text box. Click the OK button.

2. Double-click the file name, index.htm, in the Folder List pane to open the Home page.

3. Apply the Industrial theme to the Web site. Below the Select a theme list, be sure to select Background picture.

4. When FrontPage has finished applying the theme, use the Page Banner command on the Insert menu to insert a page banner with the words Whalen Metals, or the name of your company. Apply the Heading 1 style to the title. Type the text in Table 1-5, or text of your own choosing, to describe the company's support and quality points of view. When you have finished typing the text, press the ENTER key.

5. Type Whalen Metals and then press the ENTER key. Type Information on our Quality Programs: and then press the ENTER key. Press the TAB key three times and then type the names of the three quality-centered Web sites separated by a TAB character. Press the ENTER key. Use the information in Table 1-6 to create hyperlinks for the company and each of the Web sites. Press the ENTER key.

6. Type Sanjay Gupta, Director of Support Services as the author name (or substitute your name and school). Press the ENTER key.

7. Type Please e-mail questions and comments about our support and quality philosophy to sgupta@whalenmetals.com. as the last line of text (or you can substitute your e-mail address).

8. Drag through the e-mail address text to select it. Create an e-mail hyperlink to the e-mail address, sgupta@whalenmetals.com (or you can substitute your e-mail address).

9. If you have access to a Web server, publish the Web site and preview the Web site in your browser (Figure 1-90). Save the Web page. Print the Web page, write your name on the page, and hand it in to your instructor.

10. Close the Web site.

11. Quit Internet Explorer and FrontPage.

Table 1-5   Support Options Description
SUPPORT INFORMATION
When you need help with your order or our products and services, contact one of our support specialists via e-mail, the Web, or telephone. We commit to getting you in touch with a live person for support within 30 minutes of your initial contact. Most issues are resolved within an hour.
Whalen Metals practices a zero-defect quality management program. We take your concerns seriously and invite our customers to participate in our monthly quality meetings that include senior company management, vendors, and customers.

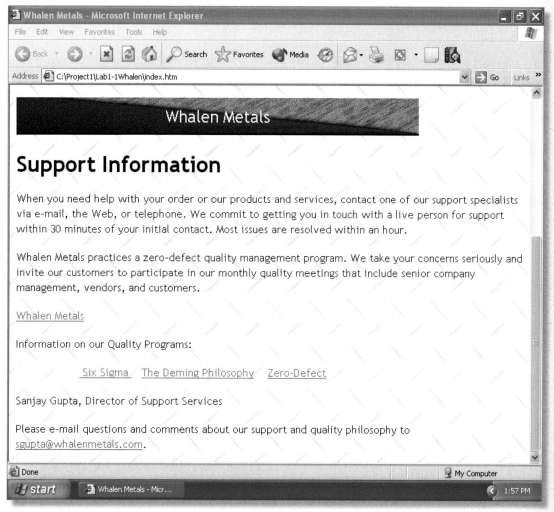

FIGURE 1-90

Table 1-6 Support Hyperlinks*	
TEXT FOR HYPERLINK	**URL FOR HYPERLINK**
Whalen Metals	http://www.whalenmetals.com
Six Sigma	http://www.sixsigma.com
The Deming Philosophy	http://deming.eng.clemson.edu/pub/den/
Zero-Defect	http://www.philcrosby.com

* If you encounter an inoperative URL in the last three links, use the Google search engine, google.com, to find a similar Web page.

2 Creating and Modifying a Personal Web Site

Problem: You have decided to develop a personal Web site with information about your favorite hobby, running. In addition to an introductory Home page, you plan to include a page of links to sites on training, equipment, clubs, and other Web sites of interest.

Instructions: Perform the following tasks.

1. Create a new Web site using the Personal Web Site template. In the Web Site Templates dialog box, click Personal Web Site and then type C:\Project1\Lab1-2Running, or a location specified by your instructor, in the Specify the location of the new Web site text box. Click the OK button.

2. On the View menu, click Navigation. Delete the Interests, Feedback, and Photo Gallery pages from the Web site.

3. Double-click the index.htm page icon in the Folder List pane to open the Home page.

4. If necessary, apply the In Motion theme, or another theme of your choosing, to the Web site. Be sure to apply the theme to all pages in the Web site and to check Vivid colors, Active graphics, and Background picture.

5. Select and delete all table cells below Favorite Links and below Weather.

6. Double-click the page banner component. In the Page Banner Properties dialog box, select the text in the Page banner text text box and then type Running My Way as the new text.

7. Select the link bar and then edit the properties to add hyperlinks to child pages under Home. Remove the check mark from the Home page check box.

8. Delete the first paragraph of placeholder text.

9. Select the placeholder text in the second paragraph and then type Looking for links to great running sites that I regularly read? Browse through my collection of favorite Web links to get information on great running resources.

10. Save the Web page. Open the About Me page. Replace all placeholder text with information about yourself and the course for which you are doing this assignment. See your instructor for relevant course information.

11. Save the Web page. Open the Favorites page.

12. Select the first paragraph of placeholder text and then type A topical listing of some of my favorite Web sites regarding running.

13. Edit the bulleted list of hyperlinks to include the sites and URLs listed in Table 1-7. Use the underlined text as the hyperlink text and then type the descriptions in the placeholder text for each hyperlink. Include any other sites of interest to you. If necessary, for the descriptions, change the style to Bulleted List by selecting Bulleted List from the Style box on the Formatting toolbar before typing the text.

14. Save the Web page.

15. Print the Home page, About Me page, and Favorites page, write your name on the pages, and hand them in to your instructor.

16. If you have access to a Web server, publish the Web site. After you test the Web pages in your browser (Figures 1-91a and 1-91b on page FP 74), close your browser, close the Web site, and then quit FrontPage.

In the Lab

HYPERLINK TEXT AND DESCRIPTION	URL
Cool Running Race calendars, race results, news, and resources.	http://www.coolrunning.com
Runner's World Online companion to a popular running magazine.	http://www.runnersworld.com
CARA Chicago Area Runners Association home page.	http://www.cararuns.org
Onrunning.com News on the professional running world.	http://www.onrunning.com
RunningResearch News Companion site to a journal devoted to the latest research on training and nutrition.	http://www.rnnews.com

Table 1-7 Bulleted List Hyperlinks *

* If you encounter an inoperative URL, use the Google search engine, google.com, to find a similar Web page.

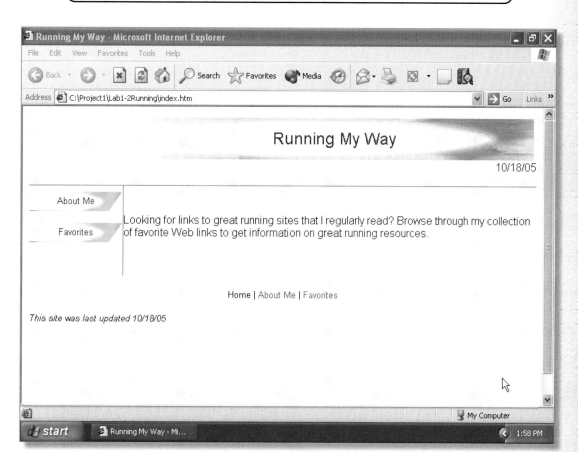

FIGURE 1-91a

(continued)

Creating and Modifying a Personal Web Site *(continued)*

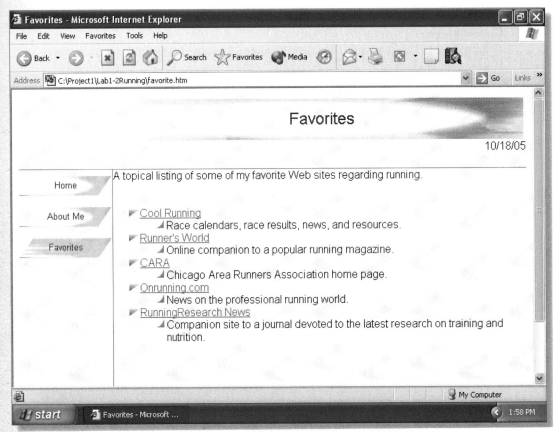

FIGURE 1-91b

3 Creating and Modifying a Corporate Presence Web Site

Problem: As the owner of Fairway Lawn Care, you want to develop a Web site that will provide customers with information about your lawn care services and your specialty landscaping services.

Instructions: Perform the following tasks.

1. Create a new Web site using the Corporate Presence Wizard template. In the Web Site Templates dialog box, click Corporate Presence Wizard and then type C:\Project1\Lab1-3Fairway, or a location specified by your instructor, in the Specify the location of the new Web site text box. Click the OK button.

2. When FrontPage displays the Corporate Presence Wizard dialog box, click the Next button. When prompted for information about the company, use the information in Table 1-8 to fill in the fields and choose which pages to include in your Web site. When you have finished, click the Finish button.

3. If necessary, when FrontPage is finished copying the template pages, click the Toggle Pane button arrow on the Standard toolbar and then click Folder List on the Toggle Pane button menu to display the Folder List pane. Open the Home page.

FIELD	INFORMATION
Table 1-8 Corporate Presence Web Site Field Information	
Main pages to include in Web Site	Products/Services
Home page information	Mission Statement
Products/Services information	0 Products 2 Services
Additional information	Capabilities list
What should appear at the top of each page	Page title Links to your main web pages
What should appear at the bottom of each page	E-mail address of your webmaster Date page was last modified
Under Construction icon	No
Full name of company	Fairway Lawn Care
Short version of name	Fairway
Company's street address	1056 Lexington Drive, Oxnard, WA 91933
Telephone and FAX numbers	888-555-3429 888-555-3430
E-mail address of your webmaster	webmaster@fairway.com
E-mail address for general information	info@fairway.com
Show Tasks View after Web site is uploaded	No

4. Open the Theme task pane by clicking Theme on the Format menu. Choose Checkers as the theme for the Web site. If necessary, click the Vivid colors, Active graphics, and Background picture check boxes. Close the Theme task pane.

5. Select the link bar component at the top of the page and then press the DELETE key. Press the BACKSPACE key twice.

6. Select the vertical link bar and, if necessary, edit the properties to include hyperlinks at the child level. Select the Home page check box and the Parent page check box.

7. Click the first paragraph to select it, click the Style box arrow on the Formatting toolbar, and then click Heading 3. Type Welcome to Fairway Lawn Care! as the new text.

8. Delete the header, Our Mission. Select the second paragraph. Type We strive to meet our customers' goals of well-maintained and manicured lawns. Whether you need a one-time mowing for your home or need your corporate campus landscaped and maintained, we have the right plan for you. Call us anytime to work with our flexible planners and managers. Let us connect you with our satisfied clients, and you can hear about our many success stories! as the new text.

9. Scroll down and select the third paragraph below the header, Contact Information. Press the DELETE key three times to delete the text and extra blank lines from the page.

10. Click the Code button. View and then print the HTML source code for the Home page. Click the Design button. Save and then print the Web page.

(continued)

In the Lab

Creating and Modifying a Corporate Presence Web Site *(continued)*

11. Open the Service 1 page by double-clicking the serv01.htm file in the Folder List pane. Double-click the page banner and replace the text in the Page banner text text box with Home Mowing.

12. Open the Service 2 page by double-clicking the serv02.htm file in the Folder List pane. Replace the text in the Page banner text text box with Business Services.

13. Open the Services page by double-clicking the services.htm file in the Folder List pane.

14. Select all of the text in the paragraph in the middle of the page. Type `Select the plan that is right for your property. We maintain your property as often as you like and in any manner you specify. Select a plan based on a weekly schedule and square footage, or work with us to develop a custom package that meets your needs and schedule.`

15. Select the two paragraphs below the paragraph entered in the previous step and delete them.

16. Print and save the Web page. The Web pages should display in the browser as shown in Figures 1-92a and 1-92b. Close the Web site and then close FrontPage. Hand in the printouts to your instructor.

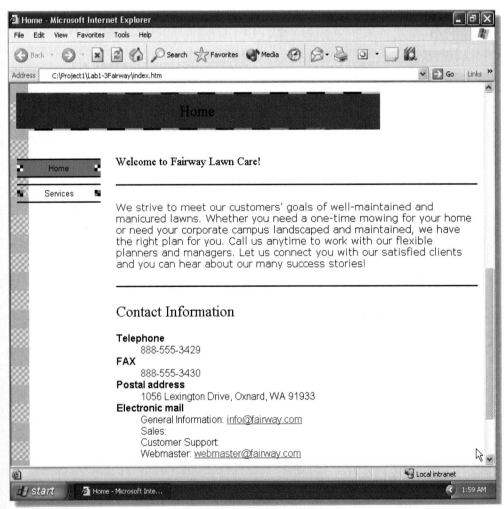

FIGURE 1-92a

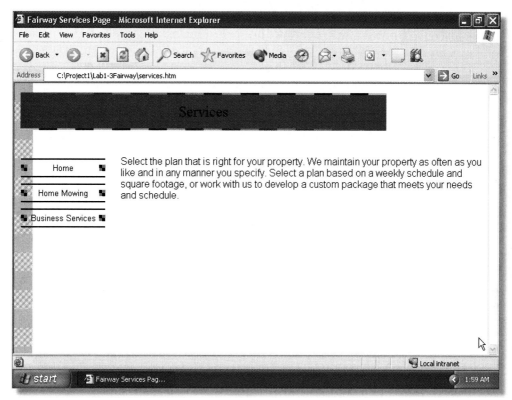

FIGURE 1-92b

Cases and Places

The difficulty of these case studies varies:
▉ are the least difficult and ▉▉ are more difficult. The last exercise is a group exercise.

1 ▉ Because of your interest in movies, you want to create a movie review Web page based on your personal reviews of movies you either like or dislike. Using the One Page Web Site template, develop a Web page that includes the following information about a movie of your choice: title, director, release year, studio, and a brief review. Use a bulleted list for these items. Center a title at the top of the page using the Center button on the Formatting toolbar. Use the Bullets button on the Formatting toolbar to add bullets to the items listed above. Include a hyperlink to your e-mail address at the bottom of the page. Optionally, apply a theme of your choice to the Web site.

2 ▉ You want to make your resume available on the Web. Using the One Page Web Site template, create a text-only Home page that includes information about your educational history and work experience. Apply the theme of your choice to the Web site. Include a hyperlink to your e-mail address at an appropriate location in the resume.

3 ▉▉ In preparation for your friend's graduation from graduate school, you were asked to develop a Web site for him. Using the Personal Web Site template, develop a Web site that includes a Home page, an Interests page, and a History page (modify the Favorites page, including the page banner). Edit the link bar properties to include child level pages, and select the Home page check box and the Parent page check box. Edit the placeholder text to include your own new text. The Home page should include an e-mail hyperlink to your Web address as the creator of the site (webmaster). You also should include a link to the e-mail address of your friend. Delete unused pages and apply a theme of your choice.

Cases and Places

4 ■■ As coordinator for your company's softball team, you have decided to develop a Web page that lists upcoming games, scores of recent games, current league standings, and highlights of noteworthy performances. Using the One Page Web Site template, develop a Web page that lists the information shown in Table 1-9 and Table 1-10. The Web page should include an e-mail hyperlink to your Web address and a hyperlink to the company's intranet page Web page at http://www.trelane.edu/intranet (you may substitute your own Web address). Use TAB characters to space the items on the page, the Font box on the Formatting toolbar, and the Underline button on the Formatting toolbar to format and lay out the page.

Table 1-9 Games and Scores		
GAME/SCORE	DATES/TIMES/RESULTS	COMMENT/HIGHLIGHTS
Upcoming Games	6:30 p.m. on July 20 at field 3, vs. Boomer's Hair Salon 7:00 p.m. on July 23 at field 2, vs. Visions Software, Inc.	We need 3 more players to commit to these games.
Recent Scores	Beat Steve's Steaks 22-4 Lost to Diesel 25-2	Sheila continues her perfect pitching record at 4-0. Despite Mario's heroic home-run, we lost big to Diesel.

Table 1-10 Current League Standings		
TEAM	WON	LOST
Ideolix	5	2
Diesel	5	2
Boomer's Hair Salon	3	3
Steve's Steaks	2	5
Visions Software, Inc.	2	5

5 ■■ **Working Together** Your team has offered to build a Web site for a local video rental store. Using the Corporate Presence Wizard template, develop a Web site that includes at least a Home page and three pages for products and services (use categories you would expect to find in a video rental store, such as movie rental, game rental, video equipment rental, and game console rental). First, develop the design for the site on paper and include a separate sheet of paper for each Web page. Have one team member review the design for proper spelling, grammar, and punctuation.

Adding a New Web Page to a Web Site

PROJECT

2

CASE PERSPECTIVE

James Keeler's personal Web site has gained attention and recognition from his friends and associates and has encouraged James to consider what he wants to see next. The current site consists primarily of text and hyperlinks. Because James describes himself as a visual person by nature, he wants to use the Internet's rich sources of unique images to enhance his Web pages to reflect his personality and activities. He wants to display photos of his school projects, some of his mentors, and a few of his favorite marketing ideas. He is concerned, however, that the significant amount of time it takes large pictures to download and display could discourage visitors from viewing his Web site. He wants to associate a brief, explanatory caption with each photo, but does not want to clutter the photo collection with too much text. He is unsure of the theme he selected for his Web pages because he thinks it might detract from the appeal of his photos.

You assure him that the photos can be added to his Web pages effortlessly, and using features that FrontPage provides will allow him to address all of his valid concerns, including the theme issue. Together, you plan the design of a new Web page that consists of a unique look and layout to add to his current Web site.

As you read through this project, you will learn about the processes involved in designing a well-planned Web page. You will learn how to manually add all of the Web page elements that were added automatically by the theme and template in the previous project. You will learn how to add a link bar and a Photo Gallery component to a Web page. Finally, you will learn how to publish changes to a Web site to a remote Web site.

MICROSOFT
Office FrontPage 2003

Adding a New Web Page to a Web Site

PROJECT

2

Introduction

Every Web page designer wants to build a high-quality Web page that is attractive, that gets the attention of new visitors, that is admired by colleagues, and that even may be imitated. This appreciation does not come from complicated or overanimated designs, but from thoughtful planning, sensitivity to viewers, and careful attention to detail. You must have a thorough understanding of the diverse community of potential viewers and the goal that you want the Web page to accomplish.

Web page development consists of three phases: design, implementation, and maintenance. **Design** consists of understanding the audience, determining the purpose of the Web page, and then selecting and organizing the individual elements that, together, will achieve that purpose. **Implementation** consists of creating the HTML statements and organizing files and folders to give substance to the design. Sometimes the design and implementation tasks are separated, with a design group rendering the design and another group responsible for the implementation. **Maintenance** consists of keeping content up to date and correcting any problems on the Web page.

Designing a Web page is an **iterative process**. Typically, this means that you would perform some analysis concerning the requirements of the Web page and then call upon your creativity to arrive at a design that satisfies those requirements regarding function, and that also is attractive.

After a Web page is designed, it is a simple matter to create it using an HTML editor, such as Microsoft FrontPage. FrontPage has many rich features that will assist you in implementing Web page designs, from the simple to the complex. In this project, you will learn some of the criteria used to arrive at well-designed Web pages and then implement the design for the Photos page shown in Figure 2-1.

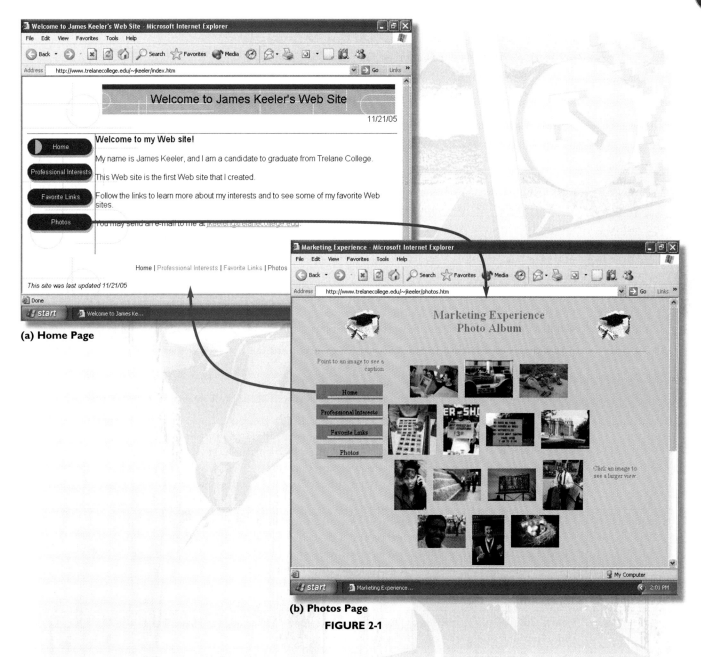

(a) Home Page

(b) Photos Page

FIGURE 2-1

Web Page Design Criteria

If you ask several experienced Web page designers what the criteria are for a good Web page design, you will get many different answers. Each designer will emphasize different elements that he or she thinks are important. A basic set of common criteria exists, however, on which all developers can agree.

When a Web page is well designed, the mechanics of the page almost disappear, enabling the users to concentrate on their research, exploration, or pleasure. Table 2-1 lists several important criteria with their associated guidelines for designing and developing Web pages. The list is by no means exhaustive.

Table 2-1	Criteria and Guidelines for Designing Web Pages
CRITERIA	GUIDELINES
Authentication	• Announce who is responsible for the existence of the Web page. • Name the sponsoring organization and author of the Web page. • Use clear, concise titles that identify or announce the purpose of the page. • List appropriate dates, such as the date written or the date the page was last changed. • List the sources for information or other data used on the Web page.
Aesthetics	• Ensure the Web page looks good and is easy to navigate. • Provide functionality and clear organization. • Select good metaphors to represent your concepts and ideas. • Use complementary color schemes. • Eliminate the use of too many animated graphics on a single page. • Avoid long paragraphs of plain text.
Performance	• Keep the pages relatively short. Long pages take time to display. • Web page design should be a compromise between many graphics versus speed of display. • Use the 7-second response rule when possible: A user will wonder if something is wrong after waiting about 7 seconds without a response.
Consistency	• Use the same colors, locations, and navigation techniques for all related pages. • Maintain a uniform look and feel for all related pages. • Utilize themes and templates to ensure consistency.
Validity	• As with any paper, story, or other literary piece, proofread the text for accuracy. • Verify all the hyperlinks to ensure they are valid. • Check the image, sound, or movie files used in the Web pages. • View the Web page using different browsers. Not every HTML trick or every file format is supported in all browsers.
Images	• Use alternate text in your Web page to provide support for text-only browsers. • Note the size of a large image next to a hyperlink so viewers can decide whether to download it. • Use thumbnail images to provide previews of larger images. • Use universally recognized images for items such as Forward and Back buttons. Remember that you have a global audience.
Hyperlinks	• Ensure that each Web page stands on its own; users can enter from any page of the Web site. • Provide hyperlinks to resources mentioned in the page. • Use clear navigation hyperlinks such as Next, Back, and Home. • At a minimum, always have a hyperlink to the site's Home page. • Limit the number of hyperlinks. • Avoid click here hyperlinks.
External files	• Note the type of file, such as .avi for compressed video files, or .jpg for image files. • Include a notation of the size of the file next to the hyperlink.

Each individual Web page should have one purpose or present one concept. Avoid splitting one concept into two parts simply to reduce the size of a page. Likewise, refrain from combining two unrelated ideas just to make a Web page larger.

To help you learn new tips and techniques, examine a number of well-designed pages. View the HTML source to see how other developers created the effects that interest you.

Each individual Web page should have one purpose or present one concept. Avoid splitting one concept into two parts simply to reduce the size of a page. Likewise, refrain from combining two unrelated ideas just to make a Web page larger. If information is designed to be read online, limit the pages to two screens, and provide links to additional information.

Many HTML style guides are accessible on the Web. Style guides can contain rules, guidelines, tips, and templates that assist you in creating Web pages. Use any Web search engine and search for the keywords, html style guide. Your school or local library also may have an HTML style guide available.

Use the criteria outlined in Table 2-1 as a guide for designing Web pages.

Web Page Composition

Although not true of all Web pages, a typical Web page is composed of three common sections: the header, the body, and the footer (Figure 2-2). The **header** can contain text or images that identify the sponsoring site, the author, or the purpose of the page. Many business Web sites place an advertisement in the header area, because this is the first part of the Web page that shows in the browser's display area. The header also can contain hyperlinks to related pages at the Web site. The header is an important part of the Web page. Viewers evaluate your site from their first impression of the header information. An appealing header piques their interest, making them want to see what else is on the page.

The **body** of the Web page contains information and other materials that initially bring visitors to the Web page. The information is conveyed through combinations of text, images, animation, and hyperlinks.

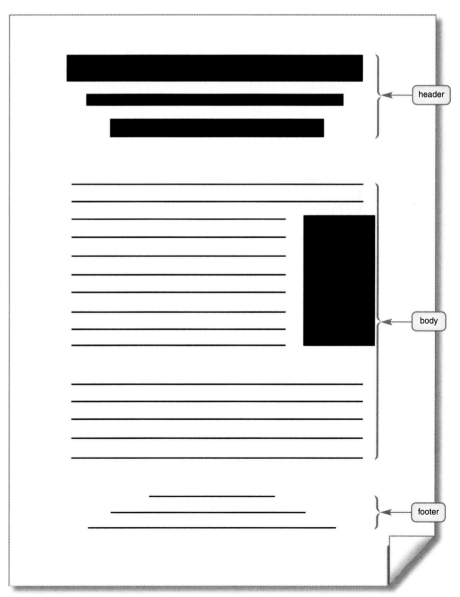

FIGURE 2-2

Q&A

Q: What is the difference between the <HEAD> or <BODY> tags and the Web page's header and body?

A: Do not confuse the header, body, and footer sections of a Web page with the <HEAD> and <BODY> tags in HTML, which are code segments. Information placed within a <HEAD> tag pair typically does not display on the Web page.

The **footer** of the Web page provides contact information and sometimes navigation controls. Here you probably can find the name and perhaps the e-mail address of the author of the Web page or other official contact person responsible for the Web site. Hyperlinks to other resources at the Web site, such as the Home page or Help information, also may be included in this section.

When designing a Web page, it is useful to divide the page into these three logical sections to ease the design process. You can focus your attention on completing one of the three sections, test it, and then proceed to the next one.

Designing the Web Page

Ideally, you create several Web page design alternatives and then discuss with other designers the merits and shortcomings of each. The leading contenders then are refined until a final design is agreed upon. In practice, however, often you will work alone and thus be responsible for these tasks yourself.

You can use several techniques, including brainstorming and word association, during the creative process. As with any artistic endeavor, form follows function. If something appears on the Web page, then it should serve some purpose. If something serves no purpose, then it should not be on the Web page.

More About

Web Page Design

Discover tips, tricks, and techniques for designing Web pages by perusing the numerous formal and informal Best of the Web sites. These sites contain links to outstanding Web pages. Use a search engine to find Best of the Web sites or visit the FrontPage 2003 More About page (scsite.com/fp2003/more) and then click Web Page Design.

Design Tip

Begin your Web page design with a single purpose in mind. If something appears on the Web page, then it should serve some purpose. If something serves no purpose, then it should not be on the Web page. Choose content that adds value, that is, content that is relative, informative, timely, accurate, and usable.

After your discussion with James, you design a Photos page, as illustrated in Figure 2-3. Although the pages previously created followed the typical page design, this one varies somewhat because it is composed primarily of pictures. Even so, you easily can identify the header and body sections and see that no footer section is used.

The header contains two images and a heading that identifies the page. The body of the page contains the desired photos arranged in a montage, each with descriptive information in the form of a ScreenTip. The navigation hyperlinks are on the left, consistent with the previous pages.

Notice the **notations** on the design document indicating special formatting requirements such as color, text size, and alignment. With the design of the page completed, you now can implement the design using FrontPage.

Adding a New Web Page to an Existing FrontPage Web Site

In Project 1 you learned that you can create a new FrontPage Web site in several ways. You can import an existing Web site from a Web server. You can use a template or wizard. Templates and wizards, such as the one used in Project 1, are great work-saving devices. As you develop customized Web sites, you will want to add new Web pages to the Web site when the need arises. To add a new Web page to an existing Web site, you start FrontPage and then open the original FrontPage Web site. The following steps start FrontPage.

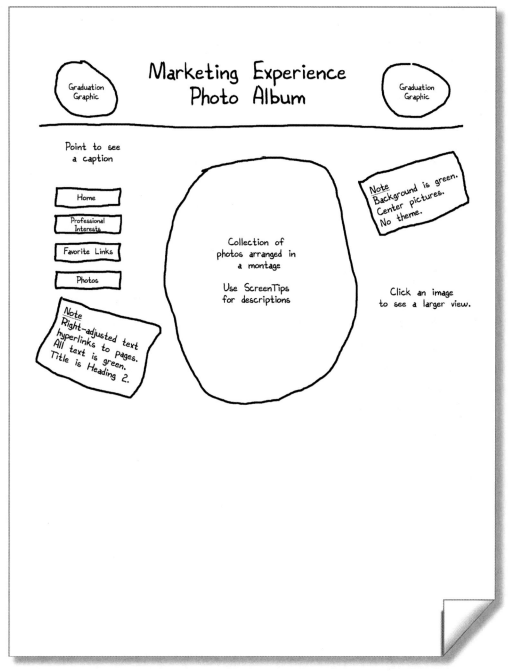

FIGURE 2-3

To Start FrontPage

1 Click the Start button on the Windows taskbar, point to All Programs on the Start menu, and then point to Microsoft Office on the All Programs submenu.

2 Click Microsoft Office FrontPage 2003 on the Microsoft Office submenu.

3 If FrontPage opened a Web site, click File on the menu bar and then click Close Site. If FrontPage opened a Web page, click File on the menu bar and then click Close.

The FrontPage window is opened and an empty page is displayed. Alternatively, FrontPage may open the last Web page or Web site that was opened in FrontPage on the computer.

Opening an Existing FrontPage Web Site

The following steps open the FrontPage Web site created in Project 1. If you did not complete Project 1, see your instructor to obtain a copy of the completed project.

To Open an Existing FrontPage Web Site

1

• **Click the Open button arrow on the Standard toolbar.**

FrontPage displays the Open menu (Figure 2-4).

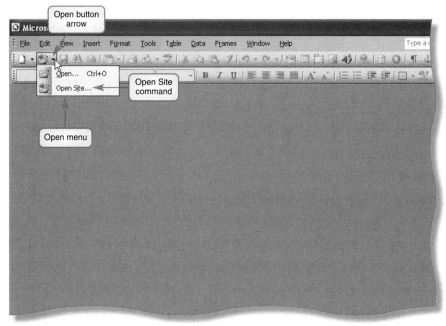

FIGURE 2-4

2

• **Click Open Site.**

• **If necessary, when the Open Site dialog box is displayed, click the Look in box arrow and select the folder location where you stored the Web site for Project 1 (e.g., C:\jkeeler).**

FrontPage displays the Open Site dialog box with the current folder selected (Figure 2-5). Use the drive and location that are appropriate for your environment. The new location is displayed in the text box.

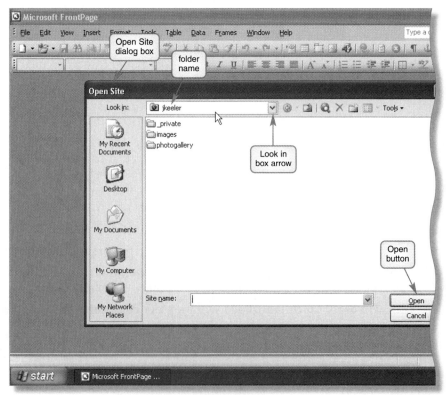

FIGURE 2-5

3

• **Click the Open button.**

• **Double-click index.htm in the Folder List pane.**

The previous Web site is loaded, and the file, index.htm, is displayed in Design view (Figure 2-6).

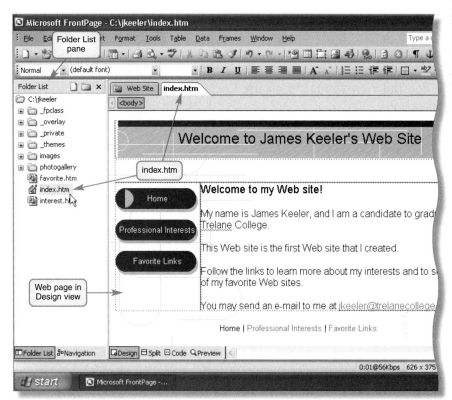

FIGURE 2-6

Adding a New Web Page

The FrontPage toolbar contains the New Page button that you can use to add a new Web page to the current Web site. A new page can be added in Design, Folders, or Navigation view. If you are using link bars or banners in your Web site, as was done in Project 1, then you should add new pages after changing to Navigation view, and then indicate the location of the new page by selecting a page icon in the Navigation pane. The new page icon will be inserted as a child below the selected page icon. This allows the link bars to be updated correctly by FrontPage and preserves the visual relationship in the graphical tree diagram in the Navigation pane.

When a new page is added in Design view, FrontPage displays the new page just as it does when an existing Web site is first opened. Such a new page does not show in the Folder List pane until it has been saved. Adding a new page in Navigation view, however, causes that page to be saved and added to the Folder List as soon as the view is refreshed.

Because link bars will be used on this page, the page should be added in Navigation view. The steps on the next page insert a new page in Navigation view in the current FrontPage Web site.

Other Ways

1. On File menu click Open Site
2. Press ALT+F, I
3. In Voice Command mode, say "File, Open Site"

To Add a New Web Page to an Existing Web Site

1

• **Click the View command on the menu bar.**

• **Click Navigation.**

FrontPage displays the Navigation view (Figure 2-7). The Home Page icon is identified by a small house figure in the lower-left corner of the icon.

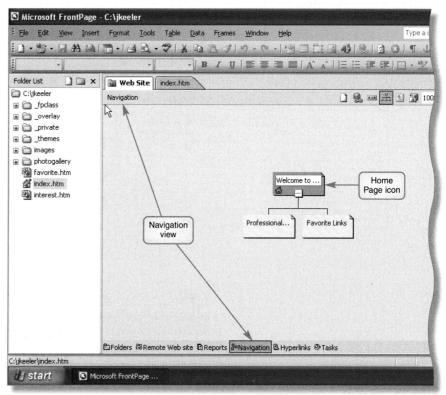

FIGURE 2-7

2

• **Right-click the Home Page icon.**

• **Point to the New command.**

FrontPage displays the New submenu (Figure 2-8).

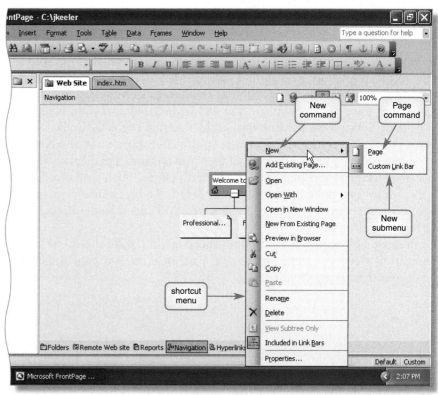

FIGURE 2-8

3

• **Click Page.**

• **When FrontPage adds the new page to the navigation structure, click View on the menu bar.**

FrontPage adds the new page to the navigation structure and displays the View menu (Figure 2-9).

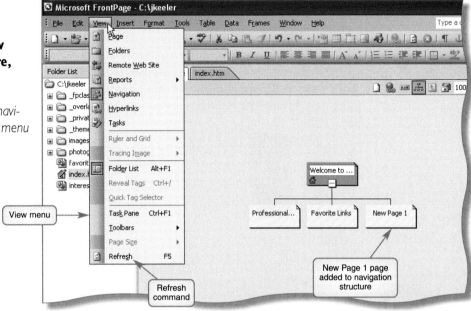

FIGURE 2-9

4

• **Click Refresh.**

FrontPage displays the new page in the Folder List pane as new_page_1.htm (Figure 2-10).

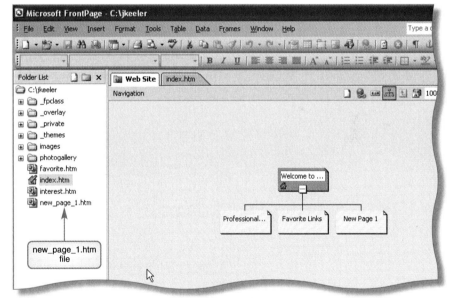

FIGURE 2-10

To control the location of the new Web page in the graphical tree diagram, you right-clicked a Web page icon to which the page was added. Because you right-clicked the top-level page, New Page 1 was added just below it, as shown in Figure 2-10. If you were to insert another page with the Home page selected, New Page 2 would be added on the same level as New Page 1. If you were to click New Page 1 and then click New Page, New Page 2 would be added below New Page 1, creating a three-level graphical tree diagram.

Other Ways

1. Click Create a new normal page button arrow on Standard toolbar, click Page
2. On the File menu click New
3. Right-click Folder List pane, click New
4. Press ALT+F, N
5. Press CTRL+N
6. In Voice Command mode, say "File, New"

Renaming a Web Page

Because a file name like new_page_1.htm is not very descriptive, you should rename the file with a more meaningful name. Because the new page is included in the navigation structure for the Web site, it was added to the Home page link bars automatically. Link bars use references to file names to locate the corresponding Web pages. Renaming files within FrontPage assures that such references are maintained, as FrontPage modifies references to the files automatically.

> *Design Tip*
>
> Use descriptive names for file names and maintain a standard for naming files. Over time and as your site includes more pages, a well-maintained organizational structure for the files in the Web site can decrease the amount of time spent on maintenance.

The following steps change the name of the newly created page.

To Rename a Web Page

1

• **Right-click the file name new_page_1.htm.**

FrontPage displays the shortcut menu (Figure 2-11).

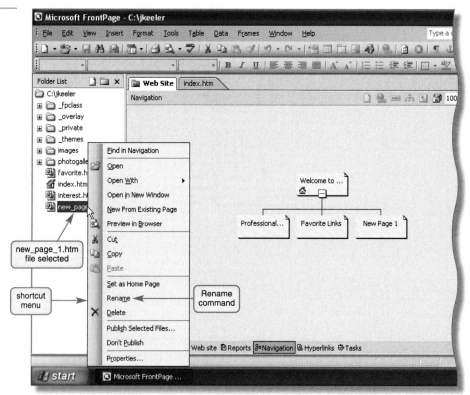

FIGURE 2-11

2

• **Click Rename on the shortcut menu.**

The new_page_1.htm file name is selected, and an edit text box is displayed around the file name (Figure 2-12).

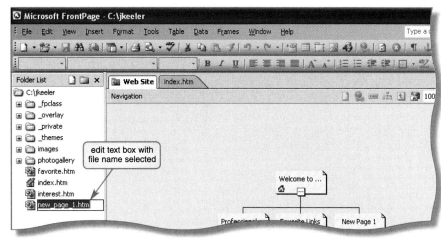

FIGURE 2-12

3

• **Type** photos.htm **as the new file name and then press the ENTER key.**

FrontPage displays a Rename dialog box during the renaming process and then closes it automatically after you press ENTER. The Folder List pane reflects the renamed file, photos.htm (Figure 2-13).

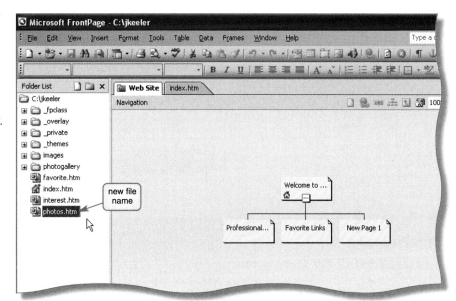

FIGURE 2-13

Other Ways

1. Click file name in Folder List pane to select it, click file name again, type new file name in edit text box

Changing the Title of a Web Page

The title of a Web page is displayed in the title bar of most browsers and in any bookmarks or favorites for that page. Although this is not the same as the page label, which is displayed in page banners and navigation bars created by FrontPage, the same text often is used by default. Each file, or page, in a Web site has its own title. The default title for a new page is New Page 1, corresponding to the default label of New Page 1 and the default file name of new_page_1.htm. You may change the title of a file without modifying its file name or label. Titles should reflect the name of the organization or purpose of the Web page.

The steps on the next page change the title of the newly created page to a name reflecting its purpose. This title will be placed on the title bar of browsers and in favorites or bookmark lists.

To Change the Title of a Web Page

1

• **Right-click the New Page 1 page icon.**

FrontPage displays the shortcut menu (Figure 2-14).

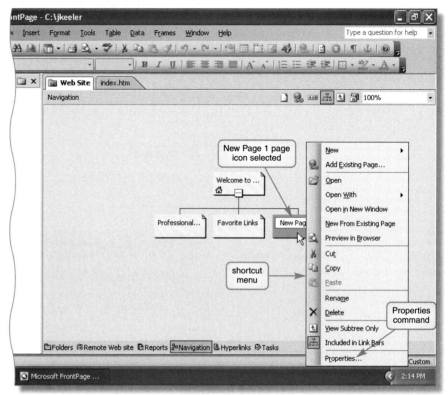

FIGURE 2-14

2

• **Click Properties.**

• **If necessary, click the General tab.**

The photos.htm Properties dialog box is displayed, and the default title is selected (Figure 2-15).

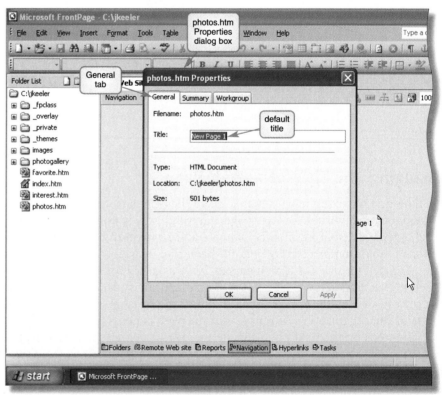

FIGURE 2-15

• **Type** Marketing Experience **in the Title text box.**

The new title replaces the old title (Figure 2-16).

• **Click the OK button.**

FrontPage closes the Page Properties dialog box. Although not visible at this point, the title has been changed.

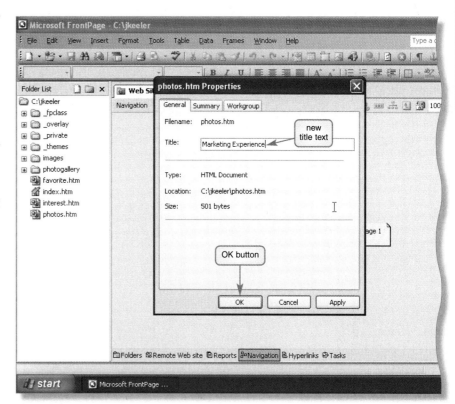

FIGURE 2-16

Although FrontPage allows you to enter very long titles, browser title bars display approximately 80 to 90 characters, so keep this limitation in mind when entering the title.

 Browser title bars display approximately 80 to 90 characters, so keep this limitation in mind when designing Web page titles.

Other Ways

1. Right-click file name in Folder List pane, click Properties on shortcut menu, type new title in Title text box in General sheet in Properties dialog box
2. Right-click Page pane, click Properties on short-cut menu, type new title in Title text box in General sheet in Properties dialog box

Changing the Page Label of a Web Page

As you have seen, changing the title of a Web page did not affect the page label. FrontPage uses the page labels displayed in Navigation view as the labels for link bars. If you change a page title, you also may want the labels on corresponding link bars to match. You can change the text that is displayed on a link bar by changing the page labels in Navigation view.

The steps on the next page change the page label of the Photos page to indicate the content of the page in the labels of link bars.

To Change the Page Label of a Web Page

1

• **Right-click the New Page 1 page icon.**

FrontPage displays the shortcut menu (Figure 2-17).

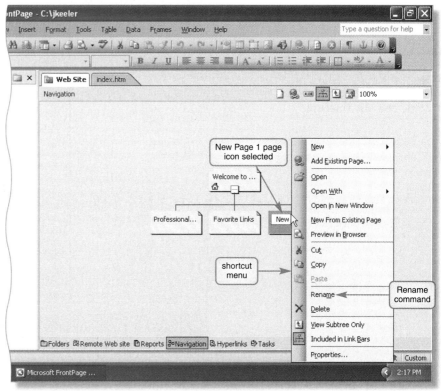

FIGURE 2-17

2

• **Click Rename.**

An edit text box is displayed around the default label, and the label is selected (Figure 2-18).

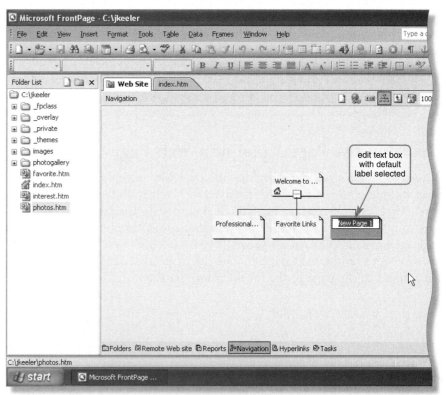

FIGURE 2-18

3

- **Type** Photos **in the edit text box.**
- **Press the ENTER key to save the new label.**

The edit text box closes, and the new label is displayed in the page icon (Figure 2-19). If a new label is longer than the room available in the page icon, then FrontPage displays ellipses to indicate that the label extends beyond the size of the icon.

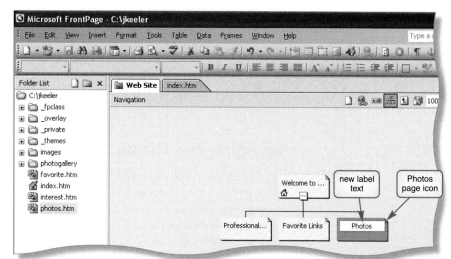

FIGURE 2-19

Other Ways

1. Click page icon to select, click text box, type new label

Editing the Web Page

The tasks required to create the Photos Web page consist of selecting the page background; inserting headings, images, and text; inserting a Photo Gallery component; and testing the page. In FrontPage, Web pages are edited in Design view. The following step edits the Photos page.

To Edit a Web Page in Design View

1

- **Double-click the Photos page icon in the Navigation pane.**

FrontPage opens the file photos.htm in Design view (Figure 2-20). The display area is empty; however, the theme for the Web site is applied to the page automatically.

Other Ways

1. Double-click photos.htm file name in Folder List pane
2. Select page icon, click Design view icon
3. Right-click in Folder List and then click Open

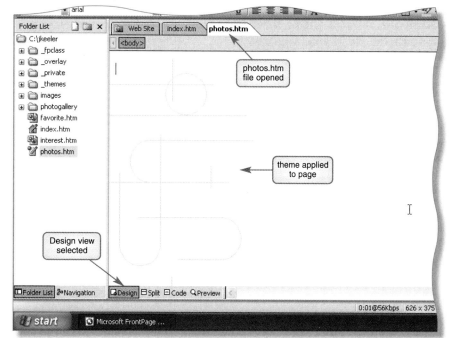

FIGURE 2-20

With the page open in Design view, you can start customizing the Web page to implement the design shown in Figure 2-3 on page FP 87. Because this Web site had a theme applied before adding the new page, the theme is applied to the new page automatically. In this case, a background color with no theme applied is desired. The first step is to remove the current theme from only this page, but not from the rest of the Web site. After the theme has been removed, the default background color will be changed.

Changing the Theme for a Single Web Page

Themes typically are applied to an entire Web site, as was done in Project 1. In some cases, a particular page in a Web site might not be presented well with the current theme, yet the theme is attractive for the remainder of the Web site. With FrontPage, it is easy to apply a different theme, or no theme at all, to an individual page in a Web site.

> *Design Tip*
>
> Generate a sense of oneness within your Web site by utilizing consistent alignment, a common graphic theme, and a common color theme. Be judicious about whether a page properly fits within the chosen scheme.

The following steps remove the current theme from the Photos page.

To Change the Theme for a Web Page

• **Click Format on the menu bar and then click Theme.**

• **Scroll the Select a theme scroll bar until the No theme selection is displayed in the list.**

FrontPage displays the Theme task pane. The Select a theme area displays the currently selected theme at the top of the list and the No theme selection is displayed at the top of the All available themes section (Figure 2-21).

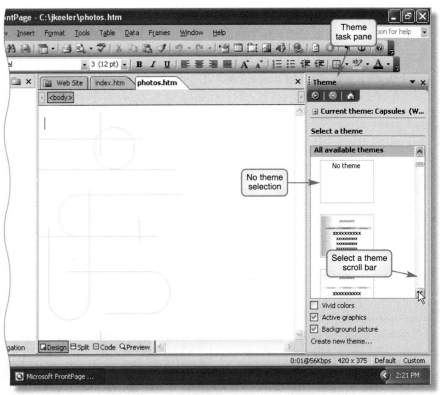

FIGURE 2-21

2

• **Click No theme.**

FrontPage displays the photos.htm page with no theme (Figure 2-22).

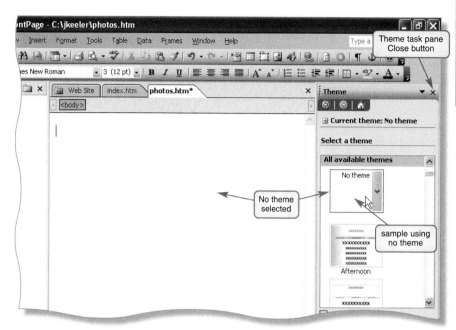

FIGURE 2-22

3

• **Click the Theme task pane Close button.**

FrontPage displays the Photos page with no theme applied (Figure 2-23).

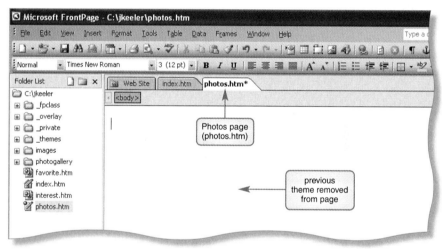

FIGURE 2-23

Other Ways
1. Press ALT+O, H
2. In Voice Command mode, say "Format, Theme"

Now that the Photos page no longer has the theme applied, you can change the default background and text colors.

Changing the Background Color of a Web Page

The background of a Web page can be a solid color, an image, or a pattern that is repeated across and down the page. You can select a color from within FrontPage, select an image or pattern stored on your local computer, or copy an image or pattern from any Web page on the World Wide Web.

Because the current theme was removed, FrontPage displays the Photos page in the default background color of white. According to the design, you are to use a solid color for the background. The steps on the next page change the background color of the Web page to a solid color.

To Change the Background Color

1

• **Click Format on the menu bar.**

FrontPage displays the Format menu (Figure 2-24). The Format menu contains commands to manage Web page formatting items such as themes, style sheets, and backgrounds.

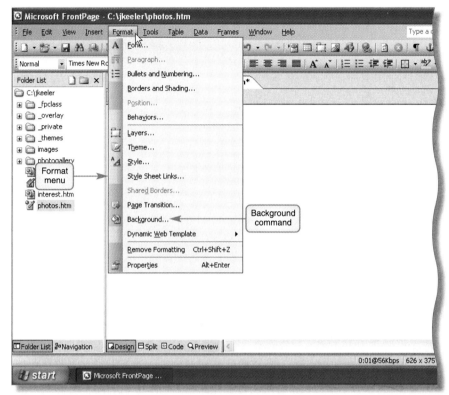

FIGURE 2-24

2

• **Click Background.**

• **If necessary, click the Formatting tab.**

FrontPage displays the Page Properties dialog box (Figure 2-25). The Formatting sheet contains settings to control the background image or color.

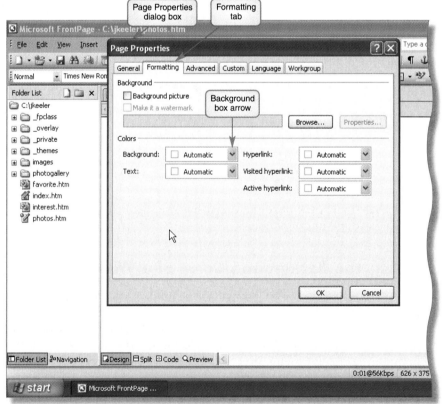

FIGURE 2-25

3

• **Click the Background box arrow.**

FrontPage displays a palette of available background colors (Figure 2-26).

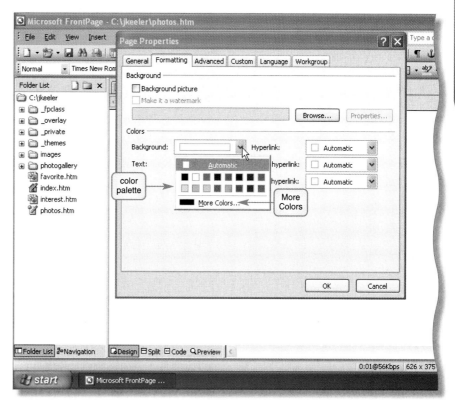

FIGURE 2-26

4

• **Click More Colors.**

• **Click the indicated color.**

FrontPage displays the More Colors dialog box (Figure 2-27). The selected color will display Hex={99,FF,CC} in the Value text box.

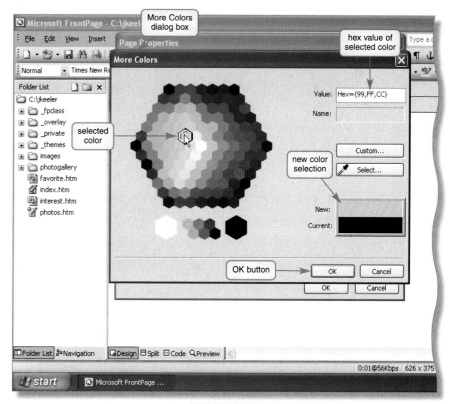

FIGURE 2-27

5

• Click the OK button.

FrontPage closes the More Colors dialog box (Figure 2-28). The Page Properties dialog box is visible with the selected color displayed in the Background box.

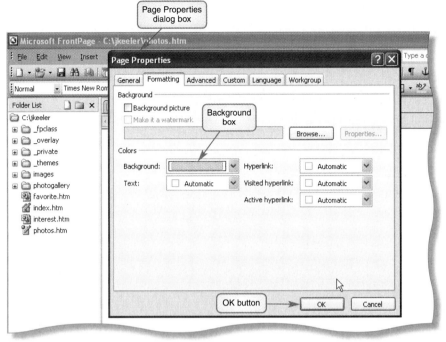

FIGURE 2-28

6

• Click the OK button in the Page Properties dialog box.

FrontPage closes the Page Properties dialog box (Figure 2-29). The Photos page is displayed with the selected color as the background color.

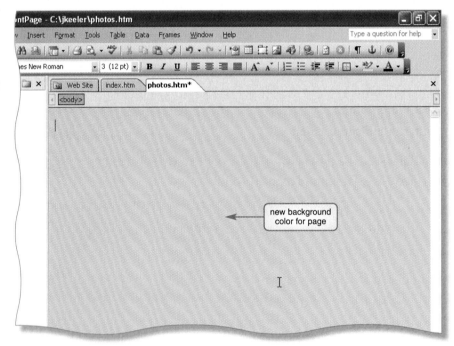

FIGURE 2-29

When you click the Background box arrow, the color palette is displayed and allows you to select the color of your choice.

Selecting More Colors on the color palette displays a More Colors dialog box (Figure 2-27 on the previous page) with additional predefined colors available. For even more colors, click the Custom button in the More Colors dialog box to display a Color dialog box (Figure 2-30) in which you can mix your own color, save it as a custom color, and then use it as the background color.

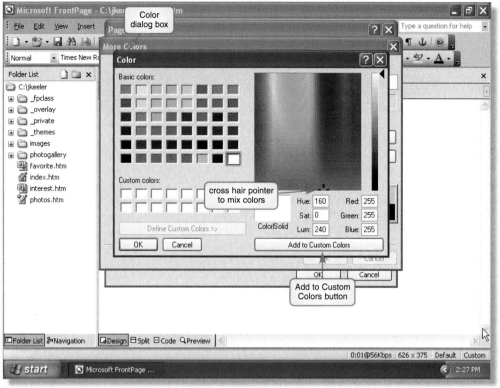

FIGURE 2-30

More About

Web Page Colors

FrontPage uses hue, saturation, and luminosity to specify colors. Hue represents a gradation of color, such as red or blue. Saturation is the amount of color in a hue. Luminosity is the brightness of a hue. Many sites offer help on selecting appropriate colors for Web pages. For more information about selecting colors for Web pages, visit the FrontPage 2003 More About page (scsite.com/fp2003/more) and then click Web Page Colors.

Inserting a Table in a Web Page

Tables are used frequently in applications to present information in a clear, concise format. Disciplines such as mathematics, engineering, and chemistry all take advantage of tables. A computer spreadsheet is laid out in the form of a table with rows and columns. Many different applications exist for which tables are an ideal solution.

An HTML table consists of one or more rows containing one or more columns. The intersection of a row and column is called a cell. Any Web page component, such as text or an image, can be placed in a cell.

Tables in a Web page help you to display any type of information that looks best in rows and columns, such as a list of products and their corresponding prices. In Web pages, tables also help you to accomplish special design effects, such as positioning of elements on a Web page.

More About

Tables

A table can have a different background color or image than the rest of the Web page. The Table Properties dialog box contains options that allow you to choose a different background color or an image file to display as a table background.

Design Tip
Before you create any table, sketch it on paper. Determine the number of rows and columns and the content that you will place in the cells. Calculate the overall width of the table and necessary width for each column.

You can create a table and insert your entire Web page in the cells. Using tables, you can define headings, sidebars, and captions and use other creative design techniques.

The Photos Web page will use a table with three rows and three columns to control the positioning of images, text, and the photo gallery (Figure 2-3 on page FP 87). The steps on the next page insert a table in a Web page.

To Insert a Table in a Web Page

1

• **Click the Insert Table button on the Standard toolbar.**

FrontPage displays the Insert Table grid (Figure 2-31). The grid is a graphical means of displaying the number of rows and columns used in a table. You can indicate how many rows and columns the table will have by clicking a cell on the grid.

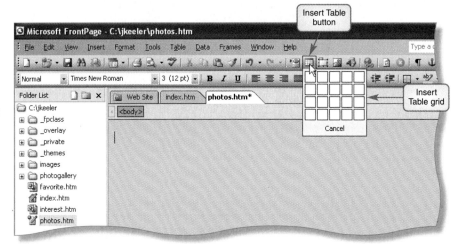

FIGURE 2-31

2

• **Point to the cell in the third row and third column to select nine squares in the grid.**

The nine squares are selected (Figure 2-32). This indicates a three-row table with three columns, for a total of nine cells.

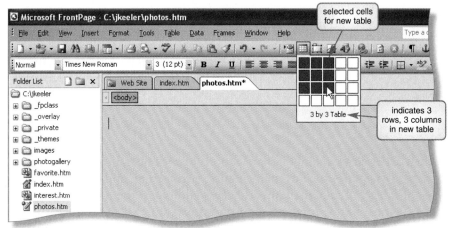

FIGURE 2-32

3

• **Click the cell in the third row and third column.**

FrontPage inserts a table in the Web page with three rows and three columns (Figure 2-33). The table extends across the width of the Web page. Each cell is the same size.

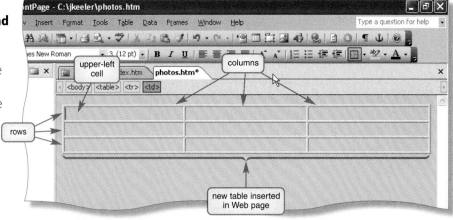

FIGURE 2-33

Other Ways

1. On Table menu click Insert, click Table
2. Press ALT+A, I, T
3. In Voice Command mode, say "Table, Insert, Table"

The Insert Table grid opens with only four rows and five columns. You can add more rows or columns simply by continuing to move the mouse through the grid. FrontPage automatically adds more rows and columns, and the Insert Table grid expands to accommodate the grid.

Extra rows can be added to the bottom of the table in the Web page by positioning the insertion point in the last column of the last row and then pressing the TAB key. You also can insert rows or columns anywhere in the table by positioning the insertion point and then clicking Insert on the Table menu and then clicking Rows or Columns. Doing so causes a dialog box to be displayed, allowing you to choose whether to insert rows or columns, the number to insert, and whether they should appear above or below the current insertion point. Finally, you can right-click any cell and then click Insert Rows on the shortcut menu to insert rows.

Merging Cells in a Table

When using a table to position items on a Web page, it is not unusual that some items span multiple cells in the table. By merging two or more cells in a table, you can set alignments that are more complex than just straight rows and columns.

The following steps merge cells in the table inserted in the previous set of steps.

To Merge Cells in a Table

1

• **Click the left cell in the middle row of the table.**

• **Hold down the SHIFT key and click the right cell in the middle row.**

• **Right-click one of the selected cells.**

The selected middle cells are highlighted, and a shortcut menu is displayed (Figure 2-34).

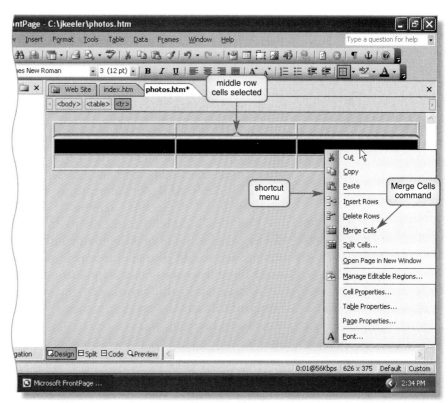

FIGURE 2-34

2

• **Click Merge Cells.**

• **Click the upper-left cell to remove the highlighting.**

The selected middle cells are merged into a single cell spanning three columns (Figure 2-35).

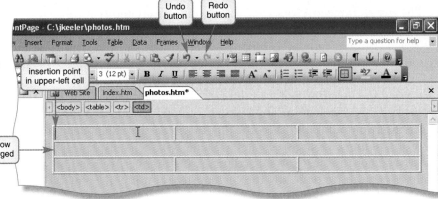

FIGURE 2-35

In addition to using the SHIFT key to choose the final cell in a selection, you also can drag through the cells to select them. The shortcut menu shown in Figure 2-34 on the previous page indicates the commands available when working with tables and table cells. Merged cells can be split again using the Split Cells command on the shortcut menu.

Undoing and Redoing Actions

Even if you take great care when creating your Web pages, you may make mistakes or you may want to make an immediate change. FrontPage provides facilities to help you undo errors with the Undo button on the Standard toolbar (Figure 2-35) or the Undo command on the Edit menu. Thus, if you make a change or a mistake, undo it using either the Undo button or the Undo command. FrontPage will reverse your action as far back as 30 consecutive actions.

Also available for quick reversal of errors and changes are the Redo button on the Standard toolbar and the Redo command on the Edit menu. Redo reverses the effect of the last Undo command. If you decide the undo is incorrect, you can click the Redo button or Redo command to restore the last change you made. Redo is available for 30 consecutive actions.

Both the Undo button and the Redo button have arrows that allow you to see the most recent undo or redo commands, respectively. This allows you to see what actions you would be undoing or redoing before actually selecting them, and to select more than one consecutive action to undo or redo.

As you work with FrontPage, you will find that using the Undo and Redo buttons facilitates the creative process. You can add and rearrange items to see if they work, knowing you can return to a previous starting point with little effort.

Inserting an Image in a Web Page

Regardless of how impressive your written message, people always respond to images. The viewer's eye is drawn naturally to a picture before reading any text. The choice and quality of images you use largely determine whether someone will take the time to read your Web page or whether they will pass it by.

Much of the Web's success is due to its capability of presenting images. Because of the impact of images on the Web, it is important to master the image options necessary to include pictures in your Web pages.

When you design a Web page, do not limit your creativity to the print environment. Where appropriate, include color, photographs, animation, video, and sound clips.

Along with the text heading, the Photos page has two images in the header. The table you inserted in earlier steps will be used to control the amount of horizontal spacing between the images and the text. The image on the left will be right-aligned in the left cell of the table. The image on the right will be left-aligned in the right cell of the table. The text, which is inserted later in the project, will be centered in the middle cell.

The goal of the images at the top of the page is to reflect the concept that the Photos page is like a computer-based photo album. Therefore, an image with an inviting cartoon caricature of a diploma is appropriate, reflecting that the pictures on the page relate to the author's academic experience. Refer to Table 2-1 on page FP 84 for criteria on the appropriate use of metaphors in your Web site designs.

FrontPage includes a library of ready-to-use images and photographs, called **clip art**, that you can insert into your Web pages. Some images probably are available on your local machine, but many more are accessible online. You also can use images from many different sources outside of FrontPage. You may use clip art from the FrontPage library or from the Data Disk to select an image for the Photos Web page.

To insert an image, you first position the insertion point at the desired location, and then select the image. The following steps insert an image in the Web page.

To Insert a Clip Art Image in a Web Page

1

• **If necessary, click the upper-left cell of the table to position the insertion point.**

• **Click Insert on the menu bar and then point to Picture.**

FrontPage displays the Insert menu and the Picture submenu (Figure 2-36).

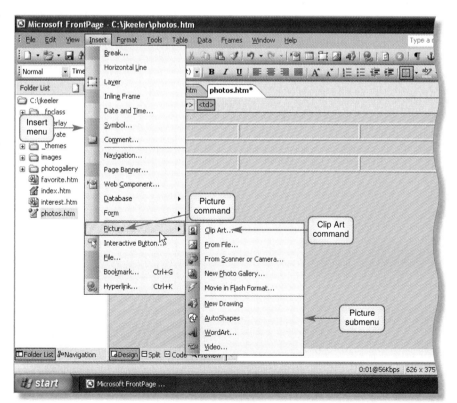

FIGURE 2-36

2

• **Click Clip Art.**

• **When the Clip Art task pane appears, type** diploma **in the Search for text box.**

FrontPage displays the Clip Art task pane (Figure 2-37). You can search for an image file or clip art file from your personal collections or collections from Office on your local computer, or from Microsoft collections on the World Wide Web.

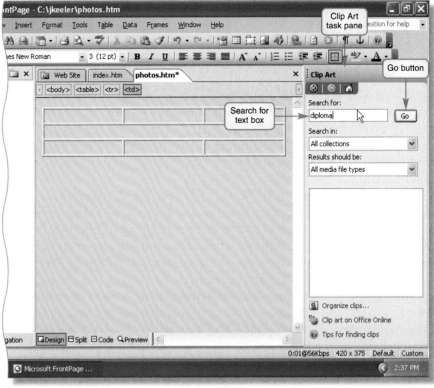

FIGURE 2-37

3

• **Click the Go button.**

FrontPage displays the results of your search as small sample preview images (Figure 2-38). Your sample images may be different.

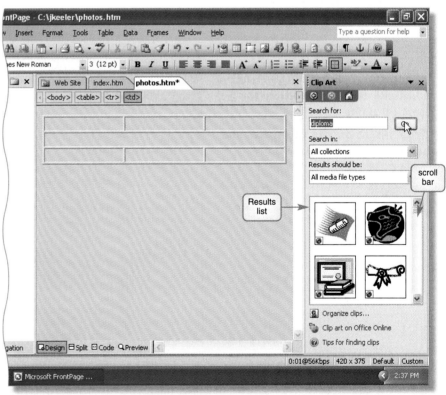

FIGURE 2-38

4

• **If necessary, scroll down the Results list until an image of a diploma is displayed, or another image of your choice.**

The image to be inserted is displayed (Figure 2-39).

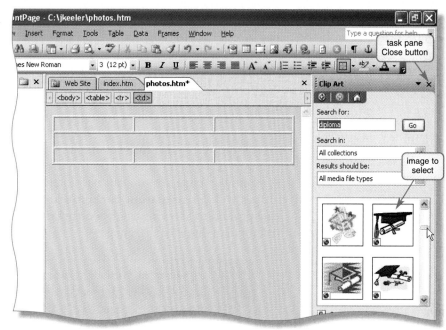

FIGURE 2-39

5

• **Point to the image.**
• **Click the box arrow and then click Insert on the shortcut menu to insert the clip art in the Web page.**
• **Click the Close button on the Clip Art task pane.**

When you point to the image, FrontPage displays a box arrow on its right. FrontPage inserts the clip art image into the upper-left cell of the table (Figure 2-40).

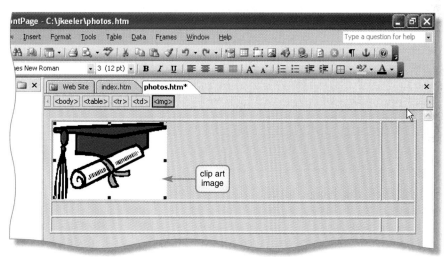

FIGURE 2-40

As you can see in Figure 2-39, many samples of clip art may be available. By default, FrontPage searches both the World Wide Web and your local machine. Typically, the number of images on your local machine is limited. To obtain a large number of images, search the World Wide Web.

Design Tip

Before downloading photos or other media from the Web, ensure that they have no copyright restrictions or royalty charges that you cannot or will not pay. Royalty charges are fees to be paid to the creator or owner of the art for its use.

Other Ways

1. On Insert menu point to Picture, click Clip Art
2. On Insert menu point to Picture, click From File
3. Press ALT+I, P, C
4. Press ALT+I, P, F
5. In Voice Command mode, say "Insert, Picture, Clip Art"

More About

Images

The more images your Web site contains, the longer it takes to download your Web pages. To count the total number of images in your Web site, point to Reports on the View menu, and then click Site Summary. In the Pictures row, the Count column lists the number of pictures in your Web site. Pictures located in hidden folders normally are not included in this report.

Replacing an Image in a Web Page

Once an image has been inserted into the Web page, you may decide that it is not as appealing as you originally thought. While many reasons to change an image may exist, replacing an image in a Web page is as easy as inserting the original image. You may replace the image simply by selecting a different image from the results of a search, or by using an image available on your local machine.

Many images used in a Web page may appear to be irregular in shape, when in fact they are rectangular. When the background color of the image is not the same as that of the Web page, the rectangular shape of the image becomes very obvious. To hide this rectangular shape, you can use images that have the same background color as your Web page, or you can use images that have a transparent background. Using images with a **transparent background** allows the color or image used in a Web page background to show through the background of the inserted image, thus hiding the rectangular shape of the image.

Design Tip

Using images with a transparent background allows the color or image used in a Web page background to show through the background of the inserted image, thus hiding the rectangular shape of the image. Cropping an image can eliminate distracting background elements and establish the focal point of the image. Discarding unwanted portions of an image also reduces its file size.

The following steps replace the image just inserted with a similar one from the local machine that has a transparent background.

To Replace a Clip Art Image in a Web Page

1

• **Right-click the image to be replaced.**

FrontPage displays a shortcut menu, and eight small boxes, called sizing handles, are displayed around the selected image (Figure 2-41).

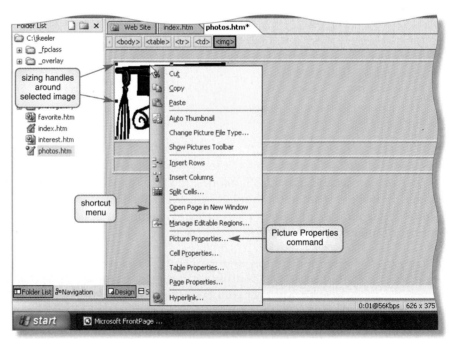

FIGURE 2-41

2

• **Click Picture Properties.**

• **If necessary, when the Picture Properties dialog box is displayed, click the General tab.**

FrontPage displays the Picture Properties dialog box. The name and location of the current image file are selected in the Picture text box (Figure 2-42).

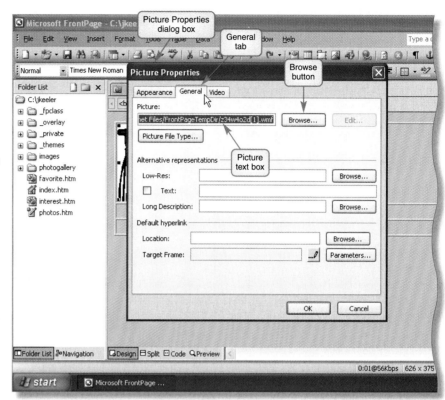

FIGURE 2-42

3

• **Click the Browse button.**

• **Insert the Data Disk in drive A.**

• **If necessary, when FrontPage displays the Picture dialog box, click the Look in box arrow and select the graduation.gif file in the Project2 folder.**

FrontPage displays the Picture dialog box with the graduation.gif file in the A:\Project2 folder selected (Figure 2-43). Use the drive and location that are appropriate for your environment.

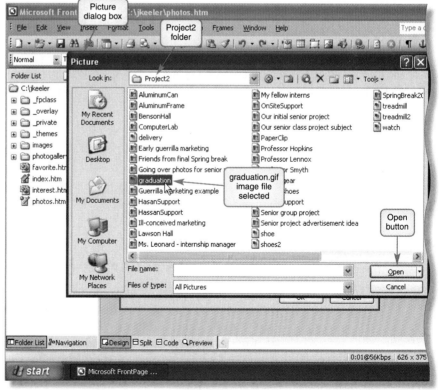

FIGURE 2-43

4

• **Click the Open button.**

FrontPage closes the Picture dialog box. FrontPage displays the replacement image file name and location in the Picture text box (Figure 2-44).

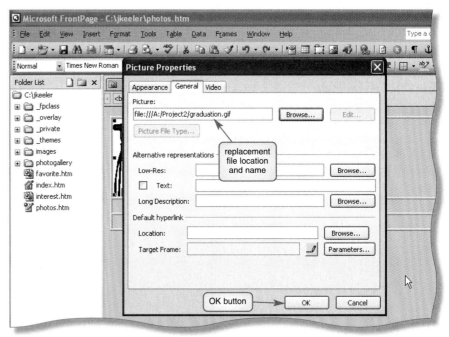

FIGURE 2-44

5

• **Click the OK button.**

• **Resize the replacement image by dragging the sizing handles to the approximate size shown in Figure 2-45.**

The selected image replaces the previous image (Figure 2-45). FrontPage displays sizing handles around the selected image. FrontPage changes the mouse pointer to a double-headed arrow when positioned on a sizing handle.

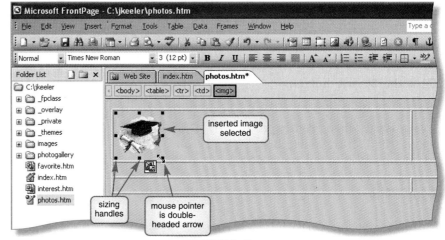

FIGURE 2-45

Other Ways

1. Open Pictures toolbar, click image, click Insert Picture From File button on Pictures toolbar

Copying and Pasting an Image in a Web Page

One of the features of Windows applications is the capability of copying information from one Windows application and inserting it in another Windows application. You can cut or copy portions of a Web page to a temporary storage area in computer memory, called the **Clipboard**, and then paste the contents of the Clipboard to other areas of the Web page. **Copy, Cut**, and **Paste** are useful when you want to move an item to another location or have the same item appearing several times in various places throughout the Web page. The clip art image you just inserted is to be inserted again, this time in the right cell of the table.

You can, of course, insert the clip art image using the steps previously shown for inserting an image. You also can copy the image to the Clipboard and then paste the image from the Clipboard to the Web page at the location of the insertion point. In this instance, the copy and paste operation would be more efficient, because you would have to maneuver through several windows to get the image from the Microsoft Clip Gallery or from an image on disk. The following steps copy and then paste the diploma image to another location in the Web page.

To Copy and Paste an Image in a Web Page

1

• **If necessary, click the clip art image to select it.**

• **Click Edit on the menu bar.**

The image is selected and the Edit menu is displayed (Figure 2-46). The Copy command copies a selected item to the Clipboard.

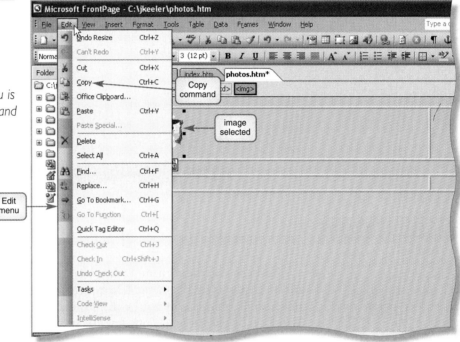

FIGURE 2-46

2

• **Click Copy and then click the upper-right cell of the table to position the insertion point.**

• **Click Edit on the menu bar.**

FrontPage displays the Edit menu (Figure 2-47). The image was copied to the Clipboard in the previous step. The Paste command inserts the contents of the Clipboard at the location of the insertion point.

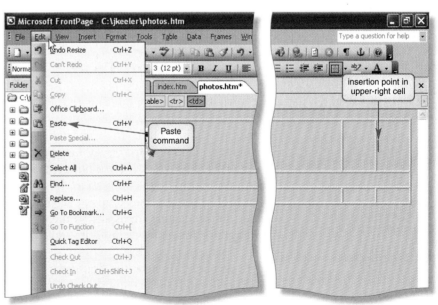

FIGURE 2-47

3

• **Click Paste.**

FrontPage copies the image on the Clipboard to the right table cell (Figure 2-48).

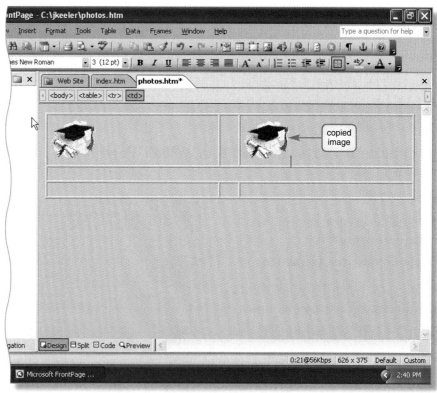

FIGURE 2-48

You can copy text or an entire table and then paste it in a similar fashion. Although the contents of the Clipboard can be inserted into other Windows applications, some objects will not be displayed as you would expect. Because many other Windows applications do not understand HTML, they cannot make an accurate copy of the three-row, three-column table if you were to try pasting it. You can, however, copy or cut and paste the clip art images and any text into other Windows applications, but you will lose any special formatting applied to the text. This again is because of the problem with translating HTML.

Using Tables to Control Alignment on a Web Page

One advantage of using tables is that they allow you to control the arrangement of items on the Web page. You can arrange, or **align**, the current text or image to the left within a table cell, to the right within a table cell, or centered in the table cell. The default alignment for newly inserted items is left-aligned.

FrontPage provides three alignment buttons on the Formatting toolbar. The Align Left button aligns an item at the left margin of the page or table cell. The Align Right button aligns items at the right margin of the page or table cell. The Center button centers items across the page or in a table cell. You simply select the paragraph or image by clicking it, and then click the appropriate alignment button on the Formatting toolbar.

To demonstrate how to align items on a Web page, the clip art image inserted in the left cell will be selected and right-aligned in the cell, which results in the clip art image aligning at the right along with text that will follow later. The following steps align an item on a Web page.

To Align Items on a Web Page

1

• **If necessary, click the clip art image in the left cell to select it.**

FrontPage shows the clip art image as selected (Figure 2-49).

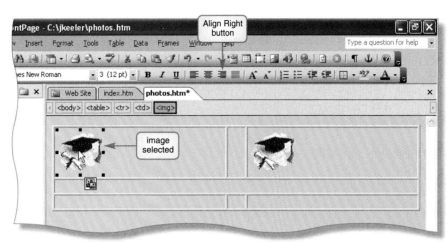

FIGURE 2-49

2

• **Click the Align Right button on the Formatting toolbar.**

FrontPage aligns the clip art image at the right margin of the table cell (Figure 2-50). The Align Right button on the Formatting toolbar is selected to denote that the image has been right-aligned.

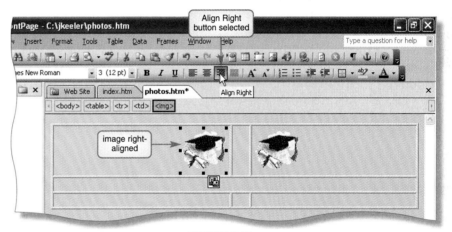

FIGURE 2-50

The image is right-aligned in the left table cell on the Web page. In later steps you use the Center button to center text and other items on the Web page.

Adjusting Table Borders

Another useful feature of tables is the capability of moving the outside borders of a table and the borders between individual cells, thus providing added flexibility in controlling spacing on the Web page.

You can adjust the borders of the table to control vertical and horizontal spacing. The bottom border can be dragged up or down to control vertical spacing. The right border can be dragged right or left to control horizontal spacing. The borders between cells also can be moved to control spacing within the table.

As shown in Figure 2-50, the clip art images do not consume all the space in their respective cells. You can adjust the borders between the cells to reduce the space in the two outside cells and increase the space in the center cell, thus providing more room for the heading. The steps on the next page adjust the borders of table cells.

To Adjust Table Cell Borders

1

• **Point to the cell border between the first and second cell in the top row.**

FrontPage changes the mouse pointer to a double-headed arrow (Figure 2-51).

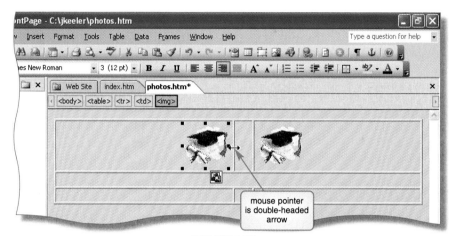

FIGURE 2-51

2

• **Drag the cell border left, to the approximate position shown in Figure 2-52, and release the mouse button.**

The cell border moves to the left (Figure 2-52).

3

• **Point to the cell border between the second and third cell in the top row.**

• **Drag the cell border right, toward the left edge of the clip art image, so that the right cell is approximately the same size as the left cell.**

The cell border moves to the right (Figure 2-53).

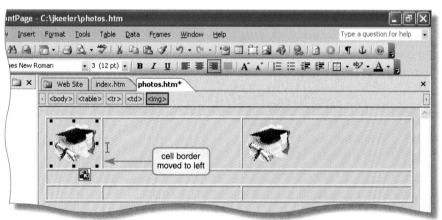

FIGURE 2-52

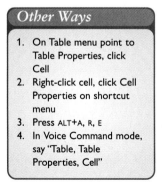

Other Ways

1. On Table menu point to Table Properties, click Cell
2. Right-click cell, click Cell Properties on shortcut menu
3. Press ALT+A, R, E
4. In Voice Command mode, say "Table, Table Properties, Cell"

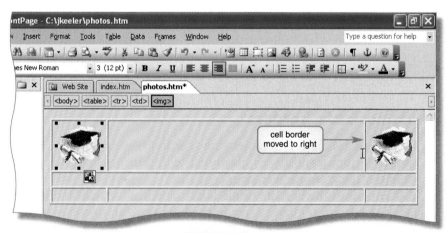

FIGURE 2-53

Moving the cell to occupy the minimum width for the images allows more space in the center cell for the Photos page heading text. You should insert the images in the table cells before adjusting the cell borders so that you can see how much space is available. Adjusting table and cell borders is a powerful way of controlling spacing on a Web page.

Modifying Table Properties

A number of table properties can be adjusted to control how the table is displayed on a Web page. FrontPage allows you to adjust the horizontal alignment of the table with respect to the Web page. FrontPage also allows you to adjust the width of the table as a percentage of the entire page, or as a specified number of pixels. A **pixel**, short for **picture element**, is the smallest addressable element on your computer screen. Instead of dragging cell borders, you also may set the cell width directly by specifying the width as a percentage of the table, or as a specified number of pixels.

Tables and the individual cells are surrounded by a default table border. You can adjust the properties of the border, such as the width, color, and use of a 3-D shadow. When using a table for spacing purposes, you most likely will not want the table borders to be seen. You can turn off the border display and adjust other table properties by using the Table Properties command on the Table menu. The following steps modify table properties.

To Modify the Properties of a Table

1

• **If necessary, click one of the cells of the table.**

• **Click Table on the menu bar and then point to Table Properties.**

FrontPage displays the Table menu and Table Properties submenu (Figure 2-54). The Table menu contains commands to manage tables. The Table Properties submenu contains commands to access properties of tables or individual cells.

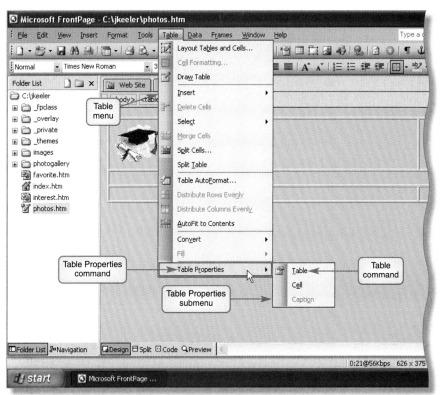

FIGURE 2-54

2

• **Click Table on the Table Properties submenu.**

• **When FrontPage displays the Table Properties dialog box, click the Alignment box down arrow in the Layout area.**

FrontPage displays the Table Properties dialog box (Figure 2-55). Options in this dialog box allow you to control various aspects of the table border and table background. The Alignment box in the Layout area allows you to control the horizontal alignment of the table on the Web page.

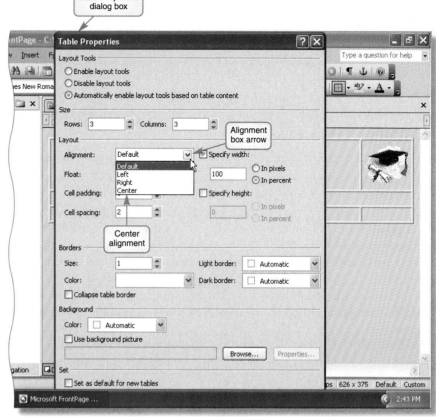

FIGURE 2-55

3

• **Click Center.**

• **If necessary, in the Layout area, click Specify width and click In pixels.**

• **Type** 688 **in the Specify width text box.**

The alignment for the table is set to Center and the width is set to 688 pixels (Figure 2-56).

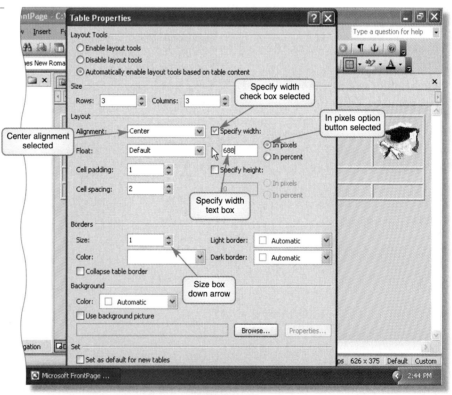

FIGURE 2-56

4

• **In the Borders area, click the Size box down arrow until zero (0) appears in the Size box.**

FrontPage displays zero (0) in the Size box, indicating that no visible border will be displayed around the table cells (Figure 2-57).

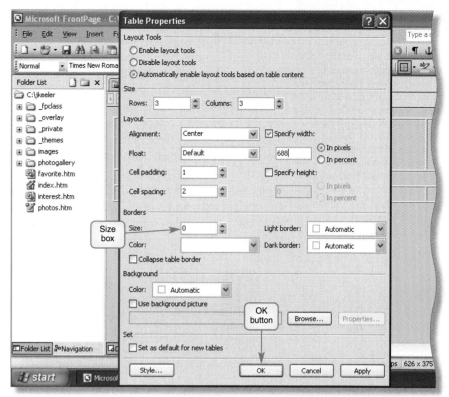

FIGURE 2-57

5

• **Click the OK button.**

The table width is set and the table border is replaced with dashed lines (Figure 2-58). These lines show you where the cell borders are and also indicate that no visible border is displayed when the browser displays the Web page.

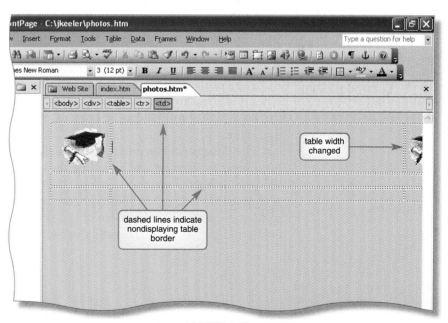

FIGURE 2-58

You have adjusted the borders around table cells and turned off the display of the table border. Now that the size of the center cell has been adjusted, the heading for the Web page can be inserted.

Other Ways

1. Right-click table, click Table Properties on shortcut menu
2. Press ALT+A, R, T
3. In Voice Command mode, say "Table, Table Properties, Table"

Inserting a Heading in a Web Page

Text on a Web page can take many forms, such as a heading, ordered and unordered lists, menus, and normal text. To this text, you can apply special formatting such as different fonts, colors, and sizes. You use the Formatting toolbar for the more frequently used formatting options.

The process of entering text using FrontPage has several steps. You might skip one or more of the steps, depending on the current settings. The first step is to select a text style. The Style box on the Formatting toolbar contains styles such as lists, menu items, headings, and normal text.

After selecting a style, you may change the font type for the text or use the font type associated with the chosen style. A **font** is another name for character set. Some commonly used fonts are Courier, Helvetica, and Arial. You change the font using the Font box on the Formatting toolbar. If a font is not available on a Web site visitor's computer, then a default font is applied in the visitor's browser.

> *Design Tip*
>
> Use common fonts in your Web pages to increase the chances of overriding default font settings and allowing the visitor to view the page in the manner in which it was designed. Type that is 10 points or smaller may not be readable to many Web page visitors.

Next, you select a color for the text. The default color is black. A text color that complements the background color or image you have chosen is preferred so your text does not fade in and out as it moves across a background image or pattern. You do not want your page to be difficult to read because of poor color selection. To change the color of text, use the Font Color button arrow on the Formatting toolbar. You can choose from a set of standard colors or from a set that matches a theme if a theme is applied, or mix your own custom colors.

The Formatting toolbar contains many text-formatting options. The Font Size box allows you to increase or decrease the size of the characters in your text. Using the Bold, Italic, and Underline buttons, you can format certain text in bold, italic, or underline.

The Photos page heading, which will be placed in the center table cell, consists of Heading 2 as its style and green for the font color. The font and font size used are the default for the style of Heading 2. The heading also is centered in the cell. The text on either side of the photo gallery will use the same font color, but will have a style of Normal and a font size of 2 (10 pt). The following steps set the style and color, and then insert the heading in the center cell.

To Add a Heading to a Web Page

1

- **If necessary, click the top center table cell to position the insertion point.**
- **Click the Style box arrow.**
- **If necessary, scroll down to Heading 2 in the Style list.**

FrontPage displays the insertion point in the top center table cell. FrontPage also displays the Style list (Figure 2-59). It contains a list of styles available for use when developing Web pages.

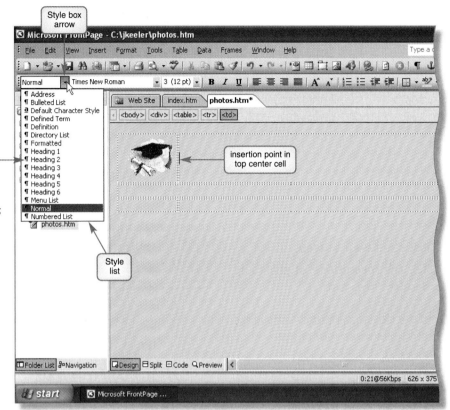

FIGURE 2-59

2

- **Click Heading 2.**
- **Click the Center button on the Formatting toolbar.**
- **Type** Marketing Experience **in the top center cell.**
- **Press SHIFT+ENTER.**
- **Type** Photo Album **to enter the remainder of the text.**

FrontPage displays the text centered in the top center table cell with a style of Heading 2 (Figure 2-60). The font and the font size associated with the style Heading 2 are displayed in the Font box and the Font Size box, respectively. The Bold button on the Formatting toolbar is selected automatically. Your font and font size may be different.

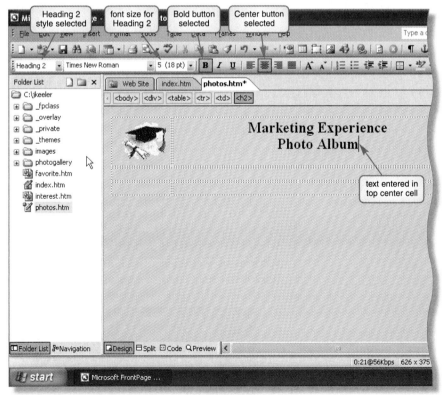

FIGURE 2-60

3

• **Drag through the text to select it.**

• **Click the Font Color button arrow.**

FrontPage displays the color palette (Figure 2-61).

FIGURE 2-61

4

• **Click the Green button.**

• **Click the second row of the table to deselect the text.**

FrontPage displays the text centered in the top center cell with a color of green (Figure 2-62).

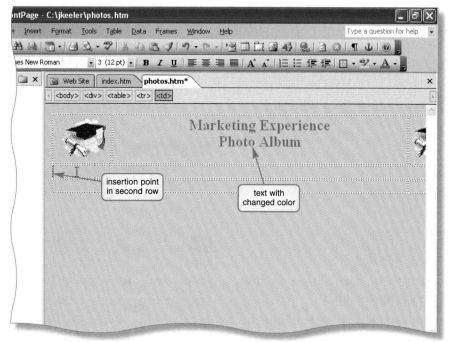

FIGURE 2-62

Other Ways

1. On Format menu click Font, click Font tab
2. Right-click text, click Font, click Font tab
3. Press ALT+ENTER
4. In Voice Command mode, say "Format, Font", click Font tab

Because the header is the part of the page that first-time viewers initially see in their browsers, it is important to format the header of the Web page so it is appealing and draws further interest. The body of the Web page keeps the viewer's attention when it is verbalized and formatted appropriately. It is customary to separate logical sections of Web pages, such as the header and body, using dividing elements called horizontal lines, or horizontal rules.

Design Tip

It is customary to separate logical sections of Web pages, such as the header and body, using dividing elements called horizontal lines, or horizontal rules. Use headers and footers on pages that comprise the main navigational structure of your site. Secondary pages need not fit a rigid design structure.

Inserting a Horizontal Rule

The use of elements such as a horizontal rule can add a special look to your pages, as well as provide the viewer with visual clues concerning the location of information on the Web page. Horizontal rules are used to break up the page into sections, and to separate elements on the page. A **horizontal rule** is a small, thin line that spans the entire Web page.

A horizontal rule will be used to separate the header section of the Web page from the body. The following steps insert a horizontal rule below the table cells containing the clip art images and heading.

To Add a Horizontal Rule to a Web Page

1

• **If necessary, click the second table row to position the insertion point.**

• **Click Insert on the menu bar.**

FrontPage displays the Insert menu (Figure 2-63). The Insert menu contains commands to insert various elements in the current Web page.

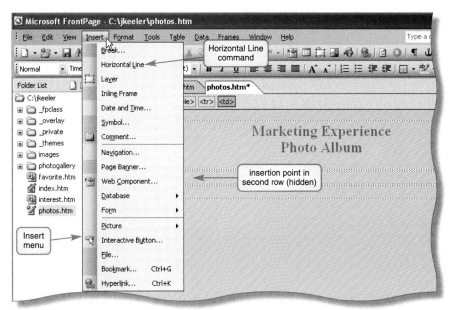

FIGURE 2-63

2

• **Click Horizontal Line.**

• **Press the DELETE key to remove the trailing blank line.**

FrontPage displays the horizontal rule in the middle row (Figure 2-64).

FIGURE 2-64

Other Ways

1. Press ALT+I, L

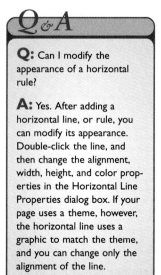

Q: Can I modify the appearance of a horizontal rule?

A: Yes. After adding a horizontal line, or rule, you can modify its appearance. Double-click the line, and then change the alignment, width, height, and color properties in the Horizontal Line Properties dialog box. If your page uses a theme, however, the horizontal line uses a graphic to match the theme, and you can change only the alignment of the line.

You can adjust the properties of the horizontal rule, such as the thickness and length, by right-clicking the horizontal rule and then clicking Horizontal Line Properties on the shortcut menu. The alignment of the horizontal rule also can be controlled using the Align Left, Center, and Align Right buttons on the Formatting toolbar.

Adding Normal Text to a Web Page

Notice in Figure 2-62 on page FP 122 that the style and font for new text reverted to the default values. This occurs whenever you move the insertion point with the mouse or arrow keys. You need to set the style, font, and color again in preparation for entering more text.

The steps for adding normal text are similar to the steps used previously to add the heading: set the style, and either use the associated font, font size, and color, or manually set these properties. According to the design, the text in the lower-left cell is to be aligned along the top edge of the cell, while the text in the right cell is to retain a default alignment. The following steps add the normal text that will be displayed on the Web page.

To Add Normal Text to a Web Page

1

• **Right-click the lower-left cell.**

FrontPage displays the shortcut menu (Figure 2-65).

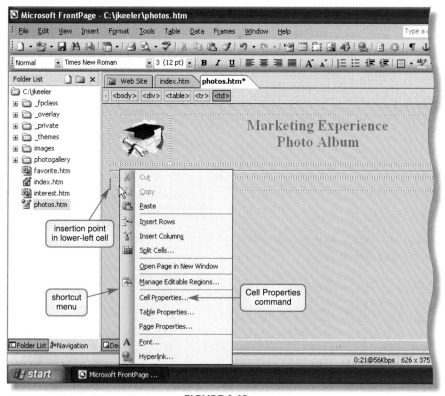

FIGURE 2-65

2

• **Click Cell Properties.**

• **When FrontPage displays the Cell Properties dialog box, click the Vertical alignment box arrow in the Layout area.**

FrontPage displays the Vertical alignment list showing the choices for vertical alignment in the cell (Figure 2-66).

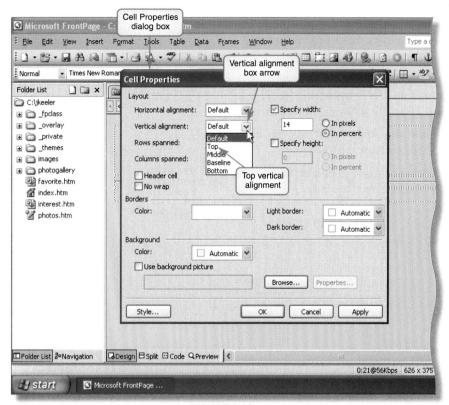

FIGURE 2-66

3

• **Click Top.**

• **Click the OK button.**

The Cell Properties dialog box closes (Figure 2-67). Although no change is visible, when an item is displayed in this cell, it will be aligned along the top cell edge.

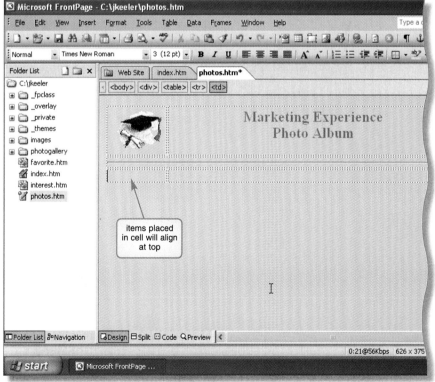

FIGURE 2-67

4

• **If necessary, click Normal in the Style list.**

• **If necessary, click the Font box arrow on the Formatting toolbar and then click Times New Roman.**

• **Click the Align Right button on the Formatting toolbar.**

• **Click the Font Size box arrow on the Formatting toolbar.**

The Style box indicates Normal style and the Font box indicates Times New Roman (Figure 2-68).

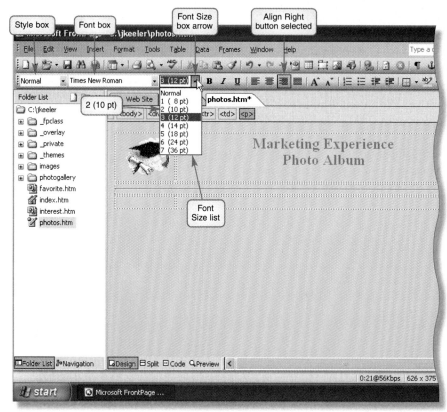

FIGURE 2-68

5

• **Click 2 (10 pt).**

• **Type** Point to an image to see a caption **in the lower-left cell.**

FrontPage displays the text entered right-aligned on the Web page (Figure 2-69).

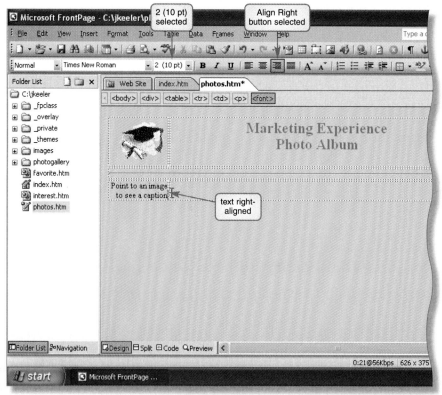

FIGURE 2-69

6

• **Drag through the entered text to select it.**

• **Click the Font Color button arrow on the Formatting toolbar and then click the Green button in the color palette.**

• **Click the bottom center cell to deselect the text.**

FrontPage displays the newly entered text with green as the font color (Figure 2-70).

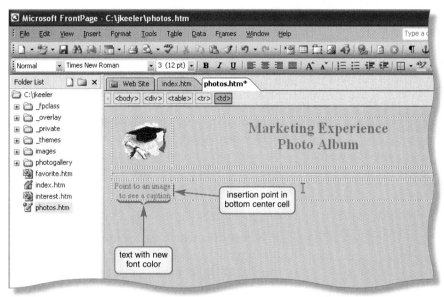

FIGURE 2-70

7

• **Click the lower-right cell to position the insertion point.**

• **If necessary, click Normal in the Style list and click Times New Roman in the Font list.**

• **Click the Font Size box arrow and then click 2 (10 pt).**

• **Type** Click an image to see a larger view **in the cell.**

8

• **Drag through the entered text to select it.**

• **Click the Font Color button arrow on the Formatting toolbar and then click the Green button in the color palette.**

• **Click the bottom center cell.**

FrontPage displays the newly entered text in Normal style, Times New Roman font, with a font size of 10 pt and a font color of green (Figure 2-71).

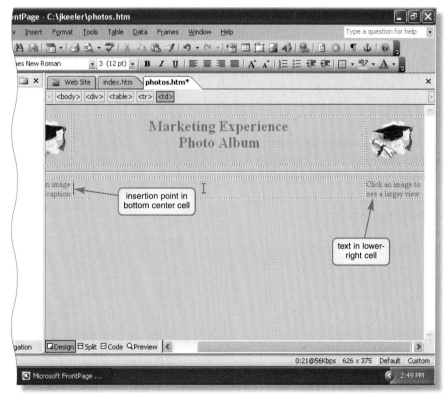

FIGURE 2-71

Other Ways

1. Select text, right-click text, click Font on short-cut menu
2. Select text, press ALT+ENTER
3. Select text, in Voice Command mode, say "Format, Font", click Font tab

You can see from the previous steps that the Formatting toolbar is very useful when entering text. You can change styles, fonts, font size, and other properties very quickly as you move through the body of the Web page.

More About

The Photo Gallery Component

The Photo Gallery component offers four layouts: Horizontal, Vertical, Montage, and Slideshow. You should examine each layout to determine which one is most appropriate for the photos you want to display.

Adding a Photo Gallery Component

One strength of Web pages is the capability to display images as well as text. Some information is better communicated in a textual form, while much fits the old adage of a picture being worth a thousand words. This is especially true when dealing with photographic clip art, because photos are meant to be seen, not just described. There are issues, however, with using photos in a Web page. First of all, the data files for photos tend to be large. Visitors to a Web page may not wait for the page to download when large pictures slow down the process. Also, when positioning text with photographs, it can be tedious and difficult to get an arrangement that is pleasing, especially when dealing with a large number of pictures.

FrontPage has a component called a Photo Gallery that presents solutions to many of these problems. A **Photo Gallery component** offers several customizable layouts for photos and provides for captions. The montage layout displays captions as ScreenTips when the mouse pointer rests on them. The pictures used in the layouts are actually thumbnail images of the original pictures, created automatically by using the Photo Gallery component. A **thumbnail image** is a small image that is a hyperlink to a larger version of the same picture. Using a thumbnail version of an image can speed up the time it takes to load a Web page, because only a smaller version is used. When you click the thumbnail image, the full-sized version of the file is loaded in your browser.

The following steps insert a Photo Gallery component.

To Add a Photo Gallery Component

1

• **If necessary, click the middle cell in the bottom row of the table to position the insertion point.**

• **Click the Center button on the Formatting toolbar.**

FrontPage displays the insertion point centered in the middle cell of the bottom table row (Figure 2-72).

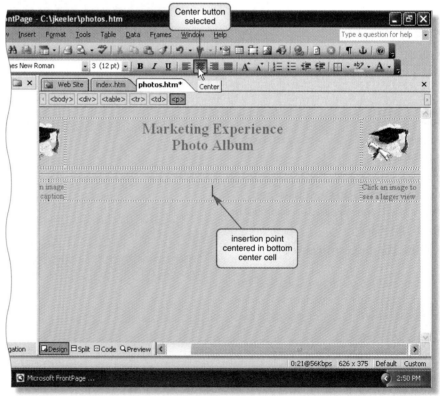

FIGURE 2-72

2

• **Click Insert on the menu bar.**

FrontPage displays the Insert menu (Figure 2-73).

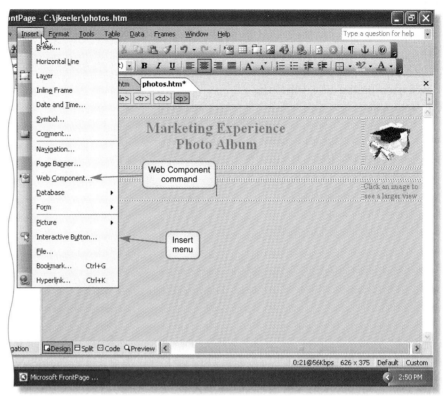

FIGURE 2-73

3

• **Click Web Component.**

• **When FrontPage displays the Insert Web Component dialog box, click Photo Gallery in the Component type list.**

• **Click the montage arrangement icon in the Choose a Photo Gallery Option list.**

FrontPage displays the Insert Web Component dialog box with the Photo Gallery component type and the montage option selected (Figure 2-74). FrontPage displays a brief description of the selected arrangement.

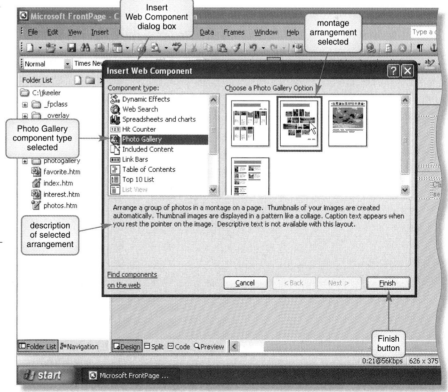

FIGURE 2-74

4

• **Click the Finish button.**

• **If necessary, when FrontPage displays the Photo Gallery Properties dialog box, click the Pictures tab.**

FrontPage displays the Photo Gallery Properties dialog box (Figure 2-75). The Pictures sheet contains settings to control the content, format, and text for a Photo Gallery.

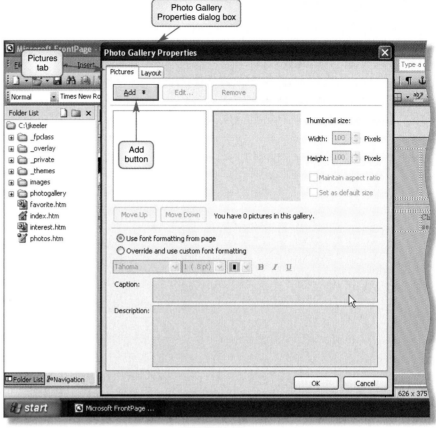

FIGURE 2-75

5

• **Click the Add button.**

FrontPage displays the Add menu (Figure 2-76). The commands on the Add menu enable you to obtain pictures from files, a scanner, or a camera.

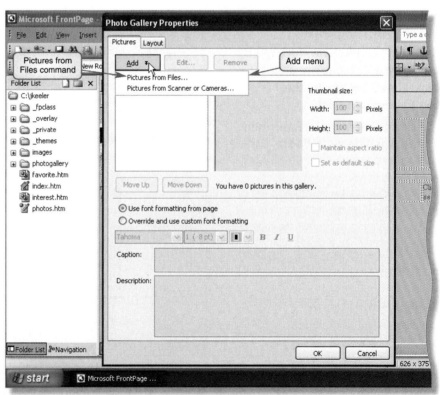

FIGURE 2-76

6

- **Click Pictures from Files.**
- **Insert the Data Disk in drive A.**
- **If necessary, when the File Open dialog box is displayed, click the Look in box arrow and select the Senior group project.jpg file in the Project2 folder.**

FrontPage displays the File Open dialog box (Figure 2-77). Use the drive and location that are appropriate for your environment.

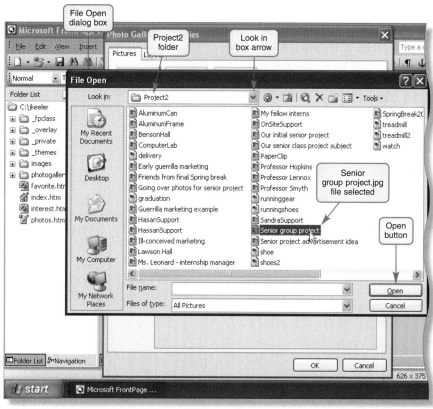

FIGURE 2-77

7

- **Click the Open button.**
- **When FrontPage closes the File Open dialog box and the Photo Gallery Properties dialog box again is visible, click the Caption text box and type** Burning the midnight oil working on our Senior group project. **in the text box.**
- **Verify that a check mark is displayed in the Maintain aspect ratio check box.**

The selected options for the Photo Gallery Properties dialog box are shown in Figure 2-78.

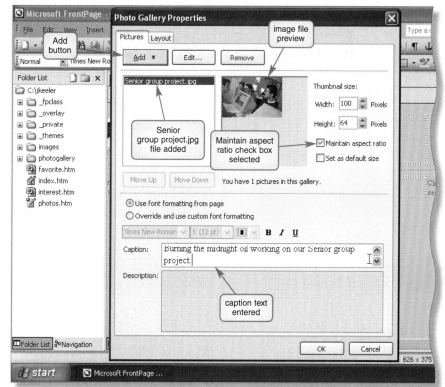

FIGURE 2-78

8

• **Repeat Step 5 through Step 7 for the photos listed in Table 2-2, typing the associated text for each photo caption.**

The remaining photos are added to the Photo Gallery list of photos (Figure 2-79). The Photo Gallery Properties dialog box indicates the number of pictures added.

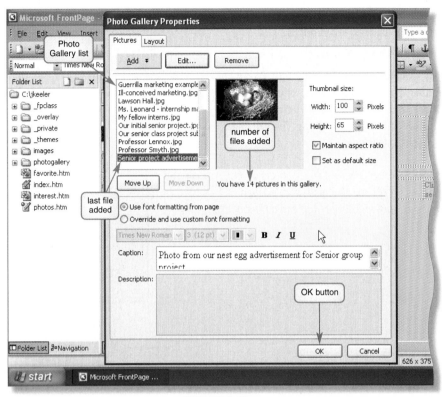

FIGURE 2-79

9

• **Click the OK button.**

• **If necessary, drag the table borders to adjust positioning of the text and images.**

The Photo Gallery Properties dialog box closes, and the Photo Gallery component generates and displays thumbnail images for the inserted photos on the Photos page (Figure 2-80).

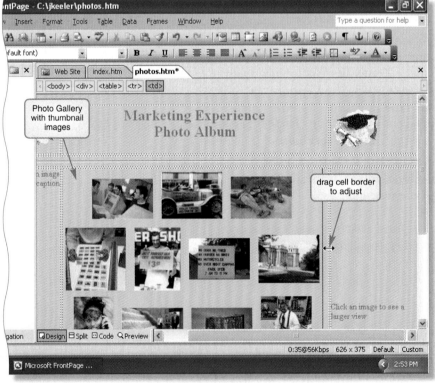

FIGURE 2-80

Other Ways

1. On the Insert menu point to Picture, click New Photo Gallery
2. Press ALT+I, P, P
3. In Voice Command mode, say "Insert, Picture, New Photo Gallery"

The thumbnail images are hyperlinks to their corresponding full-sized images. When a viewer clicks the thumbnail, the full-size image is displayed, much like a Web page would do. The browser, however, is displaying an image file, not a Web page, so hyperlinks are not available to navigate back to the previous page. The viewer must click the browser's Back button to display the previous page.

Table 2-2 Photo File Names and Captions	
PHOTO FILE NAME	CAPTION
Senior group project.jpg	Burning the midnight oil working on our Senior group project.
Early guerrilla marketing.jpg	Early guerrilla marketing attempts were innovative.
Friends from final Spring break.jpg	Relaxing for a final time before we hit the real world.
Going over photos for senior project.jpg	Inspecting photos to use in our group project.
Guerrilla marketing example.jpg	Shocking or funny. Guerrilla marketing tactics serve to set you apart.
Ill-conceived marketing.jpg	A better alternative is to focus on positives.
Lawson Hall.jpg	Where I spent half of my life for the past four years.
Ms. Leonard - internship manager.jpg	Ms. Leonard was an ideal boss. Fair yet tough.
My fellow interns.jpg	My fellow interns take a late lunch last summer.
Our initial senior project.jpg	Starting at square one for our Senior group project.
Our senior class project subject.jpg	We eventually settled on a guerrilla marketing campaign for a local barber.
Professor Lennox.jpg	My mentor for my Senior year.
Professor Smyth.jpg	Professor Smyth was the department head and my advisor.
Senior project advertisement idea.jpg	Photo from our nest egg advertisement for Senior group project.

Inserting Link Bars on a Web Page

As previously discussed, link bars are a commonly used component. The Capsules theme you applied to the Web site includes two link bars — a **vertical link bar** on the left-hand side of the page and a **horizontal link bar** on the bottom. Link bars typically are used for either child-level navigation, which allows you to move between the Home page (the parent) and the Professional Interests page or Favorite Links page (the children), or same-level navigation, which allows you to move back and forth between pages at the same level, such as the Professional Interests and Favorite Links pages. In the Personal Web site template, both link bars on a given page have the same navigation properties: links on the Home page are used for child-level navigation, and links on the child pages are set for same-level navigation. Each link bar also has an additional link to the Home page.

The steps on the next page insert a link bar component for the Photos page.

Q: Can I link to both internal and external pages with a link bar?

A: Yes. To create link bars with links both to internal pages and to pages external to your site, select the Bar with custom links bar type in the Insert Web Component dialog box.

To Add a Link Bar Component

1

• **Position the insertion point at the end of the text in the lower-left cell of the table.**

• **Press the ENTER key.**

• **Click Insert on the menu bar.**

FrontPage displays the insertion point in the left cell of the bottom table row (Figure 2-81).

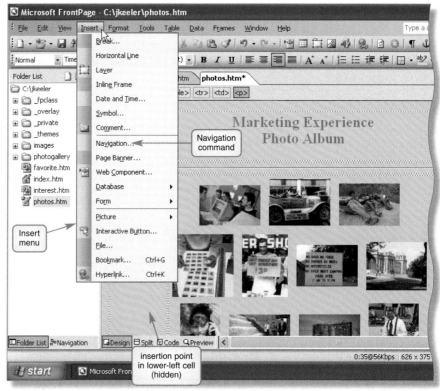

FIGURE 2-81

2

• **Click Navigation.**

• **When FrontPage displays the Insert Web Component dialog box, click Bar based on navigation structure in the Choose a bar type list.**

FrontPage displays the Insert Web Component dialog box with the Link Bars component type already selected (Figure 2-82). FrontPage displays a brief comment about the type of link bar to be added.

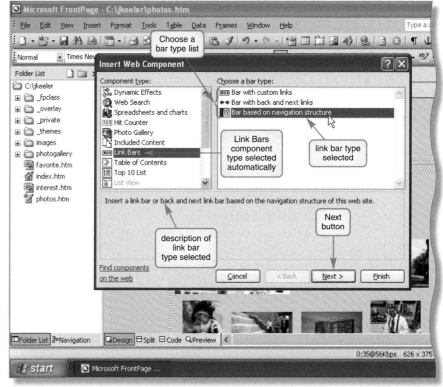

FIGURE 2-82

3

• **Click the Next button.**

• **If necessary, when FrontPage displays the Choose a bar style list in the Insert Web Component dialog box, scroll down, and then click the icon for a graphical style based on the Bars theme.**

FrontPage displays the Insert Web Component dialog box with a bar style selected based on the Bars theme (Figure 2-83). FrontPage displays a brief description of the selected style.

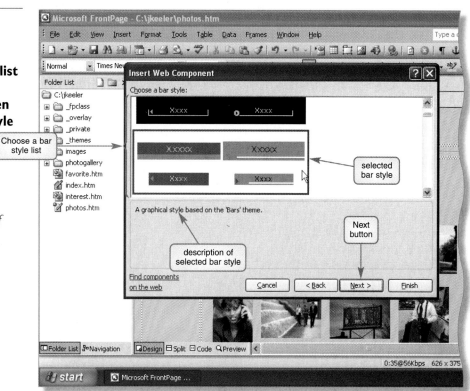

FIGURE 2-83

4

• **Click the Next button.**

• **When FrontPage displays the Choose an orientation list in the Insert Web Component dialog box, click the icon to insert the link bar with the links arranged vertically.**

FrontPage displays the Insert Web Component dialog box with a vertical link bar orientation selected (Figure 2-84). Some descriptive text indicates the arrangement to be used for the links.

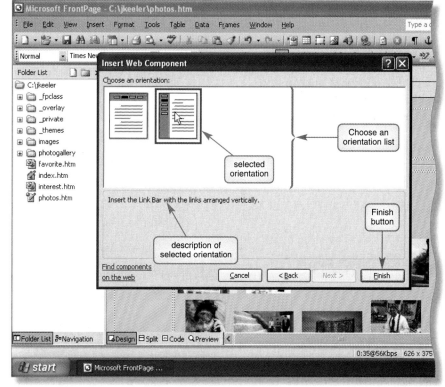

FIGURE 2-84

5

• **Click the Finish button.**

• **If necessary, when FrontPage displays the Link Bar Properties dialog box, click the General tab.**

• **Click Child pages under Home in the Hyperlinks to add to page area.**

• **Click Home page in the Additional pages area.**

FrontPage displays the Link Bar Properties dialog box with Child pages under Home and Home page selected (Figure 2-85). FrontPage displays a diagram to indicate hierarchical relationships between the page on which the link bar is displayed and the pages to which the link bar is linked.

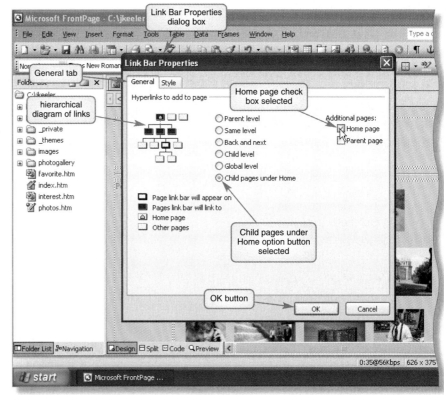

FIGURE 2-85

6

• **Click the OK button.**

• **If necessary, drag the cell borders to adjust positioning of the text.**

• **Click the Preview button and position the mouse pointer over a picture in the Photo Gallery.**

FrontPage displays the Photos page with a link bar based on the Bars theme (Figure 2-86). FrontPage displays the caption text for the indicated photo as a ScreenTip.

7

• **Click the Design button.**

Other Ways

1. On Insert menu click Web Component, click Link Bars
2. Press ALT+I, V
3. Press ALT+I, C
4. In Voice Command mode, say "Insert, Navigation"

FIGURE 2-86

Because the Photos page was added to the Web site in Navigation view — thereby establishing a navigation structure with the Photos page as a child to the Home page — FrontPage was able to create the proper links for the link bar automatically.

In addition to the Home page, the link bar you just added also links to the other child pages in the Web site — the Professional Interests page and the Favorite Links page. If you delete one of these pages from the current Web site, the link bar component automatically removes links to the deleted page from the link bars on all pages in the current Web site.

Previewing and Printing a Web Page

In Project 1, you printed the Web page without previewing it on the screen. By previewing the Web page, you can see how it will look when printed without generating a printout, or hard copy. Previewing a Web page using the Print Preview command on the File menu can save time, paper, and the frustration of waiting for a printout only to discover it is not what you want. You must be using Design view to use print preview, as this command is not accessible when using the Preview tab.

You also can print the Web page while in print preview. The following steps preview and then print the Photos Web page.

To Preview and Print a Web Page

1

• **Ready the printer according to the printer instructions.**

• **Verify that the Design button is selected.**

• **Click File on the menu bar (Figure 2-87).**

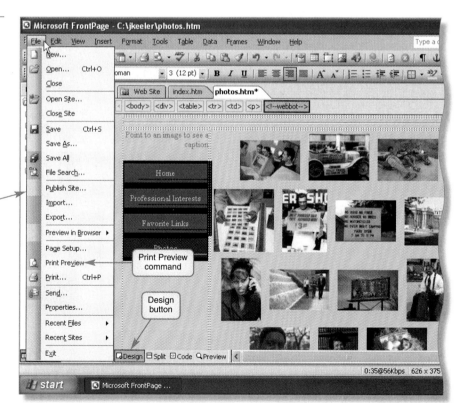

FIGURE 2-87

2

• **Click Print Preview.**

FrontPage displays a preview of the Web page in the preview pane and the mouse pointer changes to a magnifying glass when positioned over the image of the page (Figure 2-88). You may click on the image to zoom in for a closer view.

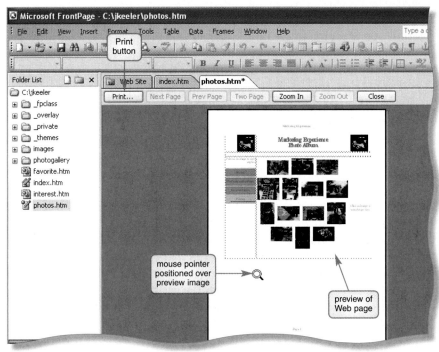

FIGURE 2-88

3

• **Click the Print button on the Print Preview toolbar.**

• **Click the OK button in the Print dialog box.**

FrontPage closes the preview pane and prints the Web page. When FrontPage completes the printing operation, retrieve the printout (Figure 2-89).

FIGURE 2-89

Other Ways

1. Press ALT+F, V
2. In Voice Command mode, say "File, Print Preview"

The Print Preview toolbar contains buttons to scroll through a multipage printout, to zoom in and out of the Web page, and to close the preview pane. You can use print preview to determine the page number of a particular page in a multipage printout and then print only that page. This allows you to print only the particular section of a long Web page on which you are working, thus saving time and paper.

Saving the Web Page and Embedded Images

Once you have finished editing the Web page, you should save it on disk. With the Photos page, the save operation consists of saving the HTML and the clip art images for the Web page. Neither the clip art images you inserted in earlier steps nor the thumbnail images created by FrontPage were physically inserted in the Photos page. FrontPage placed HTML instructions to include each clip art image file using an <IMG SRC=> tag. This tag has a reference to the file name containing the clip art image, but the image still must be saved with the Web page.

Because the thumbnail images are part of a Photo Gallery component, when the Photos page is saved, they are saved automatically in the photogallery folder in the current Web site. When the Photos Web page is saved, it contains only the HTML tags referencing the diploma clip art file and special commands referencing the Photo Gallery component. The original photo images are referenced by pages created by the Photo Gallery component in the photogallery folder. FrontPage saves the clip art and photo image files in the Web site folders as well. As a default, FrontPage saves the image files to the current folder. You may, however, want to have all images used in your Web page, except for the thumbnail images, stored in a folder separate from the actual Web page. Because FrontPage created an images folder when this new Web site was created, it makes sense to place the images in that folder. The following steps save the Photos page, along with the embedded image files.

To Save a Web Page and Embedded Images

1

• **Click the Save button on the Standard toolbar.**

FrontPage displays the Save Embedded Files dialog box (Figure 2-90). This dialog box shows the file names of the clip art images you inserted in the Web page.

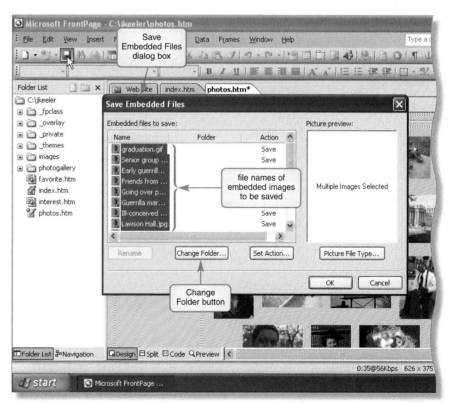

FIGURE 2-90

2

• **Click the Change Folder button.**

• **When FrontPage displays the Change Folder dialog box, click the images folder.**

FrontPage displays the Change Folder dialog box (Figure 2-91). The images folder is selected.

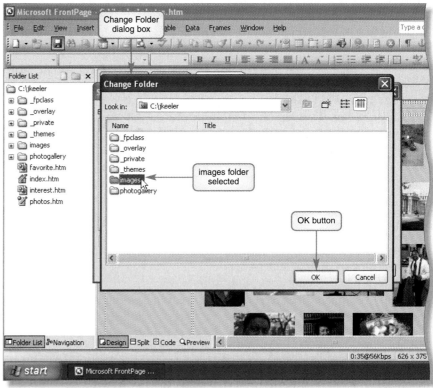

FIGURE 2-91

3

• **Click the OK button in the Change Folder dialog box.**

The Save Embedded Files dialog box indicates that the images folder will be used to store the images selected (Figure 2-92).

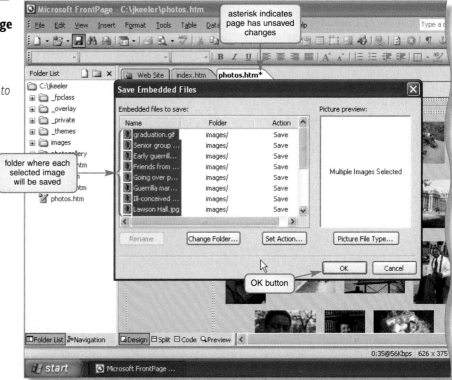

FIGURE 2-92

4

• **Click the OK button.**

The Save Embedded Files dialog box is closed and the Photos page and the clip art image files are saved (Figure 2-93).

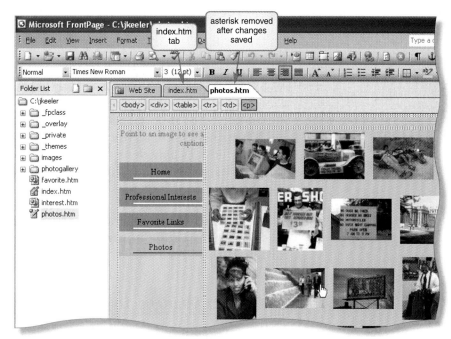

FIGURE 2-93

5

• **Click the index.htm tab to view the Home page.**

FrontPage displays the Home page with the link bar updated to include the Photos page (Figure 2-94).

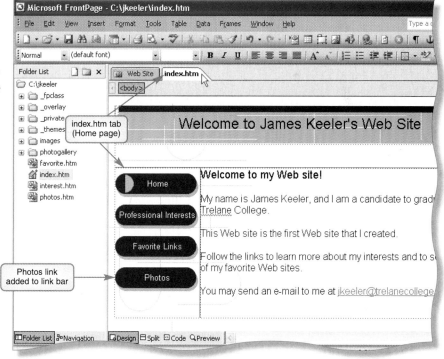

FIGURE 2-94

It is important that all clip art images be saved as part of the FrontPage Web site. These image files must be available when publishing the FrontPage Web site to a Web server. If you do not save them and then publish the FrontPage Web site, those <IMG SRC=> tags will be broken, because the files referenced by the tags will not be on the Web server. Thus, the Web page will not display properly.

Other Ways

1. On File menu click Save
2. Press ALT+F, S
3. Press CTRL+S
4. In Voice Command mode, say "File, Save"

More About

**The Quick
Reference**

For more information, see
the Quick Reference
Summary at the back of this
book, or visit the FrontPage
2003 Quick Reference Web
page (scsite.com/fp2003/qr).

Publishing Changes to an Existing FrontPage Web Site

In Project 1, James Keeler's personal Web site was published on the World Wide Web. You since have added a new Web page and the accompanying image files to the FrontPage Web site. For these new items to be available on the World Wide Web, you must publish the personal Web site again.

When you publish a FrontPage Web site that has been published before, FrontPage installs only those parts of the Web site that are new or that have changed since the last time the Web site was published. This reduces the amount of data transfer that takes place, which is good for Web sites with many folders, Web pages, and files.

The following steps summarize how to publish changes to a FrontPage Web site. Be sure to substitute your own URL or an error will occur. If you do not know what URL to use, ask your instructor.

To Publish Changes to an Existing FrontPage Web Site

1 Click the Publish Site button on the Standard toolbar. Because this Web site was published previously, FrontPage does not display the Publish Destination dialog box, but assumes that you want to publish to the same location.

2 If prompted, type your user name and password, and click the OK button.

3 Click the index.htm tab to display the Home page.

You now can view the Photos page by entering http://www.trelanecollege.edu/~jkeeler/photos.htm (use your own URL) in any browser and pressing the ENTER key. Be sure to test the hyperlink to the Home page and from the Home page to the Photos page.

Quitting Microsoft FrontPage

When you have published James Keeler's Web site, you can quit Microsoft FrontPage. The following steps quit FrontPage.

To Quit Microsoft FrontPage

1 Click File on the menu bar and then click Close Site.

2 Click the Close button on the FrontPage title bar.

Project Summary

Project 2 introduced you to the essentials of Web page development. You learned about good design criteria. Using FrontPage, you created a new Web page providing your own original content. You removed an applied theme and changed the background color of the new Web page. You inserted a table and adjusted the table properties. Using appropriate images, you inserted clip art to enhance the appearance of the Web page and later replaced the clip art with a more suitable image. Then, you added text and learned how to change formats such as style, font, font size, and alignment. Next, you inserted horizontal rules. You inserted photographs in a Photo Gallery, including captions for each picture. You learned how to insert link bars for navigation, and then you previewed your Web page before printing. Finally, you saved a Web page along with the embedded image files and published the changes to your existing Web site.

What You Should Know

Having completed this project, you should be able to perform the tasks below. The tasks are listed in the same order they were presented in this project. For a list of the buttons, menus, toolbars, and commands introduced in this project, see the Quick Reference Summary at the back of this book and refer to the Page Number column.

1. Start FrontPage   (FP 87)
2. Open an Existing FrontPage Web Site   (FP 88)
3. Add a New Web Page to an Existing Web Site (FP 90)
4. Rename a Web Page   (FP 92)
5. Change the Title of a Web Page   (FP 94)
6. Change the Page Label of a Web Page   (FP 96)
7. Edit a Web Page in Design View   (FP 97)
8. Change the Theme for a Web Page   (FP 98)
9. Change the Background Color   (FP 100)
10. Insert a Table in a Web Page   (FP 104)
11. Merge Cells in a Table   (FP 105)
12. Insert a Clip Art Image in a Web Page   (FP 107)
13. Replace a Clip Art Image in a Web Page   (FP 110)
14. Copy and Paste an Image in a Web Page   (FP 113)
15. Align Items on a Web Page   (FP 115)
16. Adjust Table Cell Borders   (FP 116)
17. Modify the Properties of a Table   (FP 117)
18. Add a Heading to a Web Page   (FP 121)
19. Add a Horizontal Rule to a Web Page   (FP 123)
20. Add Normal Text to a Web Page   (FP 124)
21. Add a Photo Gallery Component   (FP 128)
22. Add a Link Bar Component   (FP 134)
23. Preview and Print a Web Page   (FP 137)
24. Save a Web Page and Embedded Images (FP 139)
25. Publish Changes to an Existing FrontPage Web Site   (FP 142)
26. Quit Microsoft FrontPage   (FP 142)

Learn It Online

Instructions: To complete the Learn It Online exercises, start your browser, click the Address bar, and then enter the Web address scsite.com/fp2003/learn. When the FrontPage 2003 Learn It Online page is displayed, follow the instructions in the exercises below. Each exercise has instructions for printing your results, either for your own records or for submission to your instructor.

1 Project Reinforcement TF, MC, and SA

Below FrontPage Project 2, click the Project Reinforcement link. Print the quiz by clicking Print on the File menu for each page. Answer each question.

Flash Cards

Below FrontPage Project 2, click the Flash Cards link and read the instructions. Type 20 (or a number specified by your instructor) in the Number of playing cards text box, type your name in the Enter your Name text box, and then click the Flip Card button. When the flash card is displayed, read the question and then click the ANSWER box arrow to select an answer. Flip through Flash Cards. If your score is 15 (75%) correct or greater, click Print on the File menu to print your results. If your score is less than 15 (75%) correct, then redo this exercise by clicking the Replay button.

3 Practice Test

Below FrontPage Project 2, click the Practice Test link. Answer each question, enter your first and last name at the bottom of the page, and then click the Grade Test button. When the graded practice test is displayed on your screen, click Print on the File menu to print a hard copy. Continue to take practice tests until you score 80% or better.

4 Who Wants To Be a Computer Genius?

Below FrontPage Project 2, click the Computer Genius link. Read the instructions, enter your first and last name at the bottom of the page, and then click the PLAY button. When your score is displayed, click the PRINT RESULTS link to print a hard copy.

5 Wheel of Terms

Below FrontPage Project 2, click the Wheel of Terms link. Read the instructions, and then enter your first and last name and your school name. Click the PLAY button. When your score is displayed, right-click the score and then click Print on the shortcut menu to print a hard copy.

6 Crossword Puzzle Challenge

Below FrontPage Project 2, click the Crossword Puzzle Challenge link. Read the instructions, and then enter your first and last name. Click the SUBMIT button. Work the crossword puzzle. When you are finished, click the Submit button. When the crossword puzzle is redisplayed, click the Print Puzzle button to print a hard copy.

7 Tips and Tricks

Below FrontPage Project 2, click the Tips and Tricks link. Click a topic that pertains to Project 2. Right-click the information and then click Print on the shortcut menu. Construct a brief example of what the information relates to in FrontPage to confirm you understand how to use the tip or trick.

8 Newsgroups

Below FrontPage Project 2, click the Newsgroups link. Click a topic that pertains to Project 2. Print three comments.

9 Expanding Your Horizons

Below FrontPage Project 2, click the Articles for Microsoft FrontPage link. Click a topic that pertains to Project 2. Print the information. Construct a brief example of what the information relates to in FrontPage to confirm you understand the contents of the article.

10 Search Sleuth

Below FrontPage Project 2, click the Search Sleuth link. To search for a term that pertains to this project, select a term below the Project 2 title and then use the Google search engine at google.com (or any major search engine) to display and print two Web pages that present information on the term.

11 FrontPage Online Training

Below FrontPage Project 2, click the FrontPage Online Training link. When your browser displays the Microsoft Office Online Web page, click the FrontPage link. Click one of the FrontPage courses that covers one or more of the objectives listed at the beginning of the project on page FP 82. Print the first page of the course before stepping through it.

12 Office Marketplace

Below FrontPage Project 2, click the Office Marketplace link. When your browser displays the Microsoft Office Online Web page, click the Office Marketplace link. Click a topic that relates to FrontPage. Print the first page.

Apply Your Knowledge

1 Modifying a Corporate Presence Web Site

Instructions: Start FrontPage. Open the Web site, Apply 1-1Ship-It-Here, that you modified in Project 1. If you did not complete this exercise for Project 1, see your instructor for a copy of the required files.

1. If necessary, double-click the file, index.htm, in the Folder List pane to display the Ship-It-Here Home page in Design view.
2. On the Format menu, click Theme. Scroll down until you see the theme Blends and select it, or another theme as directed by your instructor. Select Vivid colors, Active graphics, and Background picture. Apply the theme to all pages in the Web site.
3. Click the graphic in the upper-left corner of the page. On the Insert menu, point to Picture and then click Clip Art. Search on the Web for a graphic depicting packaging or shipping of your choice that fits the selected theme. Replace the current image with an image of your choice. Alternatively, you may use the image, delivery.gif, in the Project2 folder on the Data Disk. See the inside back cover of this book for instructions for downloading the Data Disk or see your instructor for information on accessing the files required in this book. Drag the sizing handles to size the image appropriately.
4. Select the first paragraph that begins, We ship anything, and change the font color to red, or a color of your choice, from the theme colors.
5. Select the text in the first paragraph under the Our Destination heading that reads, to anywhere as quickly as possible. Click the Italic button on the Formatting toolbar. Click the Font Color button arrow and change the text color to blue, or a color of your choice, from the current theme.
6. Select the text after each bullet and all remaining text that is the default color (black). Change the color of the selected text to green, or a color of your choice.
7. Click the Preview button to preview the Web page. When you have finished, click the Design button.
8. Print and save the Web page and then close FrontPage. Save the embedded images if prompted. Hand in the printout to your instructor.

FIGURE 2-95

1 Modifying a Navigation Component on a Corporate Presence Web Site

Problem: The Fairway Lawn Care Web site that you began developing has an interesting and appropriate theme. Some of the pages, however, have no navigation bars — users can use only the Back button on their browsers to return to a previous Web page. You want to modify the Web site to include appropriate link bars for all pages.

Instructions: Perform the following tasks.

1. Open the Fairway Lawn Care Web site that you began in Project 1. If you did not complete that exercise for Project 1, see your instructor for a copy of the required files.

2. In the Folder List pane, double-click the file, serv01.htm, to open the Home Mowing page in Design view.

3. Click the Navigation command on the View menu to view the navigation structure of this Web site. Note that the Home Mowing and Business Services pages are shown on the same level, with the Services page as a parent to both. Double-click the Home Mowing page to display it in Design view.

4. Double-click the link bar text in the left border to open the Link Bar Properties dialog box. Note that the hyperlinks currently selected are for the child level, of which there currently are none. Furthermore, because this is a shared border, making changes here affects all other pages in the Web site. Click the Cancel button to close the Link Bar Properties dialog box.

5. Position the insertion point just before the paragraph that begins, This is a brief. On the Insert menu, click Navigation. Select a bar type based on the navigation structure. Click the Next button. Select a bar style using the page's theme. Click the Next button. Select a horizontal orientation for the link bar. Click the Finish button.

6. In the Link Bar Properties dialog box, select Back and next for hyperlinks to add to the page. Select Home page and Parent page as additional pages. Click the OK button.

7. If necessary, press the right-arrow key to deselect the link bar. Press the ENTER key. Save the changes to this page.

8. In the Folder List pane, double-click the file, serv02.htm, to open the Business Services page in Design view.

9. Position the insertion point just before the paragraph that begins, This is a brief. On the Insert menu, click Navigation. Select a bar type based on the navigation structure. Click the Next button. Select a bar style using the page's theme. Click the Next button. Select a horizontal orientation for the link bar. Click the Finish button. In the Link Bar Properties dialog box, select Back and next for hyperlinks to add to the page. Select Home page and Parent page as additional pages. Click the OK button. If necessary, press the right-arrow key to deselect the link bar. Press the ENTER key. Save the changes to this page.

10. Click the Preview tab to preview the changes made to this page. Note that the Business Services page has links for Back, Home, and Up. These link to the Home Mowing, Home, and Services pages, respectively. Click the Back button. The Home Mowing page opens. Note that the links here are almost the same, except for order and a Next button instead of a Back button. The Next button links to the Business Services page. The order and links on each page are due to the position of the page in the Web site's navigation structure.

11. Print and save the each changed Web page, and then close FrontPage. Hand in the printouts to your instructor.

In the Lab

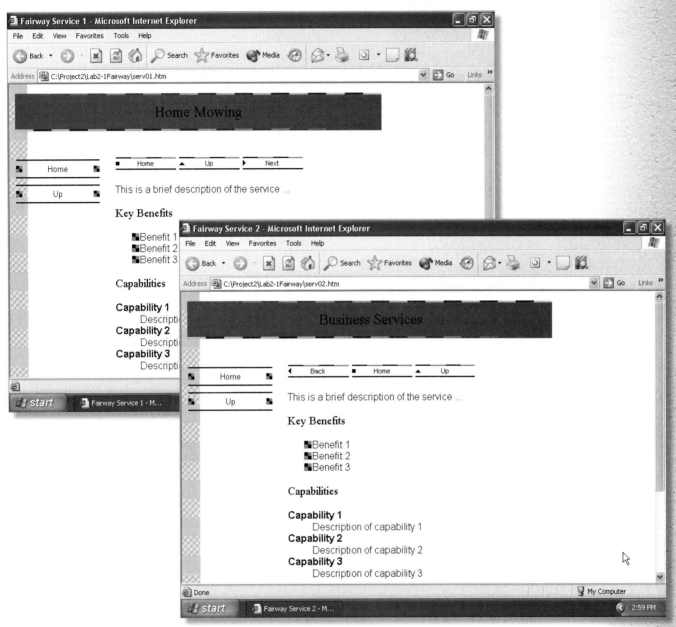

FIGURE 2-96

In the Lab

2 Modifying a Personal Web Site

Problem: Earlier, you created a personal Web site about your favorite Web sites. You have decided to add a page with links to Web pages about some of your favorite running gear.

Instructions: Perform the following tasks.

1. Open the Web site, Lab 1-2Running, that you began in Project 1. If you did not complete that exercise for Project 1, see your instructor for a copy of the required files.

2. In Navigation view, select the Home page. Right-click the Home page icon, click New, and then click Page.

3. Save the new page as gear.htm, change the page label to Running Gear, and change the page title to Running Gear. Open this page in Design view.

4. On the Insert menu, click Page Banner. When the Page Banner Properties dialog box appears, verify that Picture is selected and that the text in the Page banner text box is Running Gear. Click the OK button.

5. Position the insertion point below the newly added page banner. Click the Insert Table button on the Standard toolbar and drag through the cells to insert a 4×4 table.

6. Type Some of my favorite in the top row, first column of the table. Select the text and click the Bold button on the Formatting toolbar. Click the Align Right button. Change the font color to a color from the current theme. In the next cell to the right, insert the clip art image, runninggear.gif, from the Data Disk. Type is: in the top row, third column. Select the text, click the Bold button, and change the font color to match the text in the first cell. In the top row, fourth column, insert a clip art image of your choice representing running gear such as shoes, or you may use the file, runningshoes.gif, from the Data Disk.

7. Type Watches: in the left cell of the second row. Change the text color to a color from the theme, and make it bold and right-aligned. In the next cell to the right, insert a clip art image of your choice representing watches, or you may use the file, watch.gif, from the Data Disk. If necessary, resize the image to fit the page.

8. Type Treadmills: in the left cell of the third row. Change the text color to a color from the theme, and make it bold and right-aligned. In the next cell to the right, insert a clip art image of your choice representing a treadmill or other running equipment, or you may use the file, treadmill.gif, from the Data Disk. In the third column, insert another treadmill or running gear image of your choice, or you may use the file, treadmill2.gif, from the Data Disk.

9. Type Shoes: in the left cell of the bottom row. Change the text color to a color from the theme, and make it bold and right-aligned. In the next cell to the right, insert a clip art image of your choice representing a pedometer or other running gear, or you may use the file, shoe.gif, from the Data Disk. In the third column, insert another running gear image of your choice, or you may use the file, shoes2.gif, from the Data Disk. If necessary, resize the image to fit the page.

10. Merge the second and third cells of the second row into a single cell. Do the same for each following row.

11. Center the table alignment and specify the width as 80%. Drag the cell borders to align the text and images. Remove the table borders. Preview the Web page and adjust the alignment as needed to obtain a page similar to that shown in Figure 2-97.

12. Save the Web page. Save the embedded images to the images folder for the Web site. Print the changed Web pages and submit them to your instructor.

In the Lab

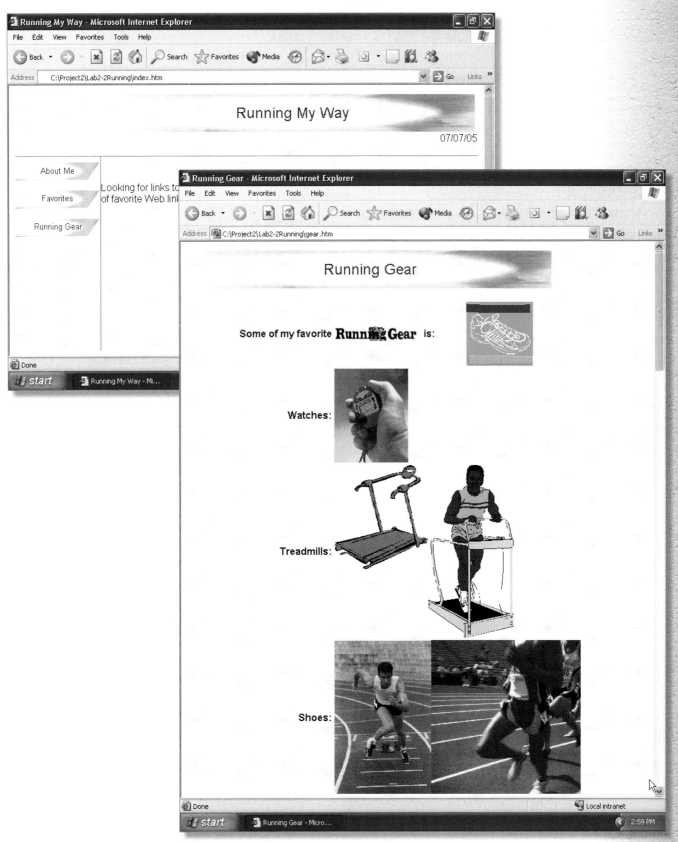

FIGURE 2-97

3 Adding a New Page and a Photo Gallery to a One-Page Web Site

Problem: Your one-page company support Web site includes a description of your company's support options, but no images of the company's product or staff. You decide to enhance the site by adding a page containing some pictures in an attractive layout.

Instructions: Using the support Web site you created in Project 1, perform the following tasks. If you did not complete this exercise in Project 1, see your instructor for a copy of the required Web site.

1. Add a new page to the current Web site navigation structure, with the current theme applied. Rename the page file as pictures.htm.
2. On the Insert menu, click Page Banner. Add a Picture Page Banner with Page banner text of Company Pictures. Click the OK button. Press the ENTER key.
3. Type, go back to. Add a link bar with a single hyperlink to the parent level.
4. Insert a Photo Gallery component. Choose the Slide Show layout. Insert the picture files, captions, and descriptions listed in Table 2-3, or personnel and product images and text of your own choosing (Figure 2-98).

Table 2-3 Support Image Files, Captions, and Descriptions

FILE NAME	CAPTION	DESCRIPTION
AluminumCan.jpg	Aluminum cans of any size and shape	We make any aluminum can to our customers' specifications.
AluminumFrame.jpg	From Aluminum framed housing...	Aluminum framed housing is our fastest growing business segment.
PaperClip.jpg	... to the smallest paperclip	But we still make the standards, such as paperclips and scissors.
SandraSupport.jpg	Billing and shipping support	24-hour support for our local and international customers alike.
HasanSupport.jpg	Hassan from specialty products support	Friendly support from people empowered to solve your problems.
OnSiteSupport.jpg	Specialists sent to your location	Industry veterans sent to your site for consulting or technical support.

5. Open the file, index.htm. At the end of the paragraph that begins, Whalen Metals practices a, type Take a look at our and then, after the text, insert a link bar with a hyperlink to the child level.
6. Save the Web pages and preview them by viewing them in your browser.
7. Print the Web pages, write your name on the pages, and give them to your instructor.
8. Close your browser and quit FrontPage. Save the embedded images if prompted.

In the Lab

FIGURE 2-98

Cases and Places

The difficulty of these case studies varies:
■ are the least difficult and ■■ are more difficult. The last exercise is a group exercise.

1 ■ In preparation for graduation, you created a text-only Web page in Project 1 to post your resume on the Web. Using that Web site, modify the text to use different font sizes for different sections, such as the title and section headings. Use bold and italics where appropriate. To position the various elements of your resume, cut and paste them into a table with no visible borders. Center the table on the Web page. Delete any bullets that remain after cutting and pasting the content to the table.

2 ■ You want to improve the appearance of the Web site you created for your movie review Web page from Project 1. Insert a two-column table with four rows per movie review. For each review, use one cell each in the left column for title, director, release year, and studio. In the right column, merge the corresponding four cells into one and place the review text for the movie in this merged cell. Do the same for all reviews completed.

3 ■ In preparation for an upcoming graduation for your friend, you were asked to develop a Web site for him. You created a personal Web site that includes a Home page, an Interests page, and a History page. Edit the History page to include a Photo Gallery of pictures from your friend's college life. Edit the caption text to provide brief descriptions of each photo. Use the exercise in Project 1 to develop the initial Web site.

4 ■■ Using clip art from the Web, enhance with appropriate images the company softball Web page that you created in Project 1. Include hyperlinks to several of your favorite sports-oriented Web sites. Use a table to position text, images, and hyperlinks. Cut and paste the existing text to insert it into the table. Apply an appropriate theme to the Web site.

5 ■■ **Working Together**   You have decided to develop a Web site to promote your chosen career, and you want to illustrate it with appropriate images. Create a new Web site with at least a parent and two child pages. Apply an appropriate theme. On one child page, add links to various sites on the Web for this career choice. On another child page, place at least five clip art images from the Web, along with text describing each image, using appropriate fonts, font sizes, and colors. Insert these within a table to arrange a pleasing presentation. Modify each page's title and label to reflect their purpose. Add a navigation bar to each page. Let child pages link to each other, as well as to the parent page.

Customizing and Managing Web Pages and Images

P R O J E C T

3

CASE PERSPECTIVE

An attractive photo collage enhances the layout of James Keeler's Photos Web page. Now, James wants to improve the visual appeal by using a lighter background and adding his favorite colors. He wants the Photos page to reflect the last date it was changed and have a counter for the number of visitors. He wants to add a graphical hyperlink on the Home page that links to the Photos page. James has created his resume in a Word document and plans to publish it to his Web site using hyperlinks to its various sections.

To manage his Web site properly, James requires a place to record ideas for new pages. He has visited Web sites with broken links and knows how frustrating it is as a visitor to be unable to navigate such a site. He needs the capability of determining whether any of the hyperlinks on his Web pages are broken. You know that FrontPage includes tools and features to help him easily change the hyperlinks, modify the theme of his choice, and incorporate data from other Office applications, such as his resume in Word. FrontPage has additional features that can help him plan and manage Web pages as well.

As you read through this project, you will learn how to customize Web pages using FrontPage's built-in themes. You also will learn about image formats used on the Web and how to enhance images for use on a Web page. You will learn how to create an image map and target a URL to the hotspot. You will learn how to insert bookmarks in a Web page to aid navigation. You also will learn how to copy text from a Word document and paste the text into a Web page. Finally, you will learn how to use FrontPage's reporting features and how to verify hyperlinks.

Customizing and Managing Web Pages and Images

P R O J E C T

Objectives

You will have mastered the material in this project when you can:

- Discuss the types of images used on the Web
- Create and apply a custom theme
- Expand an existing table
- Add a hit counter
- Add a shared border and change the navigation structure of a Web site
- Copy and paste from a Word document
- Insert bookmarks into a Web page
- Display the Pictures toolbar
- Modify image properties
- Insert an AutoShapes drawing object in FrontPage
- Create an image map hotspot
- Use a graphical image as a hyperlink
- Use FrontPage to create and view reports
- Verify the hyperlinks in a FrontPage Web site

Introduction

With the widespread use of images, graphics, and animation, it is important to take the time to learn about the types of images used on the Web and master the graphics-editing features necessary to customize Web pages. Knowing the characteristics, advantages, and disadvantages of each type of image file can help you ascertain the best type of image to use for a particular situation.

Project 3 introduces you to customizing a Web page. You will learn how to create a transparent GIF image, an image map, and bookmarks. You also will see how easy it is in FrontPage to make significant changes to an existing theme. The project shows you how to create hotspots for an image map and copy text from a Word document directly into FrontPage.

Most of the pages developed in this project are customizations of previous work. The Home page will have two new links added, one of which is an image and one of which is an AutoShapes drawing (Figure 3-1a). The links navigate the user to the Photos page, which is modified to use a customized theme (Figure 3-1b). A new page contains a resume, the text of which is copied from a Word document (Figure 3-1c). The Resume page consists of several long sections of text. You insert bookmarks to allow a user to click a hyperlink at the top of the Resume page and immediately go to the corresponding section. A shared border is added to all the pages to consistently display the last date the pages were updated.

To help you in this process, the project presents some important concepts and definitions.

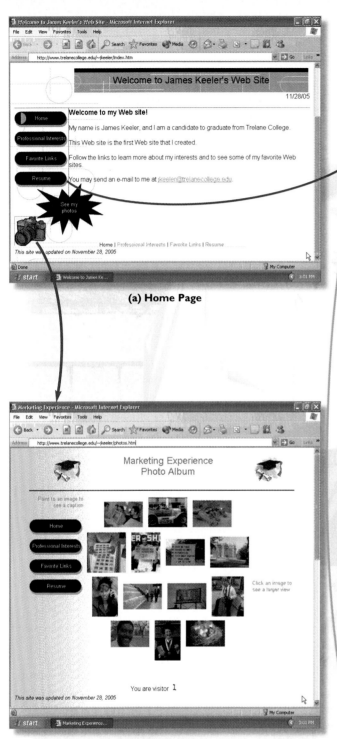

(a) Home Page

(b) Photos Page

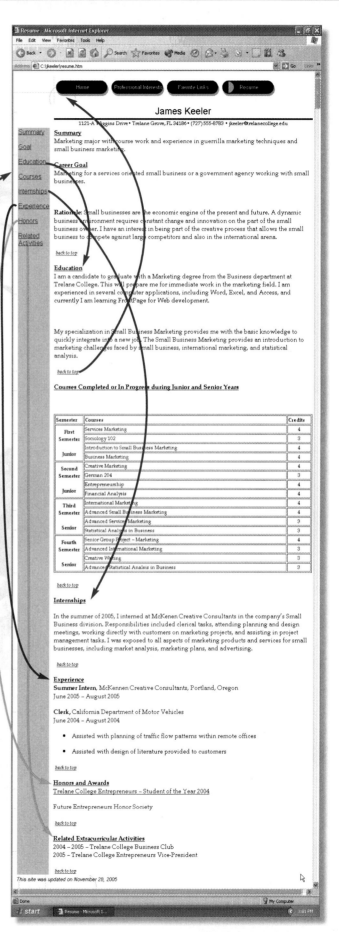

(c) Resume Page

FIGURE 3-1

Image File Formats

Many different formats are used to represent images on computers. Table 3-1 shows some of the various image file formats. Numerous graphics editors and tools are available that allow you to create and edit images. For example, you can create your own custom buttons, bullets, dividers, and background images. Most browsers display only two types of image file formats: GIF and JPEG. FrontPage can import images in several other formats, including BMP, TIF, WMF, RAS, EPS, PCX, PCD, PNG, and TGA, and then convert them to GIF or JPEG images.

Table 3-1 Image File Formats	
IMAGE FILE TYPE	**DESCRIPTION**
BMP	Windows bitmap file format — device-independent format, introduced with Windows 3.0 and increasingly supported by Windows applications.
EPS	Encapsulated PostScript file format — an extension of the PostScript file graphics format developed by Adobe Systems.
GIF	Graphic Interchange Format file format — a popular graphics exchange format used by the CompuServe Information Service and other online graphics sources. GIF is a licensed product for developers of commercial, for-profit software; however, for the nonprofit personal home page, a license agreement is not required.
JPEG	Joint Photographic Expert Group file format — used for true color, 24-bit photographic images scanned or digitized from films.
PCX	Paintbrush file format — used in Windows Paintbrush and other paint programs and supported by many desktop publishing and graphics programs.
PNG	Portable Network Graphics file format — a file format for the lossless, portable, well-compressed storage of raster images.
RAS	Sun Raster file format — the raster image file format developed by Sun Microsystems, Inc.
TGA	Targa file format — a photo-realistic image format designed for systems with a Truevision display adapter.
TIF (or TIFF)	Tagged Image File format — supported by many desktop publishing programs.
WMF	Windows Metafile format — a vector graphics format used mostly for word-processing clip art.

Q&A

Q: Should I use the PNG file format in my Web pages?

A: FrontPage allows you to import many different image file formats, including the Portable Network Graphics (PNG) format. Although FrontPage does support the PNG file format, many Web browsers cannot display PNG pictures without a special plug-in. In general, it is better to use only GIF or JPEG images in your Web pages.

Regardless of the file type, an image is displayed on a computer screen using small points of color called pixels. As you have learned, a **pixel**, or **picture element**, is the smallest addressable point on the screen. An image is formed on the screen by displaying pixels of different color. The combined group of differently colored pixels makes up the image. The **image file** contains the information needed to determine the color for each pixel used to display the image.

The **bit resolution** of an image refers to the number of bits of stored information per pixel. With an **8-bit image**, 8 bits of information are stored for each pixel. Using the binary numbering system, you can represent up to 256 numbers using 8 bits. Thus, an 8-bit image can have a maximum of 256 colors, with each number representing a different color.

A **24-bit image** can have up to 16.7 million colors. These types of images have near-photographic quality. Each pixel, however, consumes three times the storage of a pixel in an 8-bit image, which results in a larger file size for an image with the same number of pixels.

GIF Image Files

GIF stands for **Graphic Interchange Format**. GIF files (GIFs) use 8-bit resolution and support up to 256 colors. GIF files support indexed color image types, line art, and grayscale images.

Special types of GIF files, called **animated GIFs**, contain a series of images that are displayed in rapid succession, giving the appearance of movement. Special animated GIF editors are available to combine the series of images and set the display timing.

The GIF89a format contains a **transparency index**. This index allows you to specify a transparent color, which causes the background of the Web page to show through the color that has been set as transparent. If you are using line art, icons, or images such as company logos, make sure they are in the GIF89a format. You then will be able to take advantage of the transparency index.

> *Design Tip*
>
> GIF files are best suited for solid-colored images such as logos and illustrations. The 256-color limitation of GIF files makes them inappropriate for displaying photographs.

JPEG Image Files

JPEG stands for **Joint Photographic Expert Group**. The advantage to using JPEG files is the high color resolution. JPEG supports 24-bit resolution, providing up to 16.7 million possible colors. When including photographic images in your Web page, the images must use JPEG format because of the support for full color.

> *Design Tip*
>
> Each time a JPEG image is edited and saved, the image is compressed and decompressed, which degrades the image quality. You should make a copy of the original source image file and never alter the original image.

When you insert an image that is not in GIF or JPEG format, FrontPage automatically converts it to the GIF format if the image has eight or fewer bits of color. The image is converted automatically to JPEG format if the image has more than eight bits of color.

With FrontPage, you can import image files into the current FrontPage Web site, insert images in Web pages, align images with text, and create and edit image maps. The editing commands in FrontPage, such as crop, rotate, and resize, allow you to change the appearance of an image. In addition, you can change its brightness and contrast, make it black and white, or give the image beveled edges.

FrontPage can work with graphics editing programs such as the **Clip Art Gallery**, which is a tool for previewing and managing clip art, pictures, sounds, video clips, and animation. The Clip Art Gallery contains a collection of clip art and pictures you can insert into your Web pages. The Clip Art Gallery was used in Project 2 to create the Photos page.

More About

Obtaining Images

You can browse the World Wide Web and select any image to insert on your Web page. Be sure that you have permission to use the image before placing it on your FrontPage Web page as some images on the Web are copyrighted.

More About

Photographic Images

Be careful when using photographic images with 24-bit color. Many computers do not have monitors and display adapters that support 24-bit color. If you change your Windows color setting to a lower bit resolution, you can preview a Web page to see how the images look before you publish the Web page.

Modifying an Existing Web Page

Because James wanted to change his original design for the Photos page once he saw it on the computer, you decide to use the theme currently used with the other pages, and then modify elements of the theme for this page only. Applying these modifications is a simple task with FrontPage.

To modify the Photos Web page, the original Web site first must be opened. The following steps open the Photos page in the personal Web site created in Project 2. If you did not complete Project 2, see your instructor for a copy of the files required to complete this project.

To Open an Existing Page in a FrontPage Web Site

1 Click the Start button on the taskbar. Point to All Programs on the Start menu, point to Microsoft Office on the All Programs submenu, and then point to Microsoft Office FrontPage 2003.

2 Click Microsoft Office FrontPage 2003 on the Microsoft Office submenu.

3 If FrontPage opens a new_page_1.htm file, click Close on the File menu. If FrontPage opens another Web site, click Close Site on the File menu.

4 Click the Open button arrow on the Standard toolbar.

5 Click Open Site. If necessary, when FrontPage displays the Open Site dialog box, click the Look in box arrow and select the folder location where you stored the Web site for Project 2 (e.g., C:\jkeeler).

6 Click the Open button. Double-click photos.htm in the Folder List pane.

The previous Web site is loaded, and the file, photos.htm, is displayed in Page view (Figure 3-2).

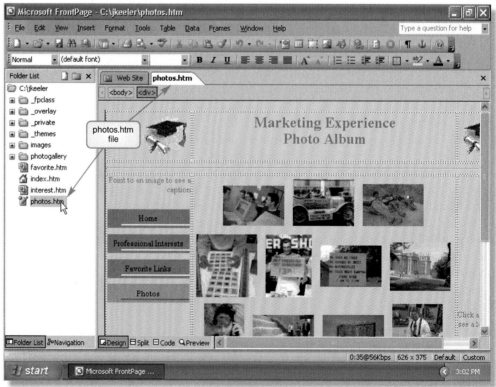

FIGURE 3-2

Creating and Applying a Customized Theme to a Web Page

Applying a theme to an existing Web page is essentially the same procedure used to apply a theme to a new Web site. When modifying a page that already contains certain graphic elements, such as a background color or image, be aware that applying a theme permanently alters such existing properties. In fact, once a theme has been applied, you cannot access the background properties of the page to apply an image or a color — they are under the control of the theme. You need to remove or modify the theme to make such changes. You effectively can remove the theme by applying a theme selection of No Theme to the Web page, as was done in Project 2. If you are not certain that you want to use a theme, you might want to make a backup copy of your FrontPage Web site by saving it in an alternate location before applying the theme.

A customized theme can be created easily by using an existing theme as a starting point, making changes to that theme, and then saving the modified theme with a new name. The following steps create and apply a customized theme to an existing Web page.

More About

The FrontPage Help System

Need Help? It is no further away than the Type a question for help box on the menu bar in the upper-right corner of the window. Click the box that contains the text, Type a question for help, type help, and then press the ENTER key. FrontPage responds with a list of topics you can click to learn about obtaining help on any FrontPage-related topic. To find out what is new in FrontPage 2003, type what is new in FrontPage in the Type a question for help box.

To Create and Apply a Customized Theme

1

• **Click Format on the menu bar and then click Theme.**

• **If necessary, when FrontPage displays the Theme task pane, scroll down and point to Capsules in the Select a theme list.**

• **Click the Capsules theme arrow next to the Capsules theme preview.**

FrontPage displays the Theme task pane and displays the shortcut menu below the Capsules theme (Figure 3-3).

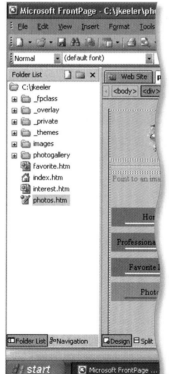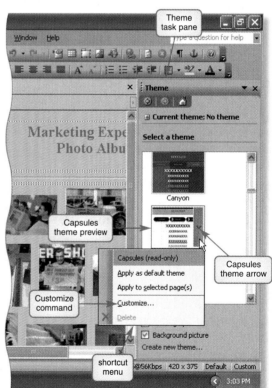

FIGURE 3-3

2

• **Click Customize.**

FrontPage displays the Customize Theme dialog box. The Preview of: Capsules area displays a sample page using the Capsules theme (Figure 3-4). FrontPage displays additional buttons that allow you to modify aspects of the theme and to save the modifications.

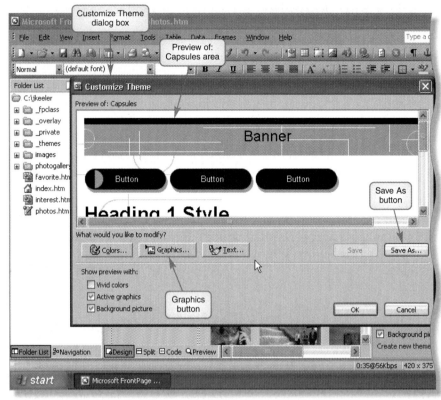

FIGURE 3-4

3

• **Click the Graphics button.**

• **If necessary, when FrontPage displays the Customize Theme dialog box, click the Item box arrow and select Background Picture from the Item list.**

• **If necessary, click the Picture tab.**

FrontPage displays the Customize Theme dialog box (Figure 3-5). FrontPage displays the item to modify in the Item list. FrontPage displays the current file used as the background picture for the theme in the Background Picture text box.

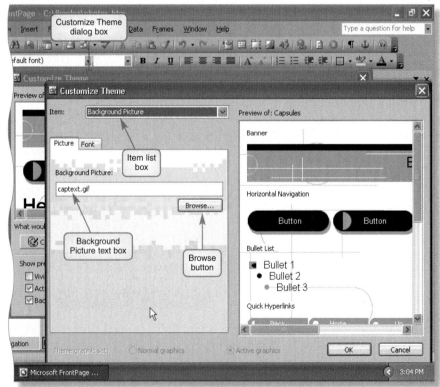

FIGURE 3-5

4

• **Click Browse.**

• **When FrontPage displays the Open File dialog box, select the newbackground file from the Project3 folder on the Data Disk.**

FrontPage displays the Open File dialog box (Figure 3-6).

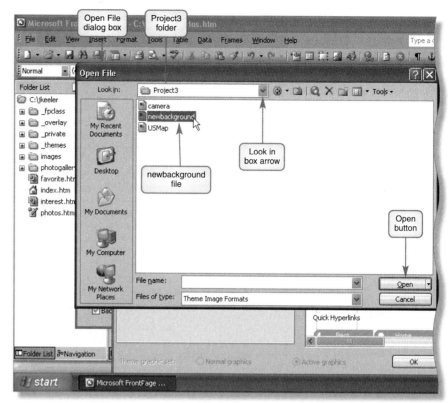

FIGURE 3-6

5

• **Click Open.**

• **Click the OK button.**

• **Click the Save As button.**

• **When FrontPage displays the Save Theme dialog box, type** Capsules Green **as the new theme title in the Enter new theme title text box.**

FrontPage displays a sample of the theme using the file, newbackground, as the background picture (Figure 3-7). FrontPage displays the new theme title in the Save Theme dialog box.

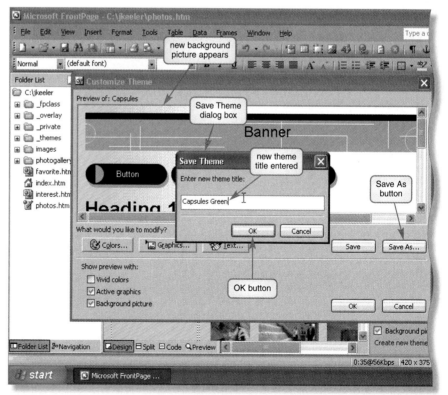

FIGURE 3-7

6

• **Click the OK button.**

FrontPage closes the Save Theme dialog box and saves the newly created theme. FrontPage displays the name of the new theme in the Preview of: area (Figure 3-8).

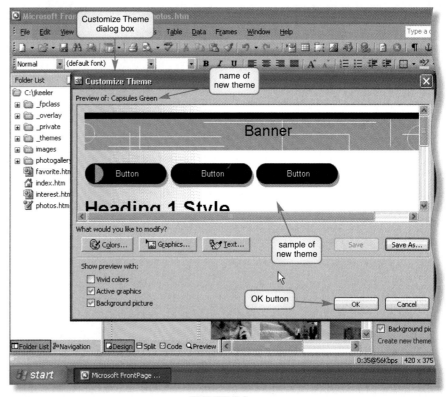

FIGURE 3-8

7

• **Click the OK button.**

• **If the Microsoft Office FrontPage dialog box appears, click the No button.**

FrontPage displays the new theme in the Select a theme list in the Theme task pane (Figure 3-9). The background picture reflects the new theme.

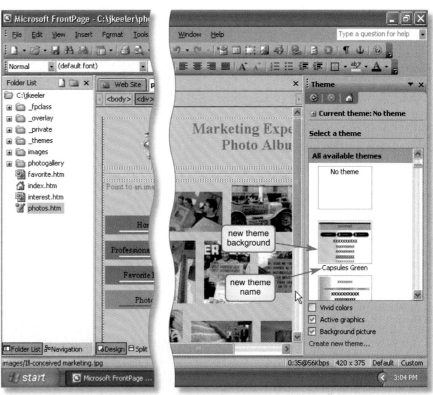

FIGURE 3-9

8

- **Click Vivid colors.**

- **Click the preview of the Capsules Green theme in the Select a theme list.**

FrontPage applies the theme to the photos.htm page (Figure 3-10).

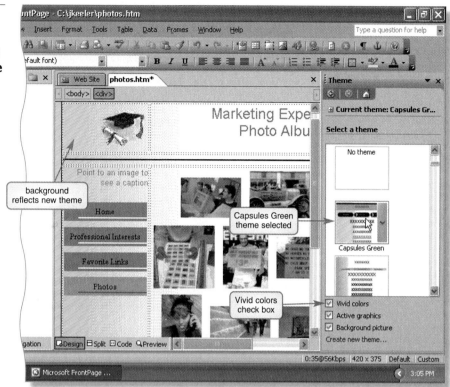

FIGURE 3-10

By saving changes to a theme as a new theme, the original theme remains unchanged. If you do not want a new theme, you simply may save the changes to the original theme.

Changing the Style of a Link Bar

When applying the new theme to the photos.htm Web page, FrontPage did not modify the link bar on the left side of the Web page to match the Capsules Green theme. To match the look of the other Web pages, the style of the link bar should be modified. The steps on the next page change the style of the link bar on the photos.htm page to match the style of the link bar on the other pages.

To Change the Style of a Link Bar

1

• **Right-click the link bar on the left side of the photos.htm Web page.**

FrontPage displays a shortcut menu (Figure 3-11).

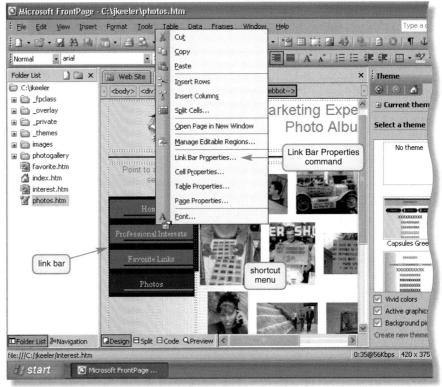

FIGURE 3-11

2

• **Click Link Bar Properties.**

• **If necessary, when FrontPage displays the Link Bar Properties dialog box, click the Style tab.**

FrontPage displays the Style sheet in the Link Bar Properties dialog box (Figure 3-12).

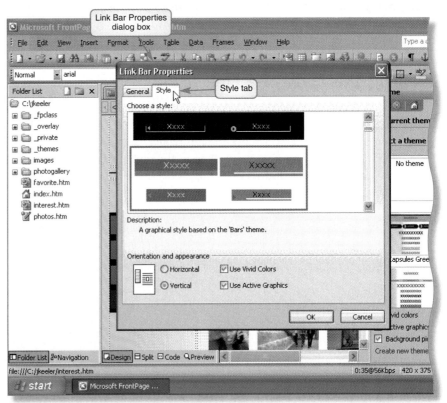

FIGURE 3-12

3

• **Scroll the Choose a style scroll bar up to display the Use Page's Theme style.**

• **Click the Use Page's Theme style.**

The Use Page's Theme style is selected in the Choose a style list box (Figure 3-13). The Use Page's Theme style indicates that the link bar should appear with the link bar style specified in the photos.htm page's style.

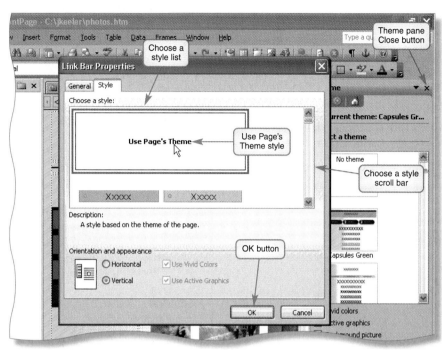

FIGURE 3-13

4

• **Click the OK button.**

• **Click the Close button on the Theme task pane.**

FrontPage displays the link bar using the Capsules Green theme's link bar style and closes the Theme task pane (Figure 3-14).

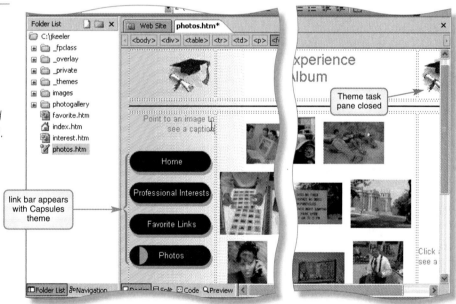

FIGURE 3-14

Expanding a Table

You may recall that tables often are used to position elements in a Web page. Items in the Photos page were placed within a table for this very reason. You already have learned how to merge table cells, and how to delete cells and even entire tables. As you make changes to the Web page, however, you may need additional rows, columns, or both, in your table. Rather than creating a new table with the required rows and columns, you can expand an existing table to accommodate new elements.

The following steps add a row to an existing table.

To Add a Row to a Table

1

• **Position the insertion point in the last row of the table.**

• **Click Table on the menu bar.**

• **Point to Insert.**

FrontPage displays the Insert submenu (Figure 3-15).

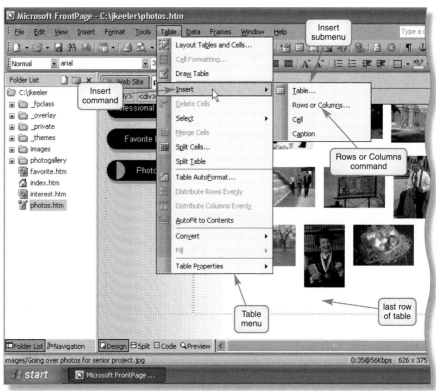

FIGURE 3-15

2

• **Click Rows or Columns.**

• **If necessary, when FrontPage displays the Insert Rows or Columns dialog box, select Rows.**

• **Verify that the Number of rows text box is set to 1 and that the location selected is Below selection.**

FrontPage displays the Insert Rows or Columns dialog box (Figure 3-16).

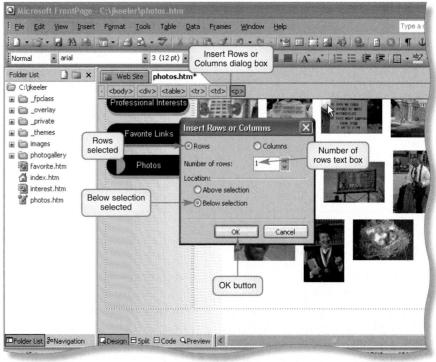

FIGURE 3-16

3

• **Click OK.**

• **Position the insertion point in the middle cell of the inserted row.**

The insertion point is positioned in the new row at the bottom of the table (Figure 3-17).

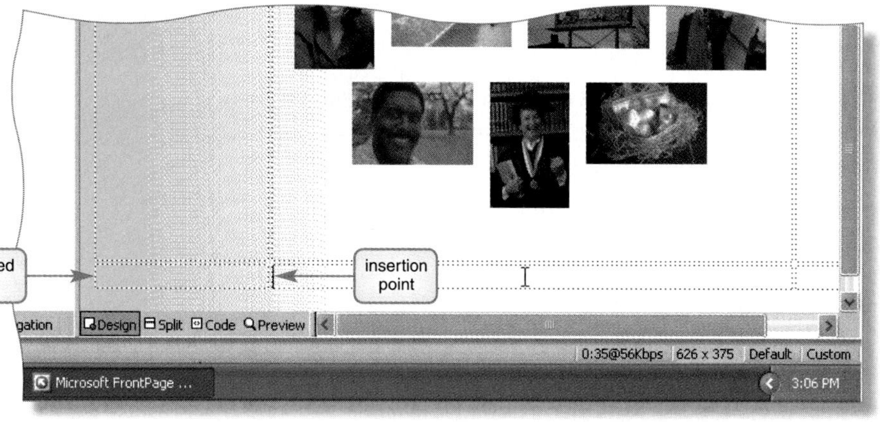

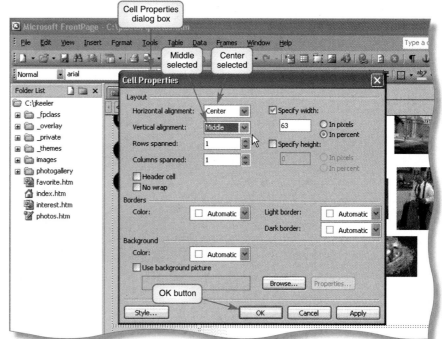

inserted row

insertion point

FIGURE 3-17

Other Ways

1. Right-click table, click Insert Rows
2. Press ALT+A, I, N
3. Click cell in table, in Voice Command mode, say "Table, Insert, Rows or Columns, OK"

Additional columns may be added to an existing table as easily as rows. Because FrontPage makes it easy to add or delete table rows and columns, you do not have to know the final dimensions of the table before you create it. You simply may modify the table size as needed.

Adding a Hit Counter Component

FrontPage provides a number of components that allow you to add common functionality to your pages easily. One feature often seen on Web pages is a hit counter. A **hit counter** is a component that displays a counter to indicate the number of times a Web page is accessed.

The following steps add a hit counter component to the Photos page.

To Add a Hit Counter

1

• **If necessary, position the insertion point in the middle cell of the last row inserted.**

• **Right-click the cell and then click Cell Properties on the shortcut menu.**

• **When FrontPage displays the Cell Properties dialog box, in the Layout area, select Center for Horizontal alignment and Middle for Vertical alignment.**

FrontPage displays the Cell Properties dialog box with Center selected for the Horizontal alignment and Middle for the Vertical alignment for the cell (Figure 3-18).

FIGURE 3-18

2

• **Click the OK button.**

• **If necessary, click the Font Color box arrow and select the Automatic font color for this theme.**

• **Type** You are visitor **and then click Insert on the menu bar. Be sure to include a space after the word, visitor.**

FrontPage inserts the text in the middle cell and displays the Insert menu (Figure 3-19).

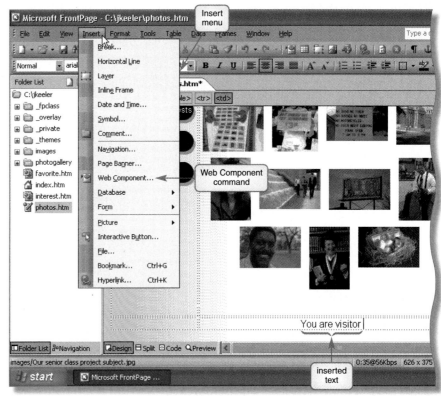

FIGURE 3-19

3

• **Click Web Component.**

• **When FrontPage displays the Insert Web Component dialog box, click Hit Counter in the Component type list.**

• **Click the second graphic in the Choose a counter style list.**

FrontPage displays the Insert Web Component dialog box with the Hit Counter component type and the counter style selected (Figure 3-20). FrontPage displays a brief description of a hit counter component.

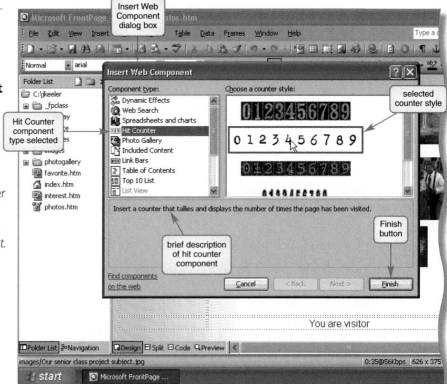

FIGURE 3-20

4

• **Click the Finish button.**

• **When FrontPage displays the Hit Counter Properties dialog box, verify that the second Counter Style is selected.**

FrontPage displays the Hit Counter Properties dialog box with the second Counter Style selected (Figure 3-21).

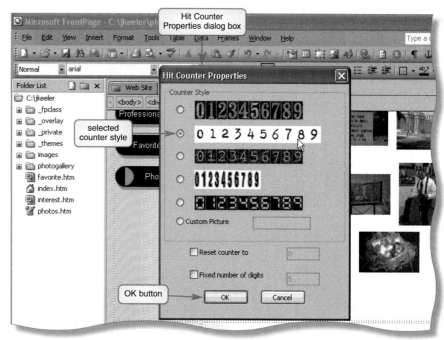

FIGURE 3-21

5

• **Click the OK button.**

FrontPage inserts a hit counter component (Figure 3-22). Placeholder text within square brackets indicates where the hit counter will be displayed when viewed on a Web server with the FrontPage Server Extensions installed.

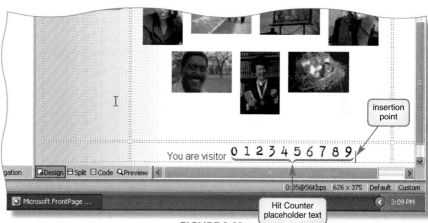

FIGURE 3-22

Other Ways

1. Press ALT+I, C
2. In Voice Command mode, say "Insert, Web Component"

When the page is viewed, either in a browser or on the Preview tab, the hit counter is displayed as a missing graphic with a textual description. To view the hit counter, the page must be published and viewed on a Web server containing the FrontPage Server Extensions. The program that actually increments and displays the graphic counter is a part of the FrontPage Server Extensions. The count itself is stored on the server in a file in the _private folder of the Web site.

Adding a Shared Border

Earlier, you learned that Web pages often have common sections that display similar, or sometimes identical, information on each page. An example of similar, but not identical, information might be link bars or page banners. In these cases, the same format and location are used on multiple pages, although the content may change from page to page. Identical information that might appear on multiple pages

Q: Can I use other content and formatting besides text in a shared border?

A: Yes. Shared borders do not have to be plain text. You independently can assign a color or even an image to the background of any shared border. Right-click the shared border and then click Border Properties.

in a Web site could be such items as a copyright notice, an e-mail address for the page author, or a date indicating when the page was last updated. Rather than duplicating this identical information for each page, it would be much easier to enter or change it in one location and then have the information propagated to all pages automatically. Placing the information within a shared border does this. A shared border provides a means for including standard content at the top, bottom, left, or right edges of a page, or for all pages, in a Web site.

Design Tip Use shared borders when multiple pages in a Web site contain identical information in the same location on the page.

The Home, Professional Interests, and Favorite Links pages each contain a line at the bottom indicating when the page was last changed. This line was inserted automatically as a result of using the Personal Web site template. Although each line displays the same information, the information is not in a shared border and could be changed on one of the pages without affecting the others, leaving the pages inconsistent. Additionally, when new pages are added to the Web site, such as the Photos page, they do not contain this line automatically. By removing this information from each individual page and inserting it into a shared border for all pages, the same information will appear on all pages currently in the Web and also on any new pages added subsequently.

By default, the Web page authoring settings in FrontPage do not allow you to add a shared border to a Web page. The capability to add shared borders must be enabled in the Page Options dialog box. The following steps turn on the ability to add shared borders to Web pages in a Web site.

To Enable Shared Borders

• **Click Tools on the menu bar.**

FrontPage displays the Tools menu (Figure 3-23).

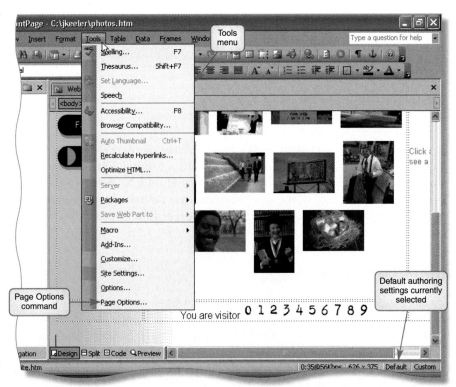

FIGURE 3-23

2
- • **Click Page Options.**
- • **If necessary, when the Page Options dialog appears, click the Authoring tab.**
- • **Click Shared Borders.**

FrontPage displays the Page Options dialog box, and a check mark appears in the Shared Borders check box (Figure 3-24).

3
- • **Click the OK button.**

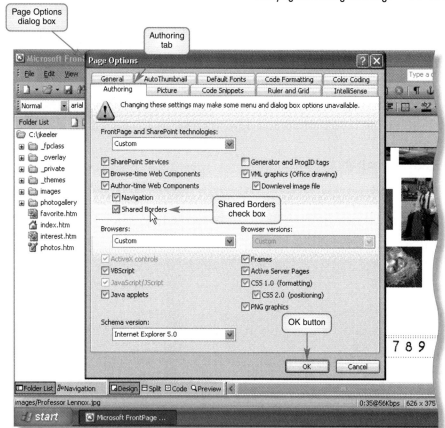

FIGURE 3-24

The Shared Borders option remains enabled for all Web pages and Web sites you create until you manually disable the option in the Page Options dialog box. After modifying the authoring settings, FrontPage displays Custom as the authoring settings in the status bar.

The steps on the next page place the date the pages were last updated into a shared border for all pages.

To Add a Shared Border

1

• **Position the insertion point below the table.**

• **Click Format on the menu bar.**

FrontPage displays the Format menu (Figure 3-25).

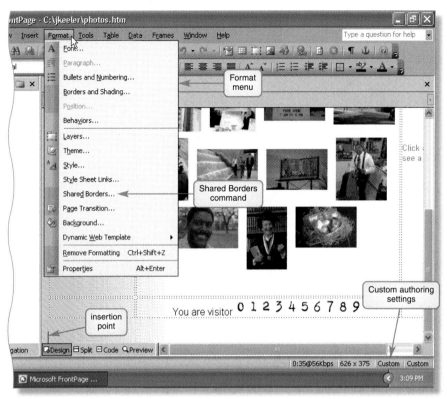

FIGURE 3-25

2

• **Click Shared Borders.**

• **When FrontPage displays the Shared Borders dialog box, verify that All pages is selected in the Apply to area.**

• **Click Bottom.**

FrontPage displays a dotted line across the bottom of the page preview graphic in the Shared Borders dialog box (Figure 3-26).

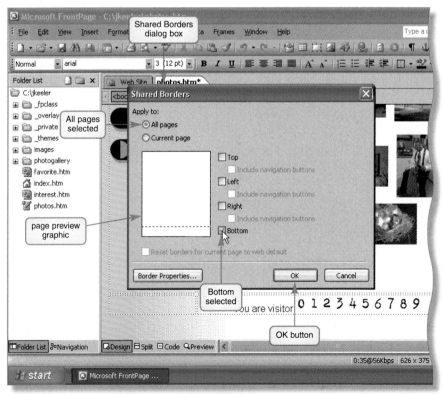

FIGURE 3-26

3

• **Click the OK button.**

A bottom shared border is inserted with a comment component as placeholder text (Figure 3-27).

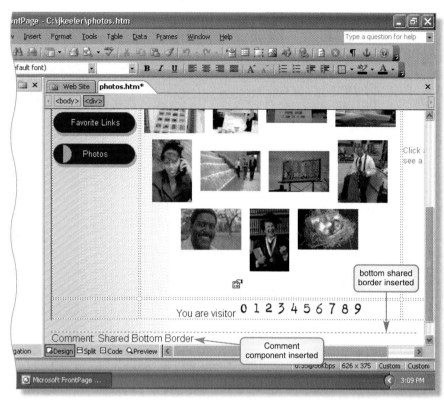

FIGURE 3-27

4

• **If necessary, scroll down to display the comment component.**

• **Click the comment component in the shared border to select it.**

• **On the Formatting toolbar, click the Font Size box arrow and select 2 (10 pt).**

• **Click the Italic button.**

• **Type** This site was updated on **and then click Insert on the menu bar. Be sure to include a space after the word, on.**

The replacement text replaces the comment component in the shared border and the Insert menu appears (Figure 3-28). Note that when the insertion point is placed within a shared border, the shared border appears as a rectangular area.

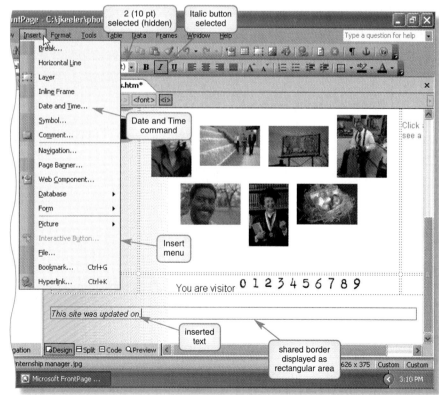

FIGURE 3-28

5

• **Click Date and Time.**

• **If necessary, when FrontPage displays the Date and Time dialog box, click Date this page was last automatically updated.**

• **Click the Date format box arrow.**

• **If necessary, scroll to the format representing a month name, a two-digit day, and a four-digit year (mmm dd, yyyy).**

FrontPage displays the Date and Time dialog box with a list of date formats (Figure 3-29).

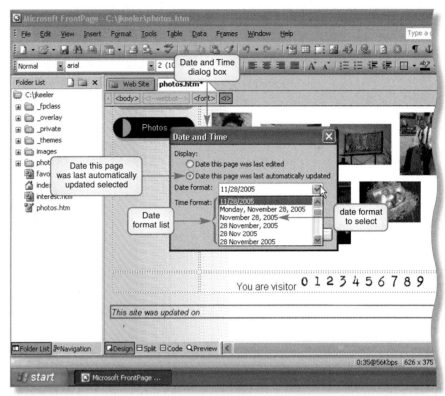

FIGURE 3-29

6

• **Click the selected date format.**

• **Verify that the Time format selected is (none).**

A long date format is selected (Figure 3-30). A time format of (none) indicates that only the date will be displayed, not a time.

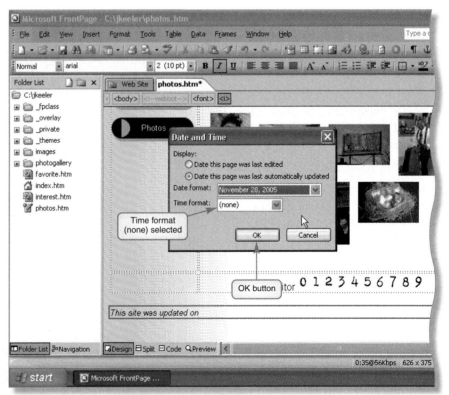

FIGURE 3-30

7

• **Click the OK button.**

• **Click the Save button on the Standard toolbar to save the changes to the page.**

FrontPage inserts a Date and Time component displaying the date that the page was last updated (Figure 3-31).

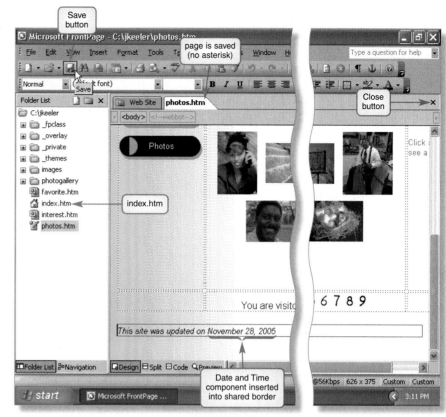

FIGURE 3-31

8

• **Click the Close button.**

• **Double-click the file name, index.htm, in the Folder List pane to open the Home page.**

• **If necessary, scroll down to the bottom of the page.**

• **Drag through the line above the shared border to select it.**

The line inserted by the Personal Web template, indicating the date that the page was last updated, is highlighted (Figure 3-32).

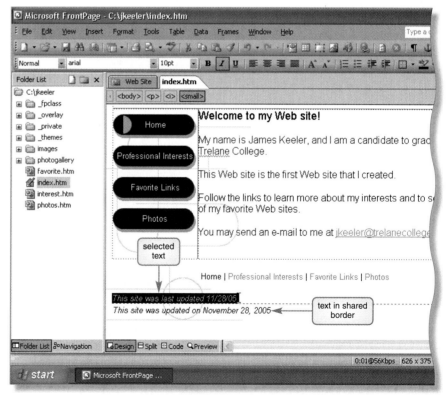

FIGURE 3-32

9

• **Press the DELETE key.**

FrontPage removes the duplicate line and only the shared border indicates the date that the page was last updated (Figure 3-33).

10

• **Save and close the Home page.**

• **Repeat Steps 8 and 9 for the Favorite Links and Professional Interests pages, saving the changes and then closing each page.**

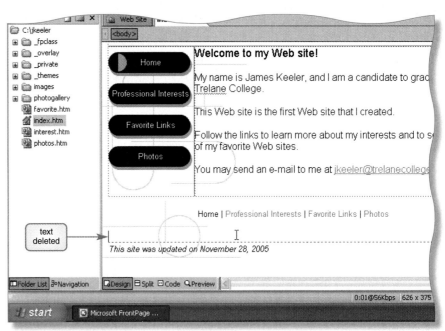

FIGURE 3-33

> **Other Ways**
>
> 1. Press ALT+O, D
> 2. In Voice Command mode, say "Format, Shared Borders"

When a shared border is inserted, FrontPage automatically includes a comment component to identify the shared border while editing in FrontPage. A **comment component** is a component that displays text visible only in FrontPage, but not when the page is viewed in a browser or on the Preview tab. Because the date last updated must be visible in a browser, the comment component is replaced with normal text.

When adding a date and time component, you have a choice of two dates to use. The Date this page was last automatically updated option reflects the date the page was last changed, either from manual editing or from a change elsewhere in the Web site that caused automatic updating. The Date this page was last edited option yields the date that the page was last saved with FrontPage.

Modifying the Navigation Structure of a Web Site

Previously, when you added a new Web page, you did so in Navigation view, so that the page was added automatically to the navigation structure of the Web site. Recall that the navigation structure affects the links that display on link bars when the link bar type is Bar based on navigation structure. If the position of a page in the navigation structure is changed, the link bars may change as well. A new page added in Page view does not display added link bars of this type until the page is saved and added to the navigation structure of the Web site.

Creating a New Page in Page View

Recall that when a Web site has a theme applied, any new page will be displayed with the theme applied automatically. Because the shared border just added was applied to all pages, it also will be applied automatically to any new page.

The following step creates a new page in Page view.

To Add a New Page in Page View

1

• **Click the Create a new normal page button on the Standard toolbar.**

FrontPage creates a new page with the current theme applied and the shared border inserted (Figure 3-34).

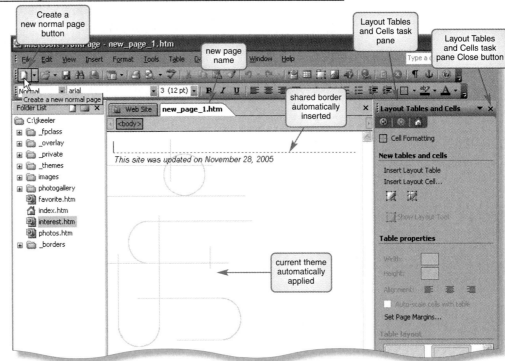

FIGURE 3-34

Although the new page has the theme of the current Web site applied, it has no hyperlinks to navigate to other pages in the Web site. A simple way to add such links is to add a Link Bar component with hyperlinks based on the navigation structure, as was done in Project 2.

The following steps add a Link Bar component to the new Web page.

To Add a Link Bar Component

1 Click Insert on the menu bar and then click Navigation.

2 Click Bar based on navigation structure in the Choose a bar type area. Click the Next button.

3 Verify that Use Page's Theme is selected and then click the Next button.

4 Verify that the horizontal arrangement is selected and then click the Finish button.

5 Click Child pages under Home. Click Home page in the Additional pages area. Click the OK button.

6 Click the Center button on the Formatting toolbar.

7 Click the Close button on the Layout Tables and Cells task pane.

The Link bar component is added, centered on the page (Figure 3-35 on the next page). A message appears indicating that the page must be added to the Navigation view for the hyperlinks to be displayed.

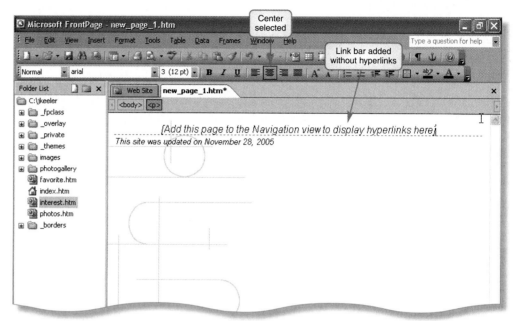

FIGURE 3-35

Modifying the Navigation Structure

When a new page was created in Page view, FrontPage automatically applied the theme and shared border. In order for a link bar based on the navigation structure to display hyperlinks, the page must be added to the navigation structure. Because visitors will access the Photos page only from the Home page, the Photo page's position in the navigation structure needs to be changed as well.

The following steps modify the navigation structure of the Web site.

To Modify the Navigation Structure

1

• **Click the Save button on the Standard toolbar.**

FrontPage displays the Save As dialog box with a default name and title for the new Web page (Figure 3-36).

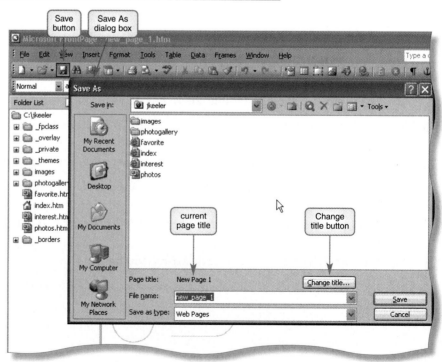

FIGURE 3-36

2

- **Click the Change title button.**
- **When FrontPage displays the Set Page Title dialog box, type** Resume.

FrontPage displays the Set Page Title dialog box with the new page title (Figure 3-37).

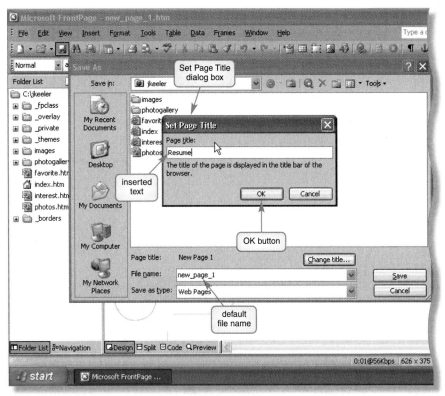

FIGURE 3-37

3

- **Click the OK button.**
- **Drag through the default file name and then type** resume **as the new file name.**

FrontPage closes the Set Page Title dialog box and displays the Save As dialog box with the new page title and new file name (Figure 3-38).

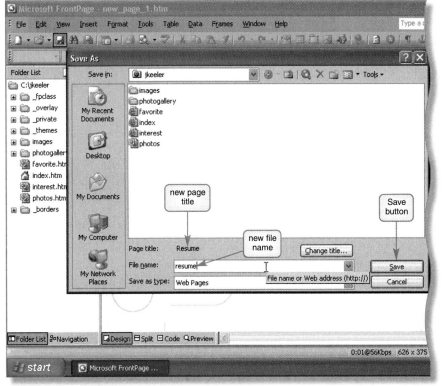

FIGURE 3-38

4

• **Click the Save button.**

FrontPage saves the new page with a file name of resume.htm (Figure 3-39). The file, resume.htm, appears in the Folder List pane.

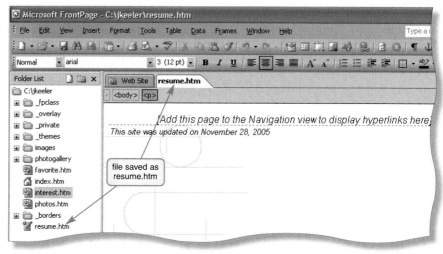

FIGURE 3-39

5

• **Click View on the menu bar and then click Navigation.**

• **Drag the file, resume.htm, from the Folder List pane and drop it under the Home page icon in the Navigation pane.**

The Resume page is added to the navigation structure of the Web site (Figure 3-40).

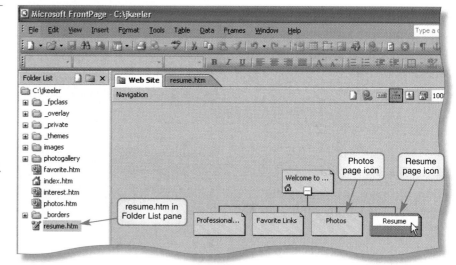

FIGURE 3-40

6

• **Drag the Photos page icon and drop it under the Professional Interests page icon in the Navigation pane.**

The Photos page no longer is displayed as a child page under the Home page and now is displayed as a child page under the Professional Interests page (Figure 3-41).

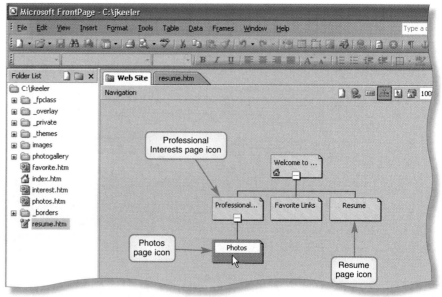

FIGURE 3-41

7

• **Double-click the Resume page file in the Folder List pane.**

FrontPage displays the Resume page in Page view with the link bar displaying hyperlinks to the Home page and to the child pages under the Home page (Figure 3-42).

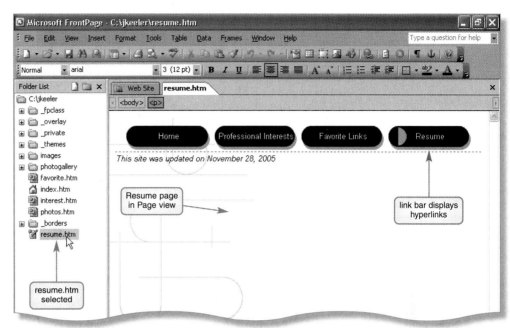

FIGURE 3-42

The Photos page also could be removed from the link bars by deleting it from the navigation structure. This would remove it from the navigation structure diagram displayed in Navigation view. By placing it under a page that does not link to child pages, the Photos page remains visible in the diagram but does not appear on any link bars. By placing the Resume page under the Home page, it appears on the link bars of other pages that link to the child pages under Home. These hyperlinks, as well as a link to the Home page, also are displayed on the Resume page.

Copy and Paste from a Word Document

You have learned that typing text in FrontPage is like typing text in a word processor. You also have learned that you can copy and paste items, such as images and text, in FrontPage. Images, text, or even tables can be copied and pasted from other Office applications into your Web pages just as easily.

The World Wide Web often is used for electronic publishing today. This means that sometimes people create Web pages to reflect what they previously produced only in a printed form, such as a resume, a scholarly paper, or even an entire book. Such a document already may exist in an electronic form, such as a Word document, but not in a form suitable for publication on the Web. Although a given word processor may allow saving a document as a Web page, the result may not appear exactly as desired. Rather than retyping a large amount of text, FrontPage allows copying the text from the document and pasting it in the Web page.

Design Tip

Copy and paste text from other documents into your Web page when the source application of the document cannot save the document in a suitable Web page format. Be sure to keep the Web page updated with any changes to the original document.

Although the text from the resume could be copied and pasted directly into a Web page, some thought should be given to the resulting presentation in a Web browser. Because the document will result in a long page, text hyperlinks should be used as an index to allow the user to navigate directly to sections of interest. A table will be used to control the positioning of both the document and the hyperlinks on the Web page. Because the current background pattern may distract the user from the text of the resume, the table background color and other properties will be modified to present the resume as a document overlaying the Web page.

The following steps create a table and modify it prior to incorporating the resume text.

To Use a Custom Background Color for a Table

1

• If necessary, position the insertion point after the horizontal link bar, on the same line containing the horizontal link bar, on the Resume page.

• Click the Insert Table button on the Standard toolbar and drag through a 3 by 3 table.

FrontPage displays the insertion point after the link bar (Figure 3-43).

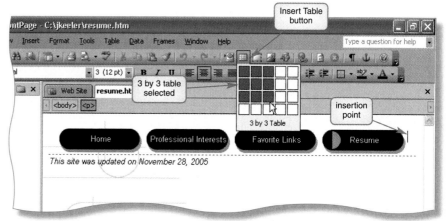

FIGURE 3-43

2

• Release the mouse button.

• When FrontPage displays the new table, right-click the left cell of the bottom row.

• Click Table Properties on the shortcut menu.

• When FrontPage displays the Table Properties dialog box, select Center in the Alignment box in the Layout area and set Size to 0 in the Borders area.

FrontPage displays the Table Properties dialog box with the alignment set to Center and the border size set to 0 (Figure 3-44).

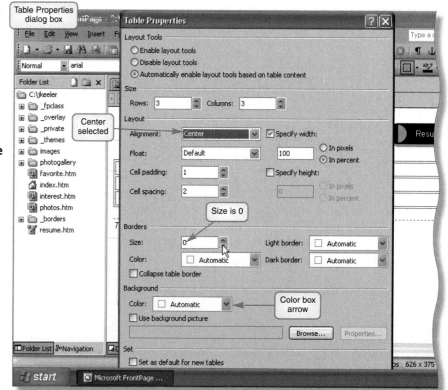

FIGURE 3-44

3

• **Click the Color box arrow in the Background area.**

• **Click More Colors.**

• **When FrontPage displays the More Colors dialog box, click the white hexagon to display a hex value in the Value text box.**

• **Drag through FF,FF,FF in the Value text box to select it.**

• **Type FC,FC,FC as the new hex value.**

FrontPage displays the new custom color hex value of FC,FC,FC (Figure 3-45).

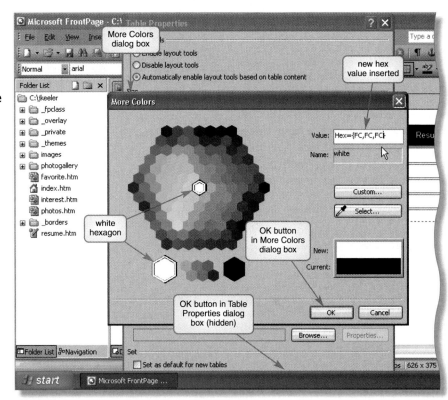

FIGURE 3-45

4

• **Click the OK button in the More Colors dialog box.**

• **Click the OK button in the Table Properties dialog box.**

FrontPage displays the table with a new background color and with dotted lines for cell borders, indicating that the borders are not displayed (Figure 3-46).

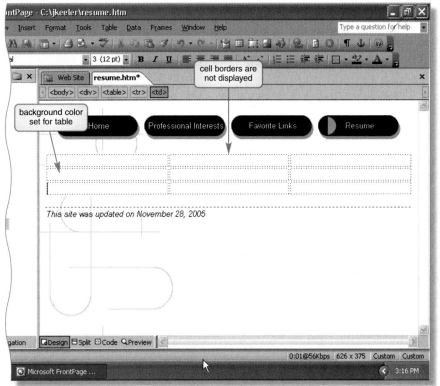

FIGURE 3-46

5

• **Right-click the left cell of the bottom row.**

• **Click Cell Properties on the shortcut menu.**

• **When FrontPage displays the Cell Properties dialog box, select Left in the Horizontal alignment box and then select Top in the Vertical alignment box in the Layout area.**

FrontPage displays the Cell Properties dialog box with the Horizontal alignment set to Left and the Vertical alignment set to Top (Figure 3-47).

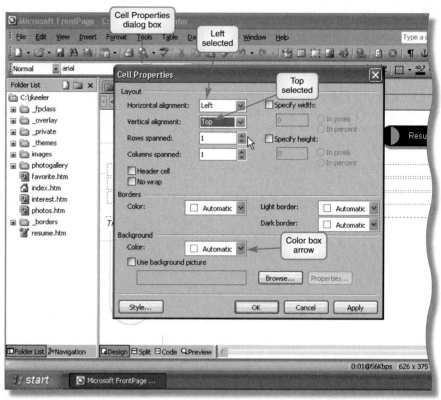

FIGURE 3-47

6

• **Click the Color box arrow in the Background area.**

• **Click More Colors.**

• **When FrontPage displays the More Colors dialog box, click the white hexagon to display a hex value in the Value text box.**

• **Drag through FF,FF,FF in the Value text box to select it.**

7

• **Type** DF,DF,DF **as the new hex value.**

• **Click the OK button in the More Colors dialog box.**

• **Click the OK button in the Cell Properties dialog box.**

FrontPage displays the cell with a background color different from that of the table (Figure 3-48).

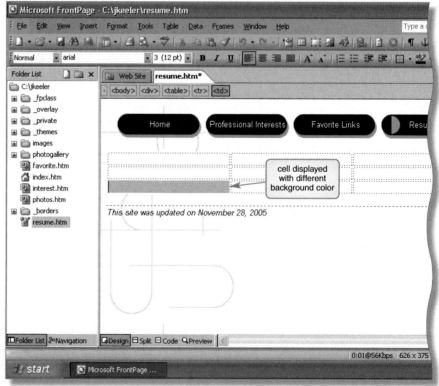

FIGURE 3-48

8

• **If necessary, click the Font Color arrow and select the Automatic font color for this theme.**

• **Type** Summary **and then press the ENTER key.**

• **Type each of the remaining text items listed in Table 3-2 on page FP 187, following each, except the last, with the ENTER key.**

The entered text appears in the lower-left cell (Figure 3-49). The cell expands as text is entered.

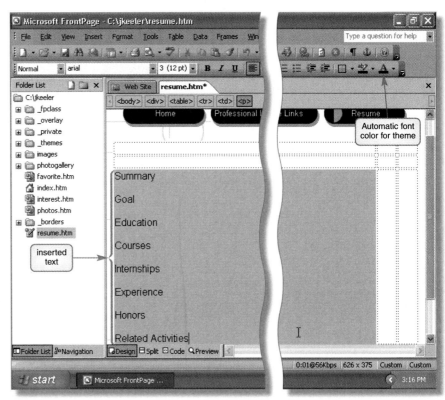

FIGURE 3-49

9

• **Drag the right borders of the left and middle columns to the left until they approximate those shown in Figure 3-50.**

• **Position the insertion point in the upper-right cell.**

Text longer than the column width automatically wraps (Figure 3-50).

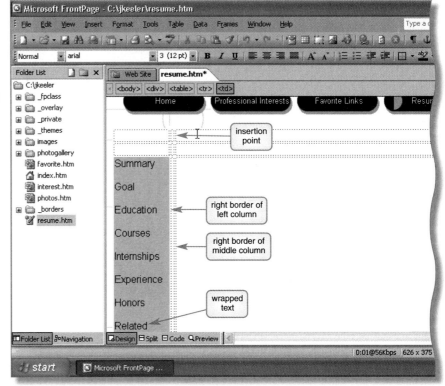

FIGURE 3-50

10

• **Hold down the SHIFT key and click the right cell in the second row to select both cells.**

• **Right-click the selected cells and then click Cell Properties on the shortcut menu.**

• **When FrontPage displays the Cell Properties dialog box, select Center in the Horizontal alignment box and then select Top in the Vertical alignment box in the Layout area.**

FrontPage displays the Cell Properties dialog box with the Horizontal alignment set to Center and the Vertical alignment set to Top (Figure 3-51).

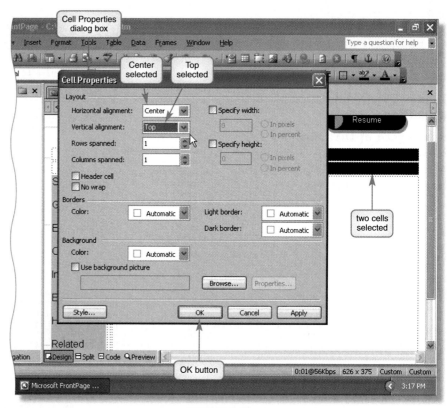

FIGURE 3-51

11

• **Click the OK button.**

• **Click the right cell in the middle row to position the insertion point.**

• **Click Format on the menu bar.**

The insertion point appears centered in the right cell of the middle row. FrontPage displays the Format menu (Figure 3-52).

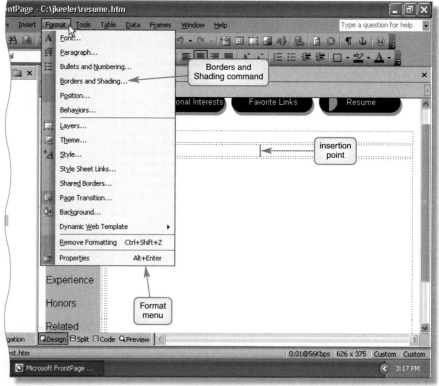

FIGURE 3-52

12

- **Click Borders and Shading.**

- **If necessary, when FrontPage displays the Borders and Shading dialog box, click the Borders tab.**

- **Click the top edge border button in the Preview area.**

FrontPage displays in the Preview area a graphic indicating where the new border will be applied (Figure 3-53).

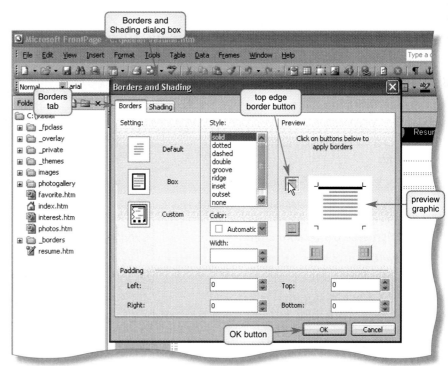

FIGURE 3-53

13

- **Click the OK button.**

- **Click the upper-right cell to position the insertion point.**

A top border is applied to the right cell of the middle row (Figure 3-54).

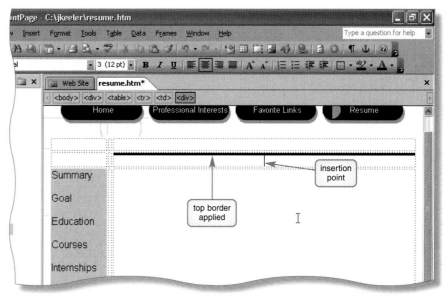

FIGURE 3-54

Although the resume could be copied and pasted directly into a Web page, using the table you just inserted will make viewing and navigating easier and more pleasant for the user. Now that the table is prepared, the steps on the next page copy text from a resume in Word and paste it into the Web page.

Other Ways

1. Press ALT+O, B
2. In Voice Command mode, say "Format, Borders and Shading"

Table 3-2	Text for Resume Index
TEXT	
Summary	Research
Goal	Experience
Education	Honors
Courses	Related Activities

To Copy and Paste from a Word Document

1

• **Click the Start button on the taskbar.**

• **Point to All Programs on the Start menu.**

• **Point to Microsoft Office on the All Programs menu.**

• **Click Microsoft Office Word 2003 on the Microsoft Office submenu.**

• **Click the Open button on the Standard toolbar.**

• **When the Open dialog box is displayed, select the file, James Keeler resume.doc, from the Project3 folder on the Data Disk.**

Word displays the Open dialog box, with the Word document file, James Keeler resume.doc, selected (Figure 3-55).

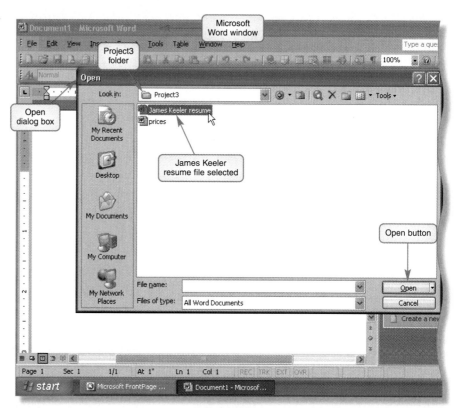

FIGURE 3-55

2

• **Click the Open button.**

• **If necessary, close the New Document task pane.**

• **If necessary, click View on the menu bar and then click Print Layout.**

• **Drag through the first line of text to select it and then press CTRL+C to copy it to the Office Clipboard.**

The Word document containing the resume is opened and is displayed in Print Layout view (Figure 3-56). The selected text is copied.

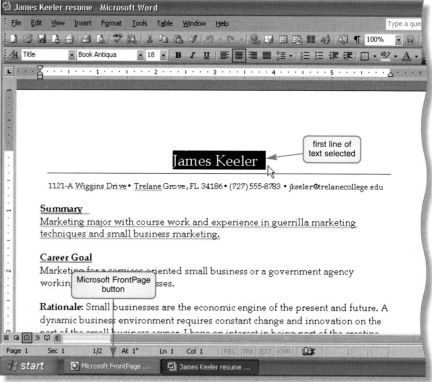

FIGURE 3-56

3

• **Click the Microsoft FrontPage button on the taskbar to switch to FrontPage.**

• **If necessary, click the upper-right cell to position the insertion point.**

• **Press CTRL+V to paste the copied text from Word into the Web page.**

• **Press the BACKSPACE key to delete the extra line.**

• **Select the text and change the font size to 5 (18 pt).**

FrontPage displays the pasted text in the Resume page in Page view (Figure 3-57).

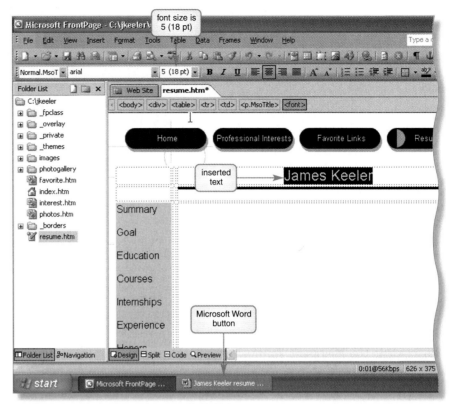

FIGURE 3-57

4

• **Click the Microsoft Word button on the taskbar to switch to Word and then drag through the second line of text to select it. Do not drag beyond the last letter in the line.**

• **Copy the text, switch to FrontPage, and then position the insertion point in the right cell of the middle row.**

• **Paste the copied text.**

5

• **If necessary, press the BACKSPACE key to delete any extra blank lines that are displayed.**

FrontPage displays the pasted text in the Resume page (Figure 3-58). The text may wrap if the width of the cell is not large enough.

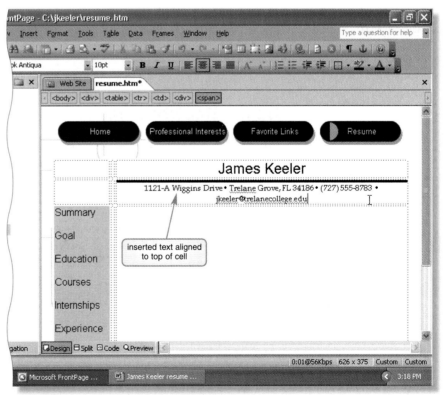

FIGURE 3-58

• **Switch to Word and then drag
through the remaining text in the
resume to select it, including the
table.**

• **Copy the text and then switch to
FrontPage.**

• **Click the lower-right cell to
position the insertion point.**

• **Paste the copied text.**

• **Press the BACKSPACE key to delete
any extra lines and spaces, but
leave one blank line at the end.**

*The remaining text is pasted in the Resume
page (Figure 3-59).*

7

• **Right-click the Microsoft Word
button on the taskbar and then
click Close on the shortcut menu.**

• **If a dialog box is displayed prompting you to save changes to the document,
click No.**

• **If necessary, select all of the pasted text and then click the Font Color button
on the Formatting toolbar to ensure that all pasted text has the same font color.**

FIGURE 3-59

Using Bookmarks

When you create a Web page, it is natural to assume that you may have to create
one or more hyperlinks from that page to another page. The ability to link from one
Web page to other pages of interest is one of the most basic and powerful features of
the World Wide Web. Not all links are created for the same purpose or in the same
manner, however. In Project 1, you created two types of links. One type provided an
e-mail link, so users could e-mail the owner of the page. Another type provided a
hyperlink from one Web page to another. You also can create a hyperlink that has a
bookmark as its destination. A **bookmark** is a location, or selected text, that you
have marked on a page.

Adding a Bookmarked Location

When designing a Web page, it is good to keep in mind how the user will
interact with that page. If there are a number of links to relatively short pieces of
information, and the user is likely to go back and forth from one page to another
visiting these links, the best design may involve placing all of the information on a
single Web page. This avoids having to reload each page as it is visited, which
increases the perceived speed at which the pages can be reached. This approach must
be balanced against having an overly large Web page, particularly if the user will not
care to visit most of it. You also may want to link the user to a place in the Web

page other than the top. This is a particular advantage when publishing a document as a Web page, because you have the ability to create hyperlinks to various sections of the document. These allow the user to move quickly from an index or table of contents to view the section of interest in the document. In a long document, particularly one containing a large amount of text, this prevents requiring the user to scroll down through the document in order to find the desired section. In both of these cases, using a bookmark can help accomplish the task.

> *Design Tip*
>
> If there are a number of links to relatively short pieces of information, and the user is likely to go back and forth from one page to another visiting these links, it may be better to place all of the information on a single Web page and use bookmarks to navigate to the short pieces of information.

The following steps bookmark a location in the current Web page.

To Bookmark a Location in a Web Page

1

• **Position the insertion point to the left of the horizontal link bar at the top of the page.**

• **Click Insert on the menu bar.**

The insertion point is positioned where the bookmark for this location is to be added. FrontPage displays the Insert menu (Figure 3-60).

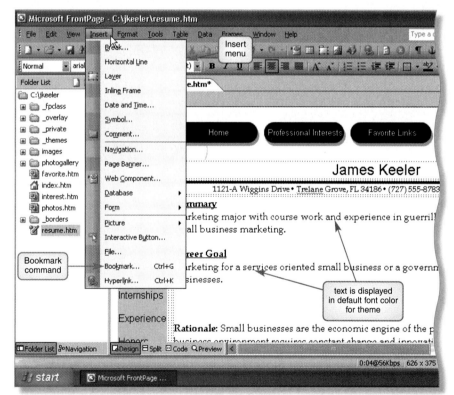

FIGURE 3-60

2

• **Click Bookmark.**

• **When FrontPage displays the Bookmark dialog box, type** Top **in the Bookmark name text box.**

FrontPage displays the Bookmark dialog box (Figure 3-61). The name of this bookmark is entered in the Bookmark name text box.

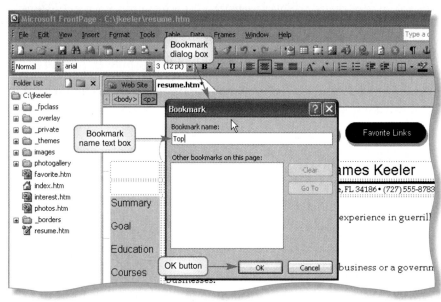

FIGURE 3-61

3

• **Click the OK button.**

• **Position the insertion point in the third row of the table, before the underlined word, Summary.**

FrontPage displays the Resume page with the bookmark flag icon, indicating the book-marked location (Figure 3-62).

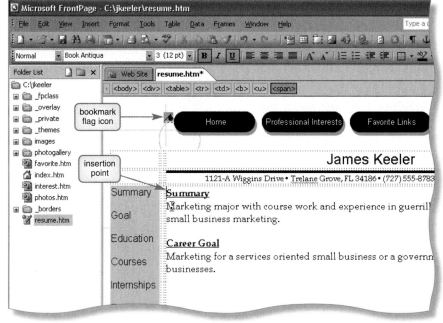

FIGURE 3-62

Adding Bookmarked Text

In FrontPage, if you bookmark a location or an image, a graphic flag icon indicates the presence of a bookmark. Text also can be bookmarked; however, it is displayed with a dashed underline. If the text was underlined previously, that under-line is not removed and is displayed normally when the page is viewed. When editing the page, however, the original underline is not visible because the dashed underline, indicating a bookmark, obscures it.

The following steps add bookmarked text to the current Web page.

To Bookmark Text in a Web Page

1

- **Drag through the underlined word, Summary, in the third row of the table to select it.**
- **Click Insert on the menu bar and then click Bookmark.**

FrontPage displays the Bookmark dialog box (Figure 3-63). The highlighted word, Summary, is the location for the bookmark that will be added. FrontPage automatically inserts the highlighted text as the default name for this bookmark in the Bookmark name text box.

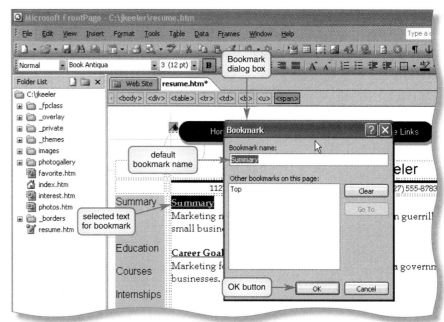

FIGURE 3-63

2

- **Click the OK button.**
- **Position the insertion point before the underlined words, Career Goal.**

FrontPage displays the Resume page, and the text, Summary, has a dashed underline, indicating that it is bookmarked (Figure 3-64).

3

- **Repeat Steps 1 through 3 to bookmark each of the remaining text items listed in Table 3-3 on the next page, selecting only the words indicated in the table. Use the default name as the bookmark name in each case.**

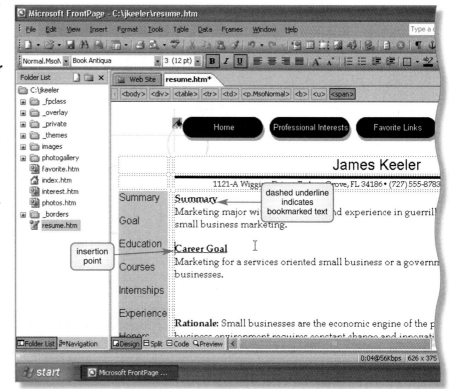

FIGURE 3-64

Other Ways
1. Press ALT+I, K
2. Press CTRL+G
3. In Voice Command mode, say "Insert, Bookmark"

More About

Hyperlinks to Bookmarks

Hyperlinks to bookmarks do not have to be located on the same Web page as the bookmarks. You easily can establish a hyperlink to a bookmark on another Web page. Click the Insert Hyperlink button on the Standard toolbar. When the Create Hyperlink dialog box displays, click the page name that contains the bookmark and then click the Bookmark button. When the Select Place in Document dialog box displays, click the desired bookmark.

Table 3-3   Text to Bookmark

BOOKMARKED TEXT
Summary
Career Goal
Education
Courses
Internships
Experience
Honors
Related Activities

Adding Hyperlinks to Bookmarks

Once the bookmarks are identified, making hyperlinks to them is done in a similar fashion as the previous hyperlinks you have created. Hyperlink addresses that target a bookmark on a page, rather than just the page itself, have the same format as a URL addressing the page, with the addition of the bookmark. A pound sign (#) preceding the bookmark name identifies a bookmark in a URL, as shown in Figure 3-68 on page FP 196.

The following steps create text hyperlinks to bookmarks in the Web page.

To Create a Hyperlink to a Bookmark

1

- **Drag through the text, Summary, in the left column of the third row in the table.**
- **Right-click the selected text.**

The text, Summary, is selected and the shortcut menu is displayed (Figure 3-65).

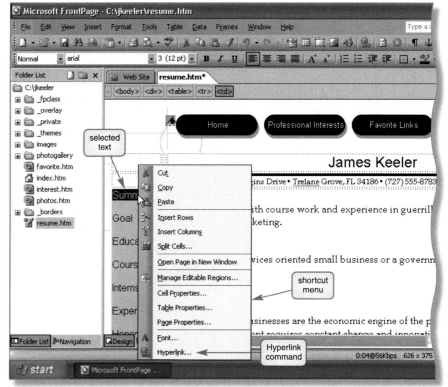

FIGURE 3-65

2

• **Click Hyperlink on the shortcut menu.**

FrontPage displays the Insert Hyperlink dialog box (Figure 3-66).

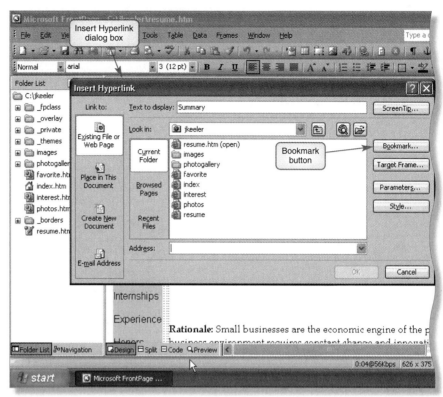

FIGURE 3-66

3

• **Click the Bookmark button.**

• **When FrontPage displays the Select Place in Document dialog box, click Summary in the list of bookmarks.**

The bookmark, Summary, is selected (Figure 3-67).

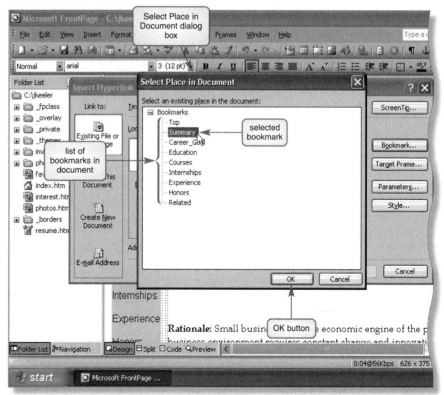

FIGURE 3-67

• Click the OK button.

The Select Place in Document dialog box is closed and the pound sign in the Address text box indicates that a bookmark will be used in the hyperlink (Figure 3-68).

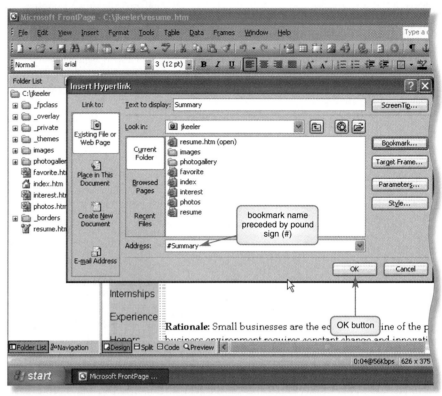

FIGURE 3-68

• Click the OK button in the Insert Hyperlink dialog box.

• Point to the hyperlink, Summary.

FrontPage displays the bookmark URL on the status bar (Figure 3-69). Because it links to a location on the same page, the full hyperlink address is not displayed.

6

• Repeat Steps 1 through 5 to create hyperlinks to each of the remaining bookmarks, as listed in Table 3-4.

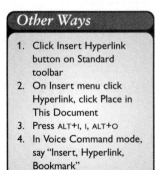

Other Ways

1. Click Insert Hyperlink button on Standard toolbar
2. On Insert menu click Hyperlink, click Place in This Document
3. Press ALT+I, I, ALT+O
4. In Voice Command mode, say "Insert, Hyperlink, Bookmark"

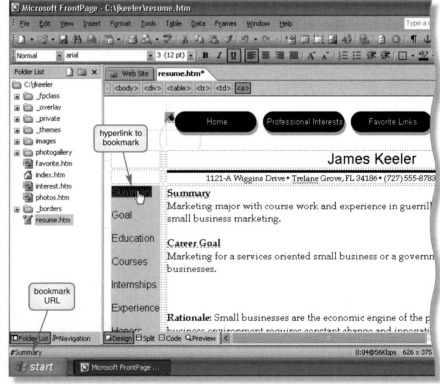

FIGURE 3-69

Once users have followed a hyperlink to a bookmark on the same Web page, they simply can scroll back to return to the previous location. If the page is very long or if the original hyperlink is not at the top of the page, however, it may be tedious for the users to find their way back. It is common to provide a back link to take the user back to the location that linked to the bookmark. Although using the Back button in the Web browser could achieve the same visible effect, there is a subtle difference. Using the browser's Back button to return removes the current page from the browser's list of recently visited links. By using a back link, the list of links the user has followed recently is preserved, even though a different page is not really loaded.

Use of a back link works if only one hyperlink targets a given bookmark. If multiple hyperlinks target the same bookmark, there is no way to determine the source of the hyperlink to which the user should be returned. Because all of the links that target your text bookmarks come from text near the top of the Web page, they may all target the same location for their back hyperlinks, the name at the top of the page. Use the following steps to create a back link for each of the text bookmarks.

Table 3-4 Bookmark Hyperlinks	
HYPERLINKED TEXT	BOOKMARK
Summary	Summary
Career Goal	Goal
Education	Education
Courses	Courses
Internships	Internships
Experience	Experience
Honors	Honors
Related Activities	Related

To Create Back Hyperlinks

1

• **Position the insertion point in the first empty line after the paragraph beginning with Rationale, after the Career Goal bookmark.**

• **Click the Font Size box arrow and then click 2 (10 pt).**

• **Click the Italic button on the Standard toolbar.**

• **Type** back to top **as text for the back hyperlink.**

The text, back to top, is inserted (Figure 3-70).

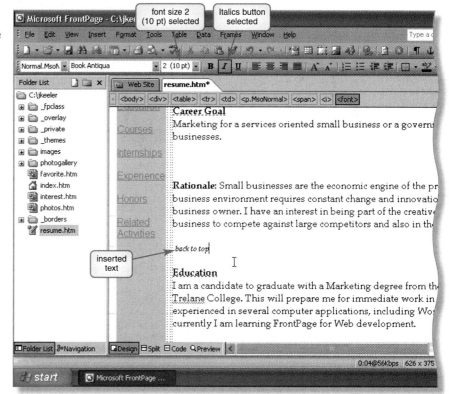

FIGURE 3-70

2

• **Drag through the text, back to top, to select it.**

• **Right-click the selected text and then click Hyperlink on the shortcut menu.**

• **When FrontPage displays the Insert Hyperlink dialog box, click the Bookmark button.**

• **When FrontPage displays the Select Place in Document dialog box, click Top in the list of bookmarks.**

The bookmark for the hyperlink is selected (Figure 3-71).

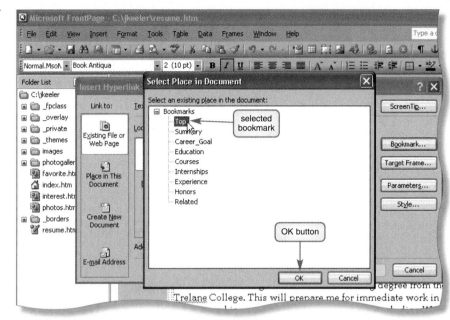

FIGURE 3-71

3

• **Click the OK button.**

• **Click the OK button in the Insert Hyperlink dialog box.**

• **Point to the hyperlink, back to top.**

FrontPage displays the bookmark URL on the status bar (Figure 3-72).

4

• **Copy and paste the hyperlink to create back hyperlinks for each of the remaining sections containing bookmarks. Do not create a back hyperlink in the cell containing the Summary bookmark at the top of the page.**

• **Insert or delete blank lines to adjust heights as needed.**

• **Save and close the Resume page.**

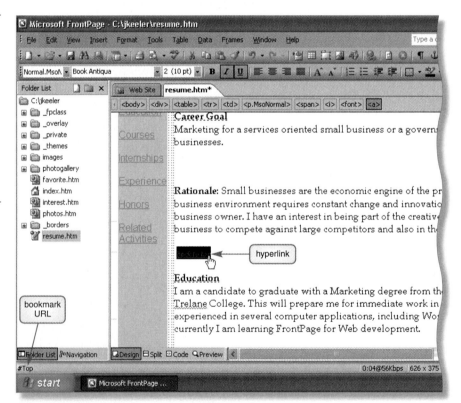

FIGURE 3-72

Because the back hyperlinks all reference the same location, the top of the page, the first back hyperlink was copied and pasted into multiple locations in the page. This saves time, rather than inserting the text and creating a hyperlink for each location separately.

Modifying an Image on a Web Page

Often, you want to use images that need some modification to be usable on a Web page. Typically, this has to do with the displayed size of the image, but also may include other properties, such as the image background or the size of the image file. FrontPage provides tools to modify these properties, thus making the images more useful.

Many images used on a Web page may appear to be irregular in shape when in fact they are rectangular. When the background color of the image is not the same as that of the Web page, the rectangular shape of the image becomes very obvious.

More About

The Pictures Toolbar

The Pictures toolbar provides a number of useful tools for images. Much as you can do with the Photo Gallery component, you can click the Auto Thumbnail button to create a thumbnail of a large image. The Auto Thumbnail button automatically inserts a hyperlink to the original, larger image.

Displaying the Pictures Toolbar

The Pictures toolbar contains a set of buttons that perform actions such as rotating the image and changing the brightness and contrast. The buttons on the Pictures toolbar may be active or inactive, depending on the type of image and its context. The Pictures toolbar can be hidden or displayed, depending on the setting on the View menu.

The following steps insert an image and display the Pictures toolbar.

To Insert an Image and Display the Pictures Toolbar

1

• **Double-click the file, index.htm, in the Folder List pane.**

• **Position the insertion point before the Home hyperlink on the bottom line.**

• **Press the ENTER key twice.**

FrontPage opens the Home page in Page view and inserts two additional blank lines (Figure 3-73).

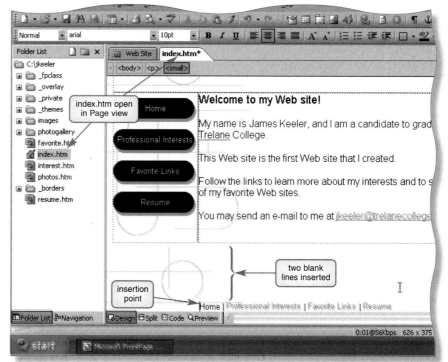

FIGURE 3-73

2

• **Click Insert on the menu bar and then point to Picture on the Insert menu.**

• **Click From File on the Picture submenu.**

• **When FrontPage displays the Picture dialog box, select the camera file from the Project3 folder on the Data Disk.**

FrontPage displays the Picture dialog box with the file, camera, selected (Figure 3-74).

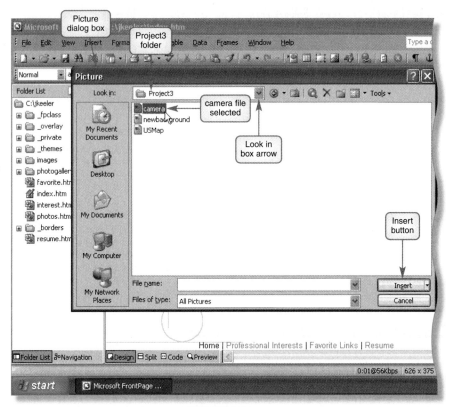

FIGURE 3-74

3

• **Click the Insert button.**

• **When the image is inserted, click the image to select it.**

• **Click View on the menu bar and then point to Toolbars on the View menu.**

FrontPage displays the Toolbars submenu (Figure 3-75). The selected check marks indicate the toolbars that currently are visible.

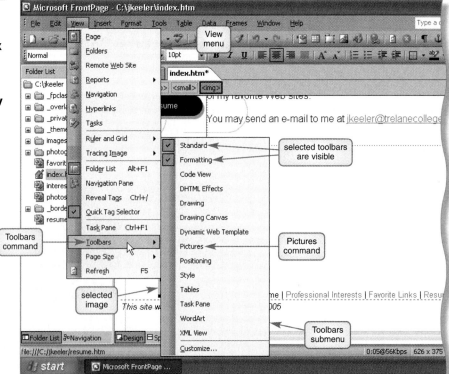

FIGURE 3-75

4

• **Click Pictures.**

FrontPage displays the Pictures toolbar (Figure 3-76).

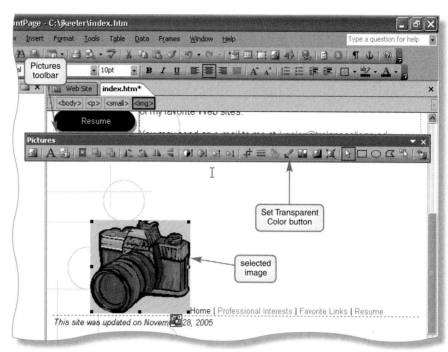

FIGURE 3-76

Other Ways

1. Press ALT+V, T, click Pictures
2. In Voice Command mode, say "View, Toolbars, Pictures"

By selecting an image and then selecting the Pictures toolbar on the Toolbars submenu, the Pictures toolbar is displayed only when an image is selected currently. If the image is deselected, the Pictures toolbar is not displayed. In order for the Pictures toolbar always to be visible on the screen, however, no image should be selected currently when the Pictures toolbar on the Toolbars submenu is chosen. In this case, the Pictures toolbar always will be displayed, whether or not an image is selected currently. All buttons are inactive, except the first, the Insert Picture From File button, until an image is selected.

Creating a Transparent Image

A **transparent image** sometimes is referred to as a **floating image** because it appears to float on the Web page. To make an image transparent, you select one of the colors in the image to be the **transparent color**. The background color or image of the page replaces the transparent color.

An image can have only one transparent color. If you select another transparent color, the first transparent color reverts to its original color. Use the Set Transparent Color button on the Pictures toolbar to make a selected color transparent. The mouse pointer changes to the Set Transparent Color pointer when the Set Transparent Color button is clicked and the mouse pointer is positioned over the image. You then click a color on the image to make it transparent.

Q&A

Q: Can I use a transparent color with an animated GIF image?

A: No. An animated GIF image consists of several images that display in rapid succession. GIF images that are animated will not allow you to select a transparent color.

Design Tip

To make an image transparent, select one of the colors in the image to be the transparent color. The transparent color is replaced by the background color, background design, or image of the page. An image can have only one transparent color.

To make an image transparent, it must be in the GIF file format. FrontPage asks you if you want to convert a JPEG image to GIF format when attempting to make a JPEG image transparent. Because GIF supports a maximum of only 256 colors, some image quality may be lost by converting from JPEG to GIF.

The procedure for making a transparent image is to select the image and then choose the transparent color using the Set Transparent Color pointer.

The following steps set the color light green around the sides of the camera image as the transparent color.

To Create a Transparent Image

1

• **If necessary, click the image to select it.**

• **Click the Set Transparent Color button on the Pictures toolbar.**

• **Position the mouse pointer over the image.**

FrontPage displays sizing handles around the image to indicate that it is selected (Figure 3-77). The mouse pointer changes to the Set Transparent Color pointer when positioned over the image.

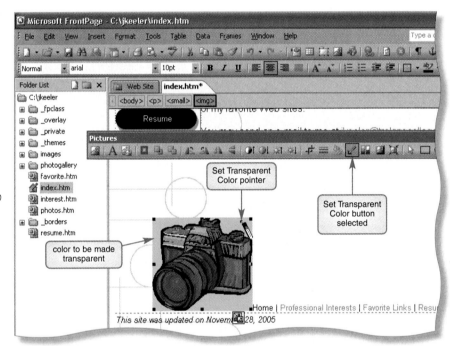

FIGURE 3-77

2

• **Click the light green color surrounding the image.**

The light green color becomes transparent and is replaced by the background (Figure 3-78). The mouse pointer is restored to the normal block arrow pointer and the Set Transparent Color button no longer is selected.

Other Ways

1. Click image, in Voice Command mode, say "Set Transparent Color"

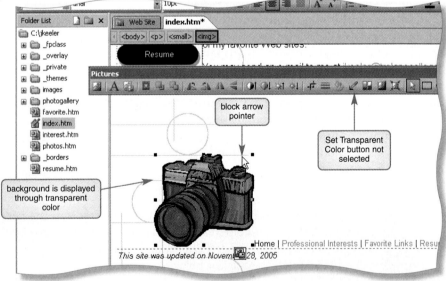

FIGURE 3-78

Care must be exercised when selecting a color to be transparent. If the color appears in other sections of the image, it will become transparent in the other sections as well, and this might have an unexpected or undesirable effect. For example, if an image containing a face includes a purple background, the result of making white the transparent color could be a face with purple eyes and purple teeth.

Resizing and Resampling an Image

Sometimes an image for a Web page is too small or too large to fit within the space set aside for it in the Web page design. The image may be resized, shrinking or stretching it, by selecting the image and dragging its handles until it becomes the desired size. This was done in Project 2 with the book image on the Photos page. The width and height of the image also may be specified directly.

Resizing an image does not automatically change the size of the image file. It changes only the HTML tags for the image, so the browser actually does the shrinking or stretching when the image is displayed. This is an advantage for small images stretched to a larger size. The small image file takes less time to load than if the file contained the image at its larger size.

Conversely, for an image you have made smaller, the file still contains the image at its original size, and it still must be loaded even though the browser displays a smaller version of the image. To take advantage of the download performance brought about by a smaller image, the image must be resampled. **Resampling** an image stores the image in the file at its new size.

When working with large image files, resample an image after adding the image to the page if the image is resized on the page. The resulting smaller file size allows the page to download faster.

Once an image has been resampled as a smaller size, it may appear better at the smaller size than before it was resampled. Once the resampled file is saved, trying to stretch it back to its original size typically results in a poorer-quality image. In both cases, this is due to the amount of information needed in the file to display the image at the given size. In the first case, too much information was provided for a smaller image. In the second, information that is needed for the larger displayed image was lost in the resampling. If you are going to resample an image but may need the larger version later, then make a backup copy.

Resampling an image becomes particularly important when inserting photographs, because the JPEG files usually are rather large. The photos used in the Photos page were not resampled, because FrontPage created the smaller thumbnail pictures for you.

Images can be resized and resampled as needed. The new images can be saved in the images folder of the project when the project is saved. If inserted images are not saved before resampling, the original images remain unchanged and are not included in the project. If the image is saved before resizing and resampling, then the saved version may be overwritten with the new one. The steps on the next page resize and resample the camera image for this project.

To Resize and Resample an Image

1

• **If necessary, click the image to select it.**

• **Use the sizing handles to resize the image to the approximate size illustrated in Figure 3-79.**

The image is resized using the sizing handles (Figure 3-79).

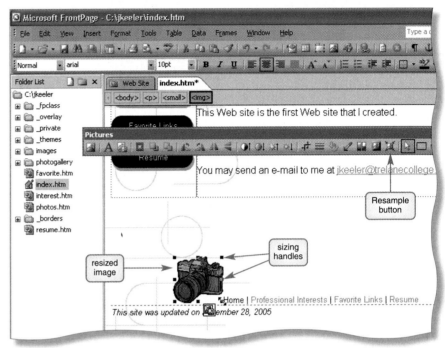

FIGURE 3-79

2

• **With the image still selected, click the Resample button on the Pictures toolbar.**

FrontPage displays the resized and resampled image (Figure 3-80).

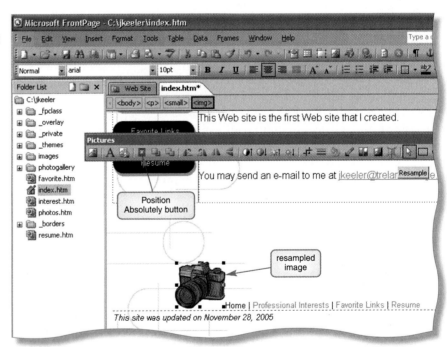

FIGURE 3-80

Other Ways

1. Click image, in Voice Command mode, say "Resample"

Once an image is resampled, it cannot be resampled again unless the size of the image is changed. The resample action can be undone, however, by clicking the Undo button.

Using Absolute Positioning with an Image

Although tables can be helpful in positioning elements on a Web page, at times even a table does not provide enough control over placement of an image. In other circumstances, using a table to position an image may prove to be difficult.

To provide more exact image placement, FrontPage supports absolute positioning for images. **Absolute positioning** refers to the ability to display page content at a specified distance from the upper-left corner of its container, which by default is the space that the Web page occupies in the browser. Unfortunately, due to differences in browsers and monitors, the results are not always consistent. Also, when an image is positioned absolutely, text and other items do not flow around the image. If a Web page's content changes, the image may need to be repositioned. Internet Explorer 6.0 and Netscape Navigator 6.0 both support absolute positioning; however, you should always verify the page in any browser that your Web site visitors are likely to use.

Design Tip

When designing a Web page that contains elements that are positioned absolutely, be sure to test the page with all browsers that Web page visitors use.

The following steps use absolute positioning with the camera image.

To Use Absolute Positioning with an Image

• **If necessary, click the image to select it.**

• **Click the Position Absolutely button on the Pictures toolbar.**

• **Position the mouse pointer over the edge of the image.**

The Position Absolutely button is selected and the pointer is displayed as a double two-headed arrow (Figure 3-81).

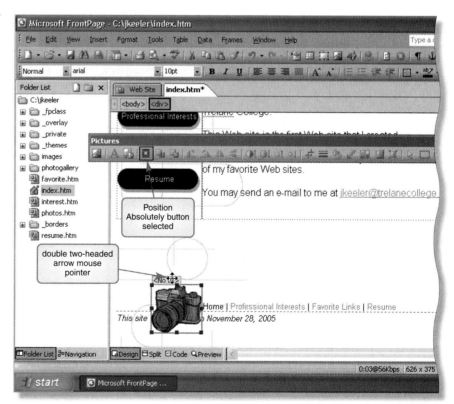

FIGURE 3-81

2

• **Drag the image to the approximate location illustrated in Figure 3-82.**

• **Click anywhere on the page off of the image to deselect the image.**

The image is repositioned (Figure 3-82).

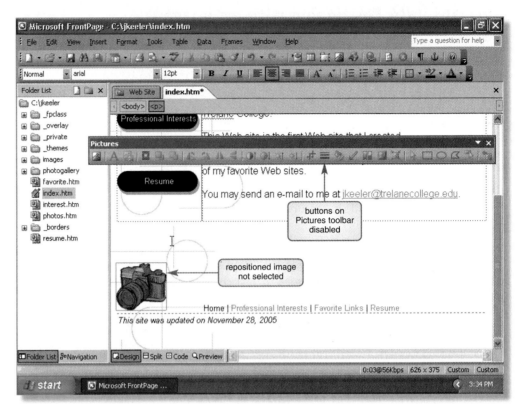

FIGURE 3-82

Other Ways

1. Click image, in Voice Command mode, say "Position Absolutely"

Inserting an AutoShapes Drawing Object

At times, finding just the right image can be time-consuming, even if it is rather simple. Users of other Microsoft Office products, such as Word and PowerPoint, are accustomed to adding drawings, as well as richly formatted text, directly to their documents. FrontPage supports drawing line graphics and rich text formatting within Web pages. The Drawing toolbar provides the ability to draw arrows, rectangles, lines, and other shapes. AutoShapes adds geometric shapes, block arrows, flowchart symbols, stars, banners, and other predrawn shapes. WordArt provides rich text formatting capabilities, such as shadowing and curving text.

The following steps add an AutoShapes object to a Web page.

To Add an AutoShapes Object

1

- **If necessary, click the Close button on the Pictures toolbar.**

- **If necessary, click View on the menu bar, point to Toolbars, and then click Drawing.**

- **Click the AutoShapes button on the Drawing toolbar.**

- **Point to Stars and Banners.**

FrontPage displays the Stars and Banners submenu (Figure 3-83).

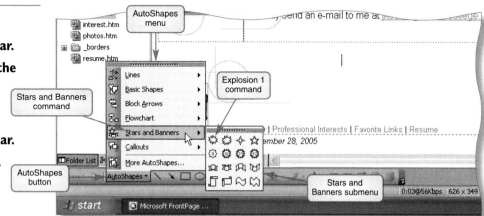

FIGURE 3-83

2

- **Click Explosion 1.**

- **Position the mouse pointer below the links bar.**

The mouse pointer changes to a cross hair (Figure 3-84).

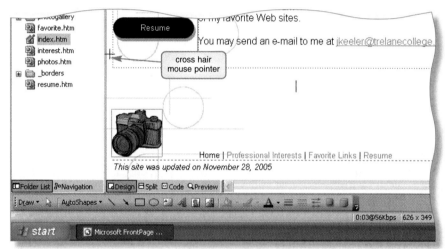

FIGURE 3-84

- **Drag the mouse pointer to the opposite corner to create a shape that is approximately the size shown in Figure 3-85.**

- **Release the mouse button.**

- **Right-click the shape and then click Add Text on the shortcut menu.**

The shape is drawn and a text box appears on the shape (Figure 3-85).

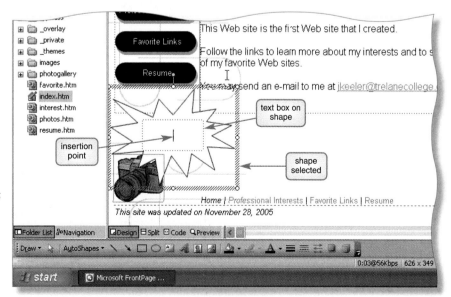

FIGURE 3-85

4

• **Click the Font Size button arrow on the Formatting toolbar and then select 2 (10 pt).**

• **Type** See my photos **in the text box on the shape.**

• **Drag through the text.**

FrontPage displays the entered text on the shape (Figure 3-86).

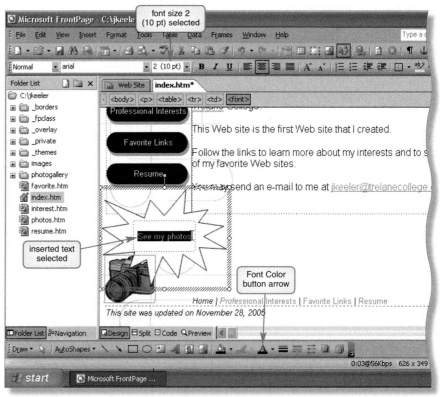

FIGURE 3-86

5

• **Click the Font Color button arrow on the Drawing toolbar.**

• **Click More Colors.**

• **When FrontPage displays the More Colors dialog box, click the title bar and drag the dialog box so it does not hide the text on the link bar buttons.**

FrontPage displays the More Colors dialog box. The dialog box is repositioned (Figure 3-87).

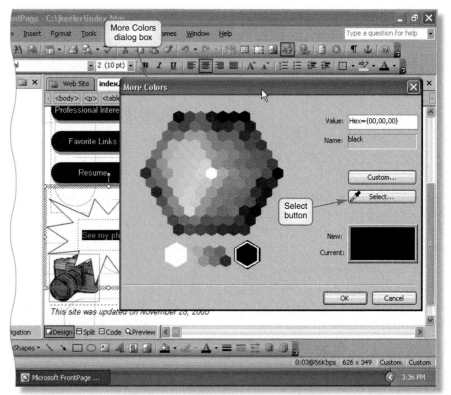

FIGURE 3-87

6

• **Click the Select button.**

• **Position the mouse pointer over the text on a Link Bar button so that the New area displays the same color as the Link Bar button text.**

FrontPage changes the mouse pointer to a dropper. The New area displays the color under the mouse pointer (Figure 3-88).

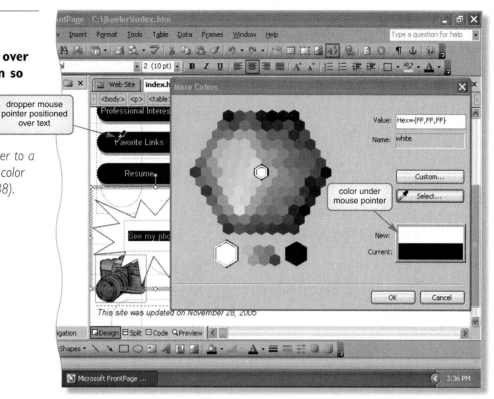

FIGURE 3-88

7

• **Click the mouse button.**

• **Click the OK button.**

• **Click the shape outside of the text box to deselect the text.**

FrontPage displays the text in the shape using the new color, which is white. Because white matches the background color of the shape, the text does not appear in the shape (Figure 3-89).

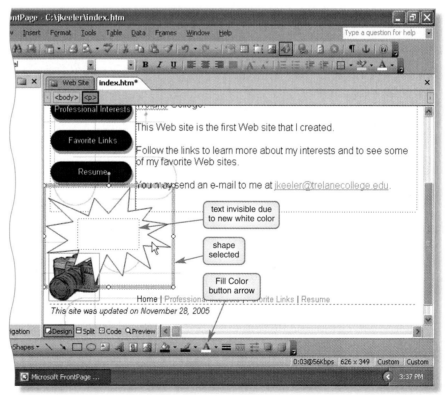

FIGURE 3-89

8

- Click the Fill Color button arrow on the Drawing toolbar.

- Click More Fill Colors.

- When FrontPage displays the More Colors dialog box, drag the dialog box so that the Link Bar buttons are visible.

- Click the Select button and then position the mouse pointer over a Link Bar button, but not over the text on a Link Bar button.

The mouse pointer is changed to a dropper and the New area displays the color under the mouse pointer (Figure 3-90).

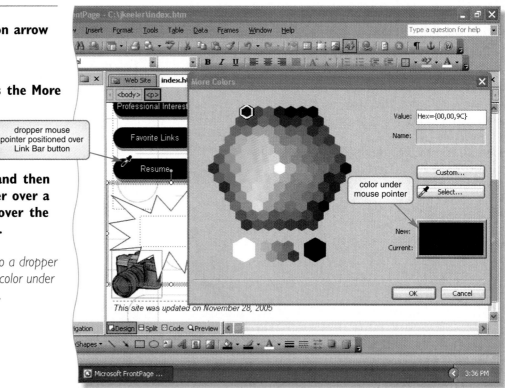

FIGURE 3-90

9

- Click the mouse button.

- Click the OK button.

- Click the Line Color button arrow on the Drawing toolbar.

FrontPage displays the shape using the selected color. The text appears because the background color of the shape no longer matches the color of the text (Figure 3-91).

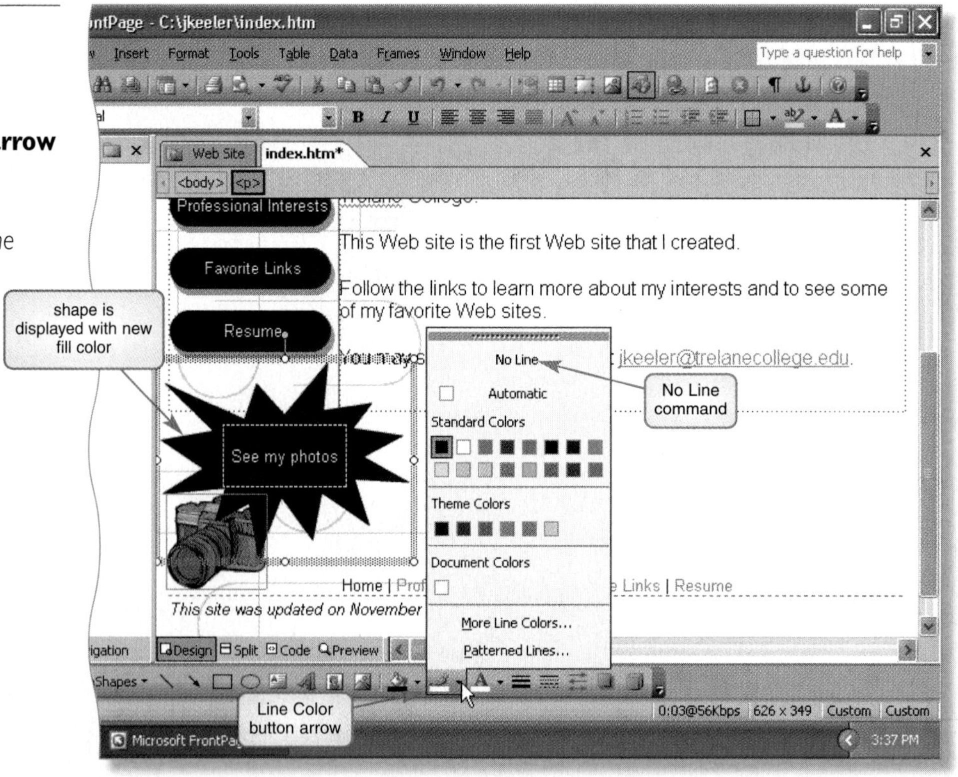

FIGURE 3-91

10

• **Click No Line.**

• **If necessary, resize the shape so that the text in the text box is fully visible.**

• **Position the pointer over the shape and then drag the shape to reposition it.**

The line around the shape is removed (Figure 3-92). When the mouse pointer is positioned over the shape, it becomes a double two-headed arrow, while if over the text, it becomes an I-beam.

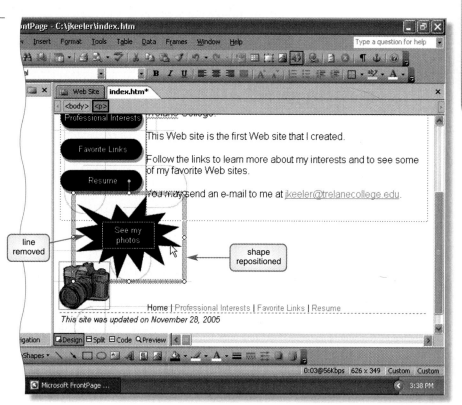

FIGURE 3-92

Other Ways

1. Press ALT+U, S, click shape
2. In Voice Command mode, say "AutoShapes, Stars and Banners, TAB, ENTER"

Besides simply creating line drawings and shapes, the Drawing toolbar includes tools to change drawing colors, add three-dimensional style effects, and add drop shadows.

These line-drawing graphics use a technology called VML (Vector Markup Language). **VML** is a way to describe images using curves, lines, and coordinates so that the instructions to draw the picture can be downloaded rather than the entire picture. A line drawing expressed in VML usually is much smaller than the same drawing stored as a GIF or JPEG file, and therefore can download more quickly.

Assigning a Hyperlink to an Image

Previous projects used text as hyperlinks, whether typed or created on a link bar. This project also will use images as hyperlinks. Now that the two images have the desired appearance, the next step is to make them function as hyperlinks.

Adding a hyperlink to the Explosion 1 shape can be accomplished in several ways. The text on the shape can be selected and assigned a hyperlink; however, this would require users to click the text, not just the shape, to activate the hyperlink.

As you have learned, many images used on a Web page may appear to be irregular in shape when in fact they are rectangular. When the Explosion 1 shape is selected, a rectangular box with sizing handles is displayed. A Web site visitor might think that clicking any area within the rectangle activates a hyperlink added to a shape. By adding a hyperlink to the shape itself, however, any location on the shape activates the hyperlink, while locations not on the shape but within the rectangular area do not. This is true even for irregular shapes, such as the Explosion 1 shape.

More About

Displaying Images

Current computers allow you to specify the bit resolution that your computer monitor will display. If the resolution is smaller than the bit resolution of an image, the image will not display properly. Right-click the desktop and then click Properties. When the Display Properties dialog box displays, click the Settings tab to see the current setting for your computer monitor.

The following steps add a hyperlink to the Explosion 1 AutoShape object.

To Add a Hyperlink to an AutoShapes Object

1

• **Right-click the Explosion 1 object.**

FrontPage displays a shortcut menu (Figure 3-93). Be sure to select the shape and not the text on the shape. If the Set AutoShape Defaults command does not appear on the shortcut menu, then the shape is not selected.

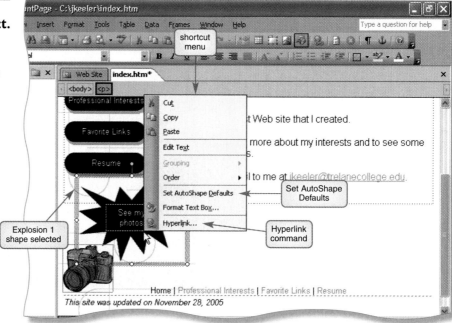

FIGURE 3-93

2

• **Click Hyperlink.**

• **If necessary, when the Insert Hyperlink dialog box appears, click the Existing File or Web Page button in the Link to bar.**

• **Select the file, photos, in the Web folder location (c:\jkeeler).**

3

• **Click the OK button.**

• **Click away from the shape to deselect it.**

• **Position the mouse pointer over the shape.**

FrontPage displays the new URL for the image hyperlink on the status bar (Figure 3-94). If the mouse pointer is positioned off of the shape, the URL does not appear.

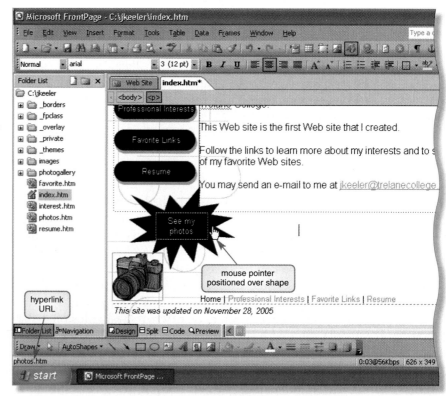

FIGURE 3-94

Adding a hyperlink to the camera image can be as simple as adding one to text. In such a case, any location within the rectangle encompassing the image will activate the hyperlink. To activate a hyperlink only from within the contours of the image, as was done with the AutoShape object, a hotspot must be defined first.

Image Maps

Rather than assign a hyperlink to an entire graphic, an image map may be used. An **image map** is a graphic image containing special areas called hotspots. A **hotspot** is a specially designated portion of the image that is set up as a hyperlink. Clicking a hotspot is the same as clicking a regular text hyperlink. The hotspot allows the Web page visitor to jump to the URL that is defined for that region of the image.

Image maps provide new ways to create interactive Web pages. They provide an alternative to plain text hyperlinks. They also allow the Web page designer to economize on images, because a single image can contain multiple hotspots and, thus, multiple hyperlinks. A well-designed image map gives the viewer clues about the destination of each hyperlink. For example, an art gallery might have an image containing a diagram of the various rooms in which different types of art are exhibited. Clicking a room displays another Web page containing images of related works of art. A college or university could have an image containing a map of the campus with hotspots defined for each building. Clicking a building would display another Web page describing the building.

When creating an image map, the use of a motif, or metaphor, for the images helps to guide the user. The image map typically replaces text hyperlinks and permits the user to navigate the Web site with less reading. For example, a campus map of different buildings might be used for obtaining navigation assistance. A bookshelf with books listing different topics might be used in a Help desk application.

Design Tip

When creating an image map, the use of a motif, or metaphor, for the images helps to guide the user. Consider image maps as a replacement for related text hyperlinks.

Defining Hotspots

To create an image map, the Web page designer first selects the image to use and then defines hotspots on the image. Finally, URLs are assigned to each hotspot.

Hotspots can be circles, rectangles, or irregularly shaped areas called polygons. Hotspots are designated using the hotspot buttons on the Pictures toolbar. For example, when the Rectangle button is clicked, the mouse pointer changes to a pencil pointer. To draw a rectangular hotspot, click and hold one corner of the desired rectangle, drag to the opposite corner, and then release the mouse button. The Insert Hyperlink dialog box automatically opens for specifying the target URL that will be assigned to the hotspot. Text can be added to an image and then hyperlinks created for the text, making it, in effect, a labeled rectangular hotspot. When adding hotspots other than as text, the Insert Hyperlink dialog box automatically appears. This is not true for text, because text may be added to an image without making it a hotspot.

The camera image only needs a single hotspot because it links only to the Photos page. Using an appropriate image, however, hotspots could be created to link to each page of interest in the Web site. The steps on the next page add a hotspot to the camera image.

More About

Image Map Hotspots

You can set a default hyperlink for any area on the image map that does not have a hotspot defined. Click the General tab in the Picture Properties dialog box.

To Add a Hotspot to an Image

1

• **If necessary, click the camera image to select it.**

• **If necessary, right-click anywhere on a toolbar and then click Pictures on the shortcut menu to display the Pictures toolbar.**

FrontPage displays the Pictures toolbar and the camera picture is selected (Figure 3-95).

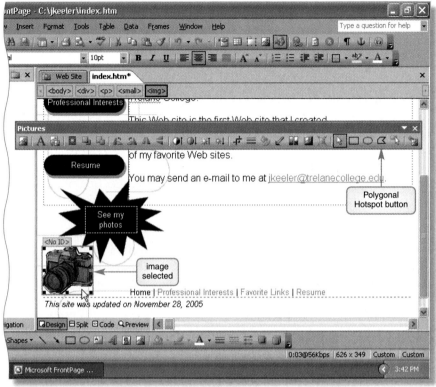

FIGURE 3-95

2

• **Click the Polygonal Hotspot button on the Pictures toolbar.**

• **Carefully draw around the perimeter of the camera image, using a single click to create a new edit point with each change of direction.**

• **When you have completed tracing around the perimeter, click the starting point to complete the hotspot.**

• **When FrontPage displays the Insert Hyperlink dialog box, click the file name, photos.**

FrontPage displays the Insert Hyperlink dialog box with the photos file selected (Figure 3-96).

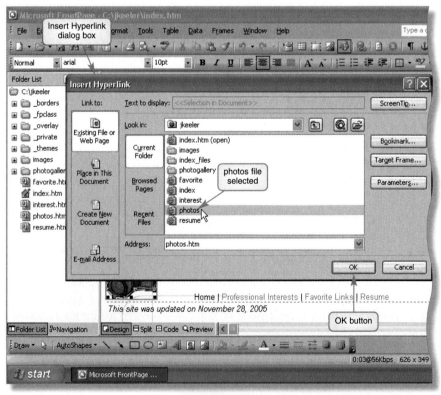

FIGURE 3-96

3

• **Click the OK button.**

• **Position the mouse pointer on the camera image.**

FrontPage displays the file name, photos.htm, on the status bar to indicate that the photos.htm file is the destination URL or the hyperlink (Figure 3-97).

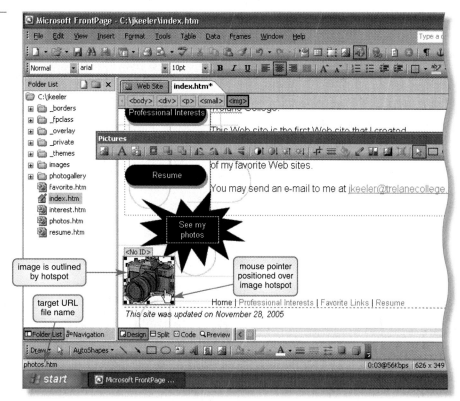

FIGURE 3-97

Other Ways

1. Click image, in Voice Command mode, say "Polygonal Hotspot"

The previous steps created a hotspot on an image map. Although this image contains only a single hotspot, it is an image map because the entire rectangular image was not used for the hyperlink. Image maps are an excellent way to present links visually in an intuitive and user-friendly fashion. Creating image maps is not hard to do, but requires some careful preparation.

Highlighting Image Map Hotspots

The hotspot on the camera image map is easy to find because there is only one and it has well-defined and intuitive boundaries. Some image maps do not have any text or image features associated with hotspots. Lines surrounding the hotspots are displayed when the image is selected. When multiple hotspots are used, or an image already has similar lines, the boundaries around each hotspot may be difficult to locate.

The Pictures toolbar includes the Highlight Hotspots button that toggles between displaying hotspots only and displaying the image and the hotspot. The steps on the next page highlight the hotspot on the camera image map.

More About

Highlighting Hotspots

When you highlight hotspots on an image, any hotspot currently not selected displays with a black outline. If a hotspot is selected, it displays as solid black.

To Highlight Hotspots on an Image Map

1

• **If necessary, click the camera image used as an image map.**

• **Click the Highlight Hotspots button on the Pictures toolbar.**

The image becomes white, and the selected hotspot is revealed as solid black (Figure 3-98). In this view, the hotspots readily are visible.

2

• **Click the Highlight Hotspots button again to remove the highlight.**

• **Click the Close button on the Pictures toolbar.**

FrontPage removes the highlight and closes the Pictures toolbar.

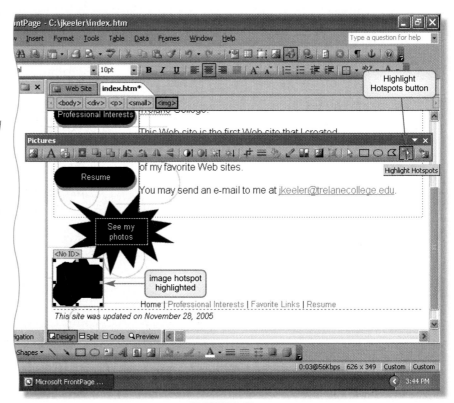

FIGURE 3-98

The Highlight Hotspots button is useful when image features make it difficult to see the hotspot outlines that are superimposed on the image.

Displaying the Hyperlinks in a FrontPage Web Site

In this and previous projects, links were created to other pages within a Web site, to Web sites not within the current Web site, and to an e-mail address. It is important to avoid having any of these hyperlinks point to nonexistent files. Hyperlinks that point to nonexistent files are referred to as **broken hyperlinks**.

Several reasons exist for encountering broken hyperlinks. The file that is the target of the hyperlink could have been deleted, renamed, moved to another folder, or moved to another Web server. The Web server on which the file resides could have had its Internet address changed, could be out of service for some period of time, or could be permanently out of service.

Design Tip

Avoid broken hyperlinks by testing the Web site before publishing the Web site, after publishing the Web site, and on a regular basis once the Web site is published.

Keeping track of broken hyperlinks in a small Web site such as James Keeler's is simple because it contains only a few hyperlinks. When developing very large Web sites, with many files and hyperlinks, however, it is very difficult to try to remember the pages that have hyperlinks, the targets where they link, and which hyperlinks are broken.

The Hyperlinks view in FrontPage alleviates this problem. For a given Web page, the Hyperlinks view displays in a graphical format the hyperlinks and their URLs, and indicates which hyperlinks are broken. The following steps display the Hyperlinks view and determine whether James Keeler's Web site has any broken hyperlinks.

To Display the Hyperlinks in a FrontPage Web Site

1

• **Make sure that you have saved all changes, saving the camera.gif file in the images folder when prompted to save the embedded image.**

• **If necessary, open the file index.htm in the Folder List pane.**

2

• **Click View on the menu bar and then click Hyperlinks.**

• **Click the plus sign on the interest.htm icon to display its links.**

FrontPage displays the Web site in Hyperlinks view (Figure 3-99). The plus sign on the interest.htm icon turns to a minus sign.

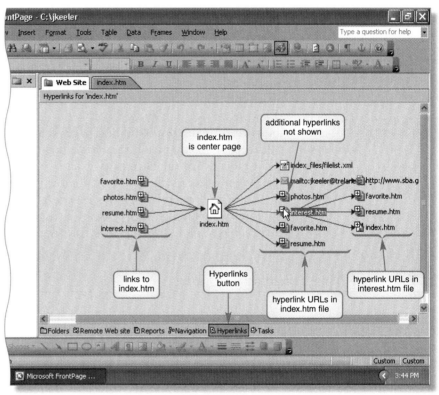

FIGURE 3-99

Other Ways

1. On View menu click Hyperlinks
2. Press ALT+V, H
3. In Voice Command mode, say "View, Hyperlinks"
4. In Voice Command mode, say "Hyperlinks"

The Hyperlinks view displays a graphical diagram of the hyperlinks in a center page. The **center page** is the page for which you want to see all hyperlinks, both to and from it, in the current FrontPage Web site. In this case it is the Home page, index.htm, which displays the hyperlinks shown in Figure 3-99. Hyperlinks exist from the Home page to the Photos page, the Professional Interests page, the Favorite Links page, and the Resume page, as well as a mailto: link. You also may see links to embedded script files or style sheets created by FrontPage. None of the hyperlinks is known to be broken. A broken hyperlink is displayed like any other hyperlink, except that it has as a broken line. A plus sign indicates additional hyperlinks that are not shown. You can view links on these pages by clicking the plus sign, as was done for the interest.htm file.

You can use Hyperlinks view to verify quickly which links, if any, are broken in the current FrontPage Web site.

Reporting on the Web Site

Even a relatively small Web site consists of many files and hyperlinks to possibly many more files, even to destinations outside of the Web site itself. Managing all of the pieces of a Web site can be a daunting task. FrontPage provides various reports to illustrate the status of the FrontPage Web site. FrontPage tracks many items in the Web site such as the number of picture files, broken hyperlinks, slow pages, recently added files, and so forth.

Viewing Reports on the Web Site

FrontPage provides a summary report on a variety of items such as uncompleted tasks and broken hyperlinks. FrontPage can generate many reports for a Web site, even if the Web site is not yet published to a server. The Web site must be opened on an appropriate server, however, to generate usage summary reports. Also, if you have made any changes to your Web pages, they should be saved before viewing reports or verifying hyperlinks.

Clicking through each file in Hyperlinks view to find broken hyperlinks displays only verified hyperlinks that are known to be broken. This can be a daunting and time-consuming task. Finding unverified hyperlinks could be even more difficult because they do not show as broken in Hyperlinks view. Another difficult task, if performed manually, is finding pages that no longer are linked and cannot be reached by starting from the Home page. The Site Summary report summarizes various statistics for the current Web site. From this report, you also can access reports for hyperlinks and files, such as the Unlinked Files report and the Broken Hyperlinks report. The Broken Hyperlinks report has multiple views available from the Site Summary, including all hyperlinks in the Web site, broken hyperlinks, and unverified hyperlinks. The following steps view the FrontPage Site Summary report.

To View the Site Summary Report

1

• **Click View on the menu bar and then point to Reports.**

FrontPage displays the View menu and Reports submenu (Figure 3-100). The selected check mark to the left of the Site Summary command on the Reports submenu indicates the report that currently is visible when in Reports view.

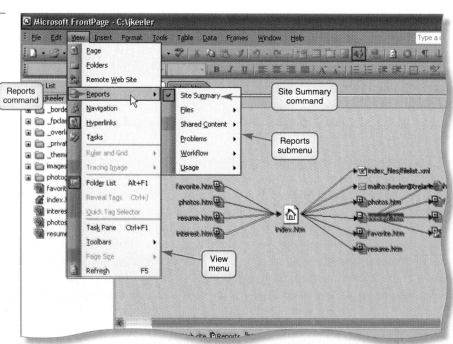

FIGURE 3-100

2

• **Click Site Summary.**

*The FrontPage window
switches to Reports view and
the Site Summary report is
displayed (Figure 3-101).*

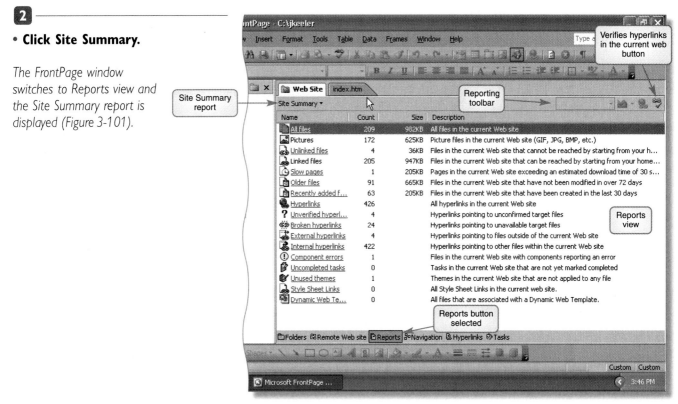

FIGURE 3-101

Verifying Hyperlinks

Just verifying that all hyperlinks in a Web site are correct is a critical and
possibly time-consuming task. FrontPage provides a means of verifying that the
hyperlinks to external destinations (destinations that are outside of the Web site)
are valid.

Hyperlinks can be verified by using the Reporting toolbar. You need to be
connected to the World Wide Web to verify external hyperlinks. The steps on the
next page use the Reporting toolbar to verify hyperlinks in the Web site.

Other Ways

1. Click Reports on
   Reporting toolbar, click
   Site Summary
2. Press ALT+V, R, M
3. In Voice Command mode,
   say "View, Reports, Site
   Summary"

More About

**Verifying
Hyperlinks**

Be aware that if you choose
to verify the status of all the
hyperlinks in the current Web
site, it could take a significant
length of time. FrontPage not
only will verify hyperlinks to
Web pages and bookmarks in
the current Web site, but
also will search the World
Wide Web to make sure the
other hyperlink targets specified in your current Web site
exist.

To Use the Reporting Toolbar to Verify Hyperlinks in the Web Site

1

• **Click View on the menu bar and then point to Reports.**

• **Point to Problems on the Reports submenu.**

FrontPage displays the Problems submenu (Figure 3-102).

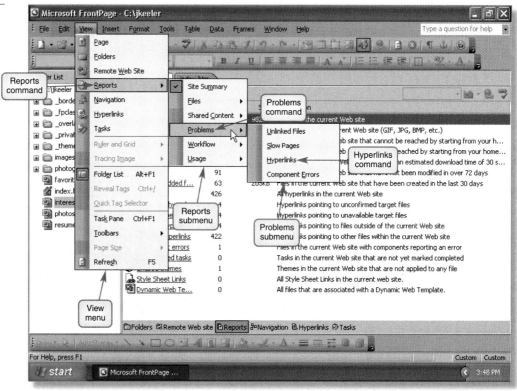

FIGURE 3-102

2

• **Click Hyperlinks.**

FrontPage displays the Reports View dialog box and the displayed report changes to the Hyperlinks report (Figure 3-103).

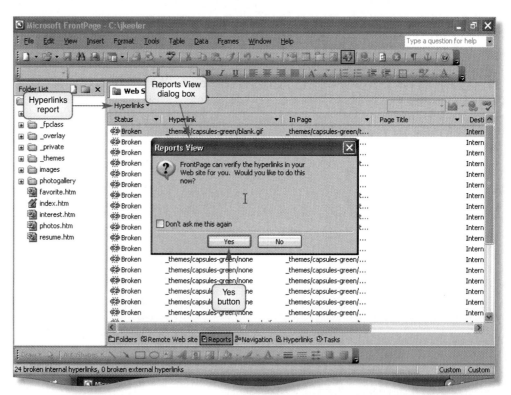

FIGURE 3-103

3

• **Click the Yes button.**

FrontPage verifies the hyperlinks and displays individual hyperlink results in the Broken Hyperlinks report (Figure 3-104). A count of broken internal and external hyperlinks is displayed on the status bar. Several of the hyperlinks in the new Capsules Green theme are broken, but the problems do not affect the Web site.

4

• **Click the index.htm tab in the document window.**

• **If you have any unsaved changes, click the Save button on the Standard toolbar.**

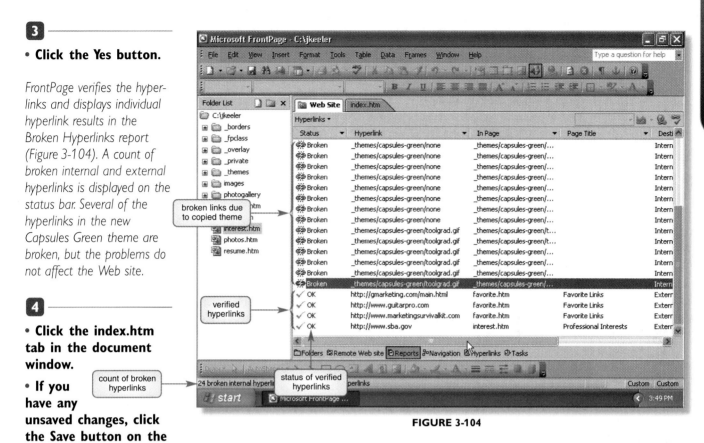

FIGURE 3-104

Other Ways

1. Press ALT+V, T, click Reporting
2. In Voice Command mode, say "View, Toolbars, Reporting"

After completing these modifications to the Web site, you should publish your changes. Remember, changes made locally do not appear to visitors to the Web site until those changes have been published.

To Publish Changes to an Existing FrontPage Web Site

1 Click the Publish Web button on the Standard toolbar. Because this Web site was published previously, FrontPage does not display the Publish Destination dialog box, but assumes that you will publish to the same location.

2 If necessary, type your user name and password. Click the OK button.

You now can view the changes by entering http://www.trelanecollege.edu/ ~jkeeler/index.htm (use your own URL) in any browser and pressing the ENTER key. Be sure to test the hyperlinks to the Photos and Resume pages and from those pages to the Home page.

Quitting Microsoft FrontPage

When you have published James Keeler's Web site, you can close the Web site and quit Microsoft FrontPage 2003. The steps on the next page close the Web site and quit FrontPage.

More About

Quick Reference

For more information, see the Quick Reference Summary at the back of this book, or visit the FrontPage 2003 Quick Reference Web page (scsite.com/fp2003/qr).

To Close a Web Site and Quit FrontPage

1 **Click File on the menu bar and then click Close Site.**

2 **Click the Close button on the right side of the FrontPage title bar.**

The FrontPage window closes and the Windows desktop is displayed.

Project Summary

Previously, you learned about essential Web page development. In Project 3, you learned how to customize your Web pages. You customized a theme, saved it for later reuse, and applied it to a single Web page. You learned about image file formats and customized images by creating a transparent image and resampling an image to change its file size. You created an image map and assigned a target URL to the hotspot. You copied text from a Word document and pasted it into a Web page. You inserted bookmarks in a Web page for easier navigation. You learned how to display the status of the hyperlinks used in the Web pages of the current FrontPage Web site. Finally, you learned how to use FrontPage reporting features and how to verify hyperlinks.

What You Should Know

Having completed this project, you should be able to perform the tasks below. The tasks are listed in the same order they were presented in this project. For a list of the buttons, menus, toolbars, and commands introduced in this project, see the Quick Reference Summary at the back of this book and refer to the Page Number column.

1. Open an Existing Page in a FrontPage Web Site (FP 158)
2. Create and Apply a Customized Theme   (FP 159)
3. Change the Style of a Link Bar   (FP 164)
4. Add a Row to a Table   (FP 166)
5. Add a Hit Counter   (FP 167)
6. Enable Shared Borders   (FP 170)
7. Add a Shared Border   (FP 172)
8. Add a New Page in Page View   (FP 177)
9. Add a Link Bar Component   (FP 177)
10. Modify the Navigation Structure   (FP 178)
11. Use a Custom Background Color for a Table (FP 182)
12. Copy and Paste from a Word Document (FP 188)
13. Bookmark a Location in a Web Page   (FP 191)
14. Bookmark Text in a Web Page   (FP 193)
15. Create a Hyperlink to a Bookmark   (FP 194)
16. Create Back Hyperlinks   (FP 197)
17. Insert an Image and Display the Pictures Toolbar (FP 199)
18. Create a Transparent Image   (FP 202)
19. Resize and Resample an Image   (FP 204)
20. Use Absolute Positioning with an Image   (FP 205)
21. Add an AutoShapes Object   (FP 207)
22. Add a Hyperlink to an AutoShapes Object (FP 212)
23. Add a Hotspot to an Image   (FP 214)
24. Highlight Hotspots on an Image Map   (FP 216)
25. Display the Hyperlinks in a FrontPage Web Site (FP 217)
26. View the Site Summary Report   (FP 218)
27. Use the Reporting Toolbar to Verify Hyperlinks in the Web Site   (FP 220)
28. Publish Changes to an Existing FrontPage Web Site   (FP 221)
29. Close a Web Site and Quit FrontPage   (FP 222)

Learn It Online

Instructions: To complete the Learn It Online exercises, start your browser, click the Address bar, and then enter the Web address scsite.com/fp2003/learn. When the FrontPage 2003 Learn It Online page is displayed, follow the instructions in the exercises below. Each exercise has instructions for printing your results, either for your own records or for submission to your instructor.

1 Project Reinforcement TF, MC, and SA

Below FrontPage Project 3, click the Project Reinforcement link. Print the quiz by clicking Print on the File menu for each page. Answer each question.

2 Flash Cards

Below FrontPage Project 3, click the Flash Cards link and read the instructions. Type 20 (or a number specified by your instructor) in the Number of playing cards text box, type your name in the Enter your Name text box, and then click the Flip Card button. When the flash card is displayed, read the question and then click the ANSWER box arrow to select an answer. Flip through Flash Cards. If your score is 15 (75%) correct or greater, click Print on the File menu to print your results. If your score is less than 15 (75%) correct, then redo this exercise by clicking the Replay button.

3 Practice Test

Below FrontPage Project 3, click the Practice Test link. Answer each question, enter your first and last name at the bottom of the page, and then click the Grade Test button. When the graded practice test is displayed on your screen, click Print on the File menu to print a hard copy. Continue to take practice tests until you score 80% or better.

4 Who Wants To Be a Computer Genius?

Below FrontPage Project 3, click the Computer Genius link. Read the instructions, enter your first and last name at the bottom of the page, and then click the PLAY button. When your score is displayed, click the PRINT RESULTS link to print a hard copy.

5 Wheel of Terms

Below FrontPage Project 3, click the Wheel of Terms link. Read the instructions, and then enter your first and last name and your school name. Click the PLAY button. When your score is displayed, right-click the score and then click Print on the shortcut menu to print a hard copy.

6 Crossword Puzzle Challenge

Below FrontPage Project 3, click the Crossword Puzzle Challenge link. Read the instructions, and then enter your first and last name. Click the SUBMIT button. Work the crossword puzzle. When you are finished, click the Submit button. When the crossword puzzle is redisplayed, click the Print Puzzle button to print a hard copy.

7 Tips and Tricks

Below FrontPage Project 3, click the Tips and Tricks link. Click a topic that pertains to Project 3. Right-click the information and then click Print on the shortcut menu. Construct a brief example of what the information relates to in FrontPage to confirm you understand how to use the tip or trick.

8 Newsgroups

Below FrontPage Project 3, click the Newsgroups link. Click a topic that pertains to Project 3. Print three comments.

9 Expanding Your Horizons

Below FrontPage Project 3, click the Articles for Microsoft FrontPage link. Click a topic that pertains to Project 3. Print the information. Construct a brief example of what the information relates to in FrontPage to confirm you understand the contents of the article.

10 Search Sleuth

Below FrontPage Project 3, click the Search Sleuth link. To search for a term that pertains to this project, select a term below the Project 3 title and then use the Google search engine at google.com (or any major search engine) to display and print two Web pages that present information on the term.

11 FrontPage Online Training

Below FrontPage Project 3, click the FrontPage Online Training link. When your browser displays the Microsoft Office Online Web page, click the FrontPage link. Click one of the FrontPage courses that covers one or more of the objectives listed at the beginning of the project on page FP 154. Print the first page of the course before stepping through it.

12 Office Marketplace

Below FrontPage Project 3, click the Office Marketplace link. When your browser displays the Microsoft Office Online Web page, click the Office Marketplace link. Click a topic that relates to FrontPage. Print the first page.

Apply Your Knowledge

1 Customizing a Web Page Using AutoShapes and Color

Instructions: Start FrontPage. Open the Ship-It-Here Web site that you modified in Project 2. If you did not complete this exercise for Project 2, see your instructor for a copy of the required files.

1. If necessary, double-click the file, index.htm, in the Folder List pane to display the Ship-It-Here Home page in Page view.

2. On the Format menu, click Theme. When the Theme task pane appears, select the current Web site default theme in the Select a theme list and then click Customize on the shortcut menu. When the Customize Theme dialog box is displayed, click the Colors button.

3. If necessary, when the second Customize Theme dialog box is displayed, click the Color Schemes tab and, if necessary, scroll down and click the color scheme for Eclipse. Verify that Vivid colors is selected. Click the OK button.

4. Verify that Vivid colors and Active graphics are selected in the Customize Theme dialog box. If necessary, click Background picture so that it does not contain a check mark. Click Save As and save the new theme as Custom Eclipse, or a name of your choice. Click OK. Click the OK button in the Customize Theme dialog box. Apply the theme to all pages in the Web site.

5. Click the AutoShapes button on the Drawing toolbar. Point to Stars and Banners, and then click 5-Point Star. Position the mouse pointer centered under the links bar. Drag the mouse pointer to the opposite corner to create a small star shape. Release the mouse button. Click the Fill Color button arrow on the Drawing toolbar. Click Green on the color palette. Create two additional stars to the left and to the right of the original, positioned a little lower than the original star image.

6. Click the AutoShapes button on the Drawing toolbar, point to Stars and Banners, and then click Curved Down Ribbon. Position the mouse pointer under the star images. Drag the mouse pointer to the opposite corner to create a ribbon banner shape. Release the mouse button.

7. Right-click the ribbon shape. Click Add Text on the shortcut menu. Click the Font Size button arrow on the Formatting toolbar and then select 2 (10 pt). Type International! in the text box on the shape. Drag through the text and then click the Font Color button arrow on the Drawing toolbar. Click White on the color palette. Click the Fill Color button arrow on the Drawing toolbar and then click Red.

8. Click the Text Box button on the Drawing toolbar. Position the mouse pointer under the ribbon image. Drag the mouse pointer to the opposite corner to create a text box and then release the mouse button. Using font size 2 (10 pt), type We now ship to over 100 countries overnight with the lowest rates in the business. in the text box. If necessary, drag the sizing handles so all of the text is visible. Drag through the text and then click the Font Color button arrow on the Drawing toolbar. Click Red on the color palette. Click the text box to select it. Click the Fill Color button arrow. Click No Fill.

9. In the upper-left corner of the Web page, click the delivery man image to select it. If the Pictures toolbar is not displayed, point to Toolbars on the View menu and then click Pictures on the Toolbars submenu. When the Pictures toolbar is displayed, click the Set Transparent Color button. Click the white area on the image to make it transparent.

10. Click the Preview tab to preview the Web page. When you have finished, click the Normal tab.

11. Print and save the Web page. When prompted to save the modified image, save it in the images folder, overwriting the previous version. Close the Web site and then close FrontPage. When viewed in a Web browser, the Web page appears as shown in Figure 3-105.

Apply Your Knowledge

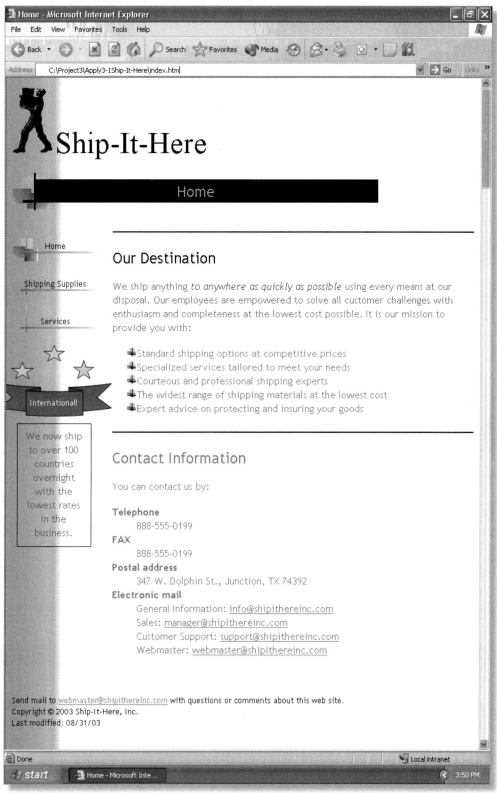

FIGURE 3-105

In the Lab

1 Adding Link Bars and Creating Bookmarks in a Table Copied from Word

Problem: The owner of Fairway Lawn Care wants to add a price list for various standard services. The list currently exists in a Word document. Because the list is rather long, you want to create hyperlinks that direct the visitor to the various sections of interest.

Instructions: Perform the following tasks.

1. Open the Lab2-2Fairway site that you modified in Project 2. If you did not complete that exercise for Project 2, see your instructor for a copy of the required files.

2. In Navigation view, add a new page under the Services page and then drag the new page icon to the left of the Home Mowing page icon. Right-click the New Page 1 icon and then click Rename on the shortcut menu. Type Price Sheet as the new page title. Double-click the Price Sheet icon to open the page in Page view. Rename the page as prices.htm in the Folder List pane.

3. Click the link bar on the left side of the page and press the DELETE key to delete the link bar. Click the line below the page title, click the Center button on the Formatting toolbar, and insert a link bar based on navigation structure. Use the page's theme as the link bar style and select a horizontal orientation for the bar. In the Link Bar Properties dialog box, select Back and next for hyperlinks. Select Home page and Parent page as additional pages. Click the OK button. If necessary, press the RIGHT ARROW key to deselect the link bar. Press the ENTER key.

4. Create a 2 by 3 table and, beginning with the upper-left cell, enter the hyperlink text from the first column in Table 3-5 into all the cells across the first row, and then the three columns of the second row. In the Table Properties dialog box, set the Alignment to Center, the border size to 0, and, if necessary, click Specify width so that it does not contain a check mark. Drag the table borders to prevent the text from wrapping. Position the insertion point after the table. On the Insert menu, click Horizontal Line.

Table 3-5 Hyperlink Text for Section Headings	
HYPERLINK TEXT	**SECTION HEADING**
Mowing	MOWING
Shrub Trimming	SHRUB TRIMMING
Debris Removal	DEBRIS REMOVAL
Tree Trimming	TREE TRIMMING
Fertilizing	FERTILIZING
Leaf Cleanup	LEAF CLEANUP

5. Using Microsoft Word, open the file, prices.doc, on the Data Disk. See the inside back cover of this book for instructions for downloading the Data Disk or see your instructor for information on accessing the files required in this book. Click in the table and then click Table on the menu bar. Point to Select and then click Table on the Select submenu. Press CTRL+C to copy the table. Switch back to FrontPage. Position the insertion point under the horizontal line and then press CTRL+V to paste the copied table.

6. Click the page banner at the top of the page and then click the Center button on the Formatting toolbar.

7. Position the insertion point to the left of the horizontal link bar at the top of the page. Insert a bookmark. When the Bookmark dialog box is displayed, type Top in the Bookmark name text box. Click the OK button.

8. Select the section heading, MOWING, in the pasted table and insert a bookmark using the default name for the bookmark name. Select the text, Mowing, in the upper-left cell in the table above the horizontal line. Create a hyperlink to the MOWING bookmark. Repeat this process for each of the remaining section headings and the corresponding text in each cell of the top table as listed in Table 3-5.

In the Lab

9. Beginning with the second section heading, SHRUB TRIMMING, position the insertion point to the right of the bookmarked section heading. Insert a space, type back to top, and then insert spaces before this text to align it to the right side of the column. Select the text just inserted and insert a hyperlink to the Top bookmark. Copy and paste this hyperlink after each subsequent section heading, inserting spaces as needed to align the hyperlink to the right of the column.

10. Save the changes to this page. Preview the changes in your browser. Print the Web page, close the Web site, and then close FrontPage. The new Web page should be displayed in a browser as shown in Figure 3-106.

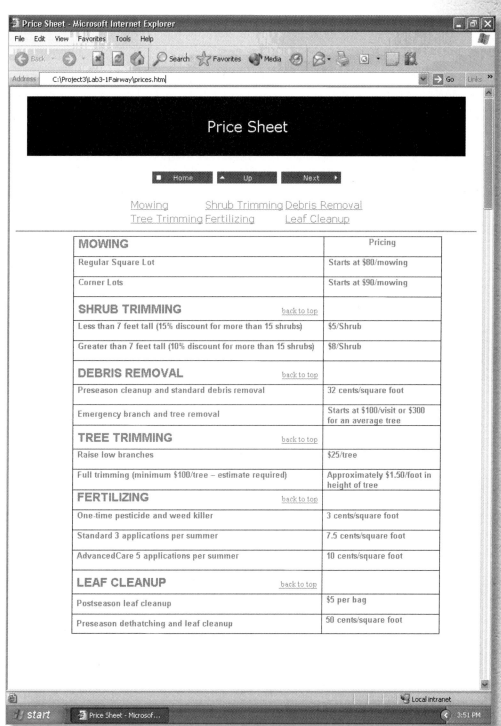

FIGURE 3-106

2 Expanding an Existing Table

Problem: Earlier, you added a Web page about running gear to your personal Web site; however, that page had none of the items common on the other pages, such as navigation links or the date last updated. You decide to add these items to your running gear Web page.

Instructions: Perform the following tasks.

1. Open the Web site Lab2-2Running that you modified in Project 2. If you did not complete that exercise for Project 2, see your instructor for a copy of the required files.
2. Open the gear.htm Web page in Design view. Click the table used to position elements on the page. Add a new row at the top and a new column at the left of the table. Merge the four rightmost cells in the top row just added. Merge the cells in rows two through five in the left column just added.
3. Click the page banner at the top of the page and drag it into the merged cells in the top row of the table. Delete the blank line remaining above the table.
4. In the merged cells of the left column, insert a vertical navigation bar with links to the Home page and children under Home. Adjust table cell widths as necessary and set the vertical alignment of the cell with the link bar to Top (see Figure 3-107).
5. Add a shared border for all pages at the bottom of the page. Type `This site was last updated on` in place of the comment component text and insert a Date and Time component for the date last updated. Edit the other pages in the Web site to remove similar information not in the shared border.
6. Save the changes to the Web pages. Print the running gear Web page, close the Web site, and then close FrontPage.

In the Lab

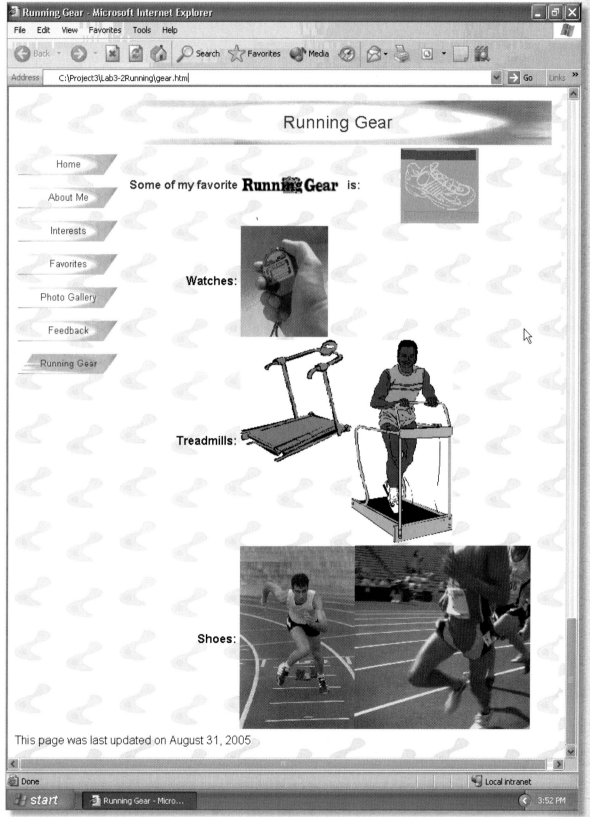

FIGURE 3-107

In the Lab

3 Creating an Image Map

Problem: The Whalen Metal support Web site includes links to pages for several regions of the United States. You decide to add an image map so visitors can click on a map of the regions.

Instructions: Using the support Web site that you modified in Project 2, perform the following tasks. If you did not complete this exercise in Project 2, see your instructor for a copy of the required files.

1. Open the Web site and position the insertion point after the link that reads, Zero-Defect. Press SHIFT+ENTER and then type Click on a region to e-mail your regional support manager.
2. Insert an image of a United States map using the file, USMap.gif, from the Project3 folder on the Data Disk, or another image as directed by your instructor. See the inside back cover of this book for instructions for downloading the Data Disk or see your instructor for information on accessing the files required in this book. Resize and move the image so that it fits appropriately on the Web page. Resample the image.
3. Click the map image, open the Pictures toolbar, and draw a polygonal hotspot approximately around the northeastern states. If necessary, when the Insert Hyperlink dialog box is displayed, click E-mail Address in the Link to area and type dmartin@whalenmetals.com as the e-mail address. Click the OK button.
4. Repeat Step 3 for the northwestern states, including Alaska, and type smurrant@whalenmetals.com as the e-mail address. Repeat Step 3 for the southeastern states, including Hawaii, and type bbrown@whalenmetals.com as the e-mail address. Click the Highlight Hotspots button on the Pictures toolbar to see the hotspot outlines. Click the Highlight Hotspots button again to remove the highlighting.
5. If necessary, click the image to select it. Set the background color as the transparent color for the image.
6. Add a shared border at the bottom of the page and apply it to all pages. Remove the comment component from the shared border. Move the name and e-mail information at the bottom of the page into the shared border.
7. Save the Web page. When prompted to save the image file, save the image in the images folder of the Web site. Verify all the hyperlinks in the Web site.
8. Preview the pages in your browser and then print the Web pages. The Web page should appear in your browser as shown in Figure 3-108.
9. Close your browser, close the Web site, and quit FrontPage.

In the Lab

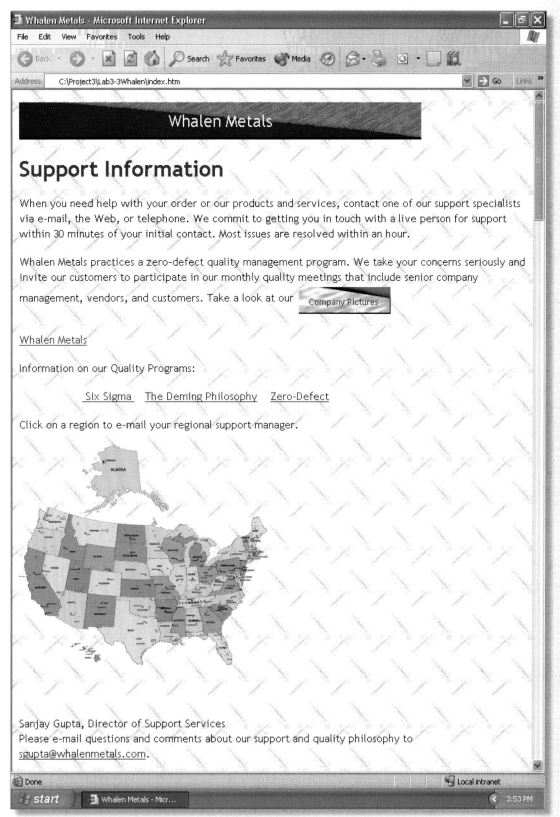

FIGURE 3-108

Cases and Places

The difficulty of these case studies varies:
■ are the least difficult and ■■ are more difficult. The last exercise is a group exercise.

1 ■ You want to make it easy for visitors to navigate to the different sections of the resume Web page that you created in Project 2. Create bookmarks for each section heading. Add a column to the left side of the table that contains the resume and then place hyperlinks in that column to each of the various bookmarked sections.

2 ■ Open the Web site that you created for your movie review Web page, and that you modified in Project 2. Add a shared bottom border for all pages and place in it your name, your e-mail address, and a date component for when the Web site was updated. Remove the portion of any Web page that already contains an e-mail address hyperlink.

3 ■■ Add a new page, titled Time Line, to the personal Web site that you created for your friend's graduation in Project 2. On the new page, draw a time line using AutoShapes, such as a rectangle, for each event of note, beginning with events listed on the History page. Use lines to connect each shape and use text and fill colors appropriately. Add a hyperlink from the rectangle for the first event (your friend starts school) to the Home page and make links for any other friends or events that have their own Web sites.

4 ■■ Modify the theme for the company softball Web page that you updated in Project 2. Search the Web for replacement graphics and modify the theme, replacing buttons, background picture, and bullets as needed. Add a marquee Web component to display announcements about upcoming games.

5 ■■ **Working Together** Develop a Web page that lists all of the instructors in your department at school. Include a brief description of the courses taught by each instructor under each instructor's name. Add bookmarks for each instructor, and at the top of the page, create links to each of the bookmarks. Check with the department for other enhancements, such as links to personal pages for each professor. Ask the department to supply you with any needed faculty photos and appropriate graphics.

MICROSOFT
Office FrontPage 2003

Creating a Stand-Alone Web Page Using a Layout Table

CASE PERSPECTIVE

As James Keeler approaches his graduation, he plans to relinquish his extracurricular leadership positions to others. As president of the Future Entrepreneurs Honor Society, he must find a willing replacement to lead the club. James has decided to create a Web page that lists the requirements and duties for the president of the club. He has asked that you develop this page for him and provides you with a Word document that contains the content for the Web page.

The Webmaster for the school's extracurricular activities Web site provided the following guidelines. He wants only a single Web page that can be linked from one of the existing activities Web pages, and he has indicated that the design need not correspond to any of the templates included with FrontPage.

The design includes pages in which the content is surrounded by a thin border and is over a yellow background. Additionally, the borders have rounded corners and include a shadow outside the right and bottom border.

With your knowledge of FrontPage, you know that you quickly can create a Web page that meets the requirements of the design using layout tables and cells.

As you read through this Table feature, you will learn how to use layout tables to format a Web page. You will learn how to modify a layout table's structure to meet your needs. You will learn how to modify layout cells within a layout table and create effects such as shadowing and rounded corners.

Objectives

You will have mastered the material in this project when you can:

- Create a stand-alone Web page
- Use a layout table to design a Web page
- Format layout cells in a layout table with rounded corners, shadows, and borders

Introduction

Tables created using the Insert Table button on the Standard toolbar are useful for creating Web pages that are simple in format or contain tabular data. Templates provide another way to lay out the contents of a Web page. **Layout tables** provide a third method for creating the overall framework of a Web page's layout. Layout tables consist of layout cells arranged in rows and columns. **Layout cells** are the regions in the framework that include the content, such as text, images, or other elements.

Layout tables provide exact control over the location of content on Web pages. The use of layout tables provides the ability to create Web pages that resemble the layout of a newspaper page. Headers, a body, columns, and footers can be laid out precisely before or after content on the page is added. Content includes titles, images, text, and Web components. Figure 1 on the next page shows that the Web page developed in this project includes content in a header and the body. Empty columns and rows of layout cells surround and separate the content in a specific manner. The content for the body of the Web page is provided in a Word document.

The layout cells containing the header and body include formatting such as a shadow, rounded corners, and a background color. A layout cell also can include a header and footer. The cells containing the title and body in Figure 1 include rounded corners, a shadow on the right and bottom of the second cell, and a background color. The layout cells that surround these cells do not include formatting and appear as empty space on the Web page, but in fact are a part of the formatting because they provide the positioning for the cells that include the content.

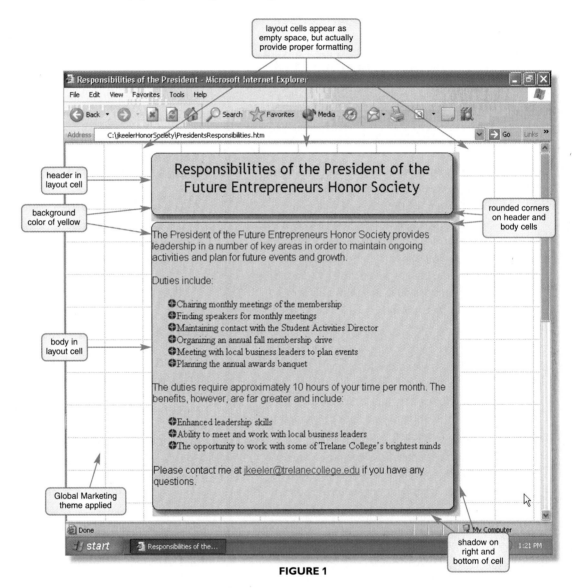

FIGURE 1

Creating a Web Page with a Layout Table

The previous projects in this book discussed the development of Web sites. FrontPage also provides for the development of individual Web pages that can be published as individual pages or incorporated into a Web site at a later time. The following steps start FrontPage and create a new Web page.

To Start FrontPage and Create a New Web Page

1 Click the Start button on the Windows taskbar, point to All Programs on the Start menu, and then point to Microsoft Office on the All Programs submenu.

2 Click Microsoft Office FrontPage 2003 on the Microsoft Office submenu.

3 If FrontPage has opened a previously opened Web site, click File on the menu bar and then click Close Site.

4 If a new Web page named new_page_1.htm is not displayed in Design view, click the Create a new normal page button on the Standard toolbar to create a new Web page.

5 If a task pane appears, click the Close button on the task pane.

The FrontPage window is opened and an empty page is displayed. The Web Site tab is not displayed because only a Web page is opened in FrontPage.

Adding a Layout Table to a Web Page

FrontPage provides eleven predefined layout tables. When using a layout table, you select the layout table that most closely resembles the overall design of the Web page. A layout table may include a header, a footer, one or more columns, corners, and cells on the left or right of the layout table. Each area may contain content or be used simply to provide positioning of other elements of the Web page. After adding the predefined layout table to the Web page, FrontPage allows for the modification of the layout cells that compose the layout table. FrontPage also allows you to add additional layout cells, merge layout cells, or remove layout cells from the layout table.

The Web page developed in this feature, President's Responsibilities Web page, requires a header and a body. The Centered Header, and Centered Body layout table provides the necessary framework for the required content. The steps on the next page add a theme to the new_page_1.htm Web page and then add the Centered Header, and Centered Body layout table to the new_page_1.htm Web page.

More About

Creating a New Web Page

Use the New command on the File menu to create a new page using the New task pane. The New task pane allows you to choose a template for the new page or to create a new page from an existing Web page.

Q&A

Q: Can I nest the layout table templates?

A: No. While standard tables can be nested, you can apply only one layout table template to a Web page. That is, you cannot embed a layout table template from the Layout Tables and Cells task pane within another layout table.

To Add a Layout Table to a Web Page

1

• **Click Format on the menu bar.**

• **Click Theme.**

• **When FrontPage displays the Theme task pane, scroll to Global Marketing in the Select a theme list.**

The Theme task pane is displayed (Figure 2).

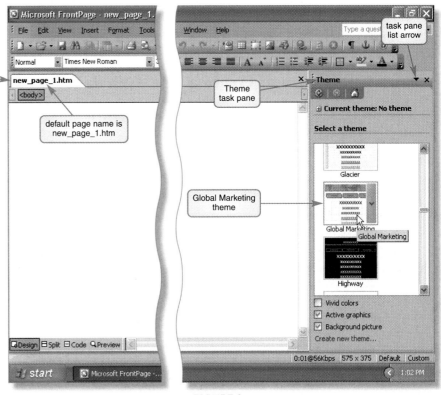

Web Site tab does not appear

default page name is new_page_1.htm

task pane list arrow

Theme task pane

Global Marketing theme

FIGURE 2

2

• **Click Global Marketing in the Select a theme list.**

• **Click the task pane list arrow.**

FrontPage applies the selected theme to the Web page and displays the task pane menu (Figure 3).

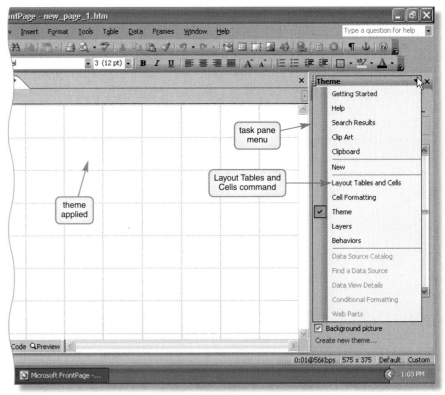

task pane menu

Layout Tables and Cells command

theme applied

FIGURE 3

3

• **Click Layout Tables and Cells.**

FrontPage displays the Layout Tables and Cells task pane (Figure 4).

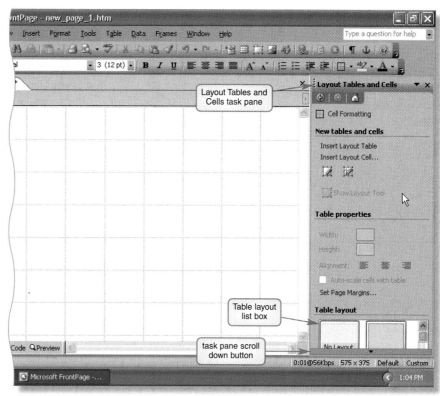

FIGURE 4

4

• **Click the task pane down scroll arrow to scroll through the task pane.**

• **Use the scroll bar on the Table layout list to scroll through the Table layout list until the Centered Header, and Centered Body table layout appears.**

FrontPage displays the lower portion of the Layout Tables and Cells task pane. The Centered Header, and Centered Body table layout appears in the Table layout list (Figure 5).

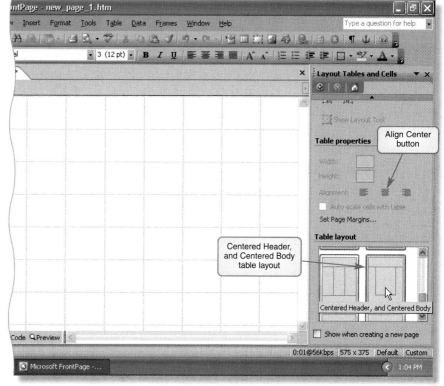

FIGURE 5

5

- **Click Centered Header, and Centered Body.**

- **Click the Align Center button in the Table properties area.**

FrontPage adds the layout table and layout cells to the Web page. Height and width labels appear in the layout cells (Figure 6). The table dimensions may vary depending on your screen resolution.

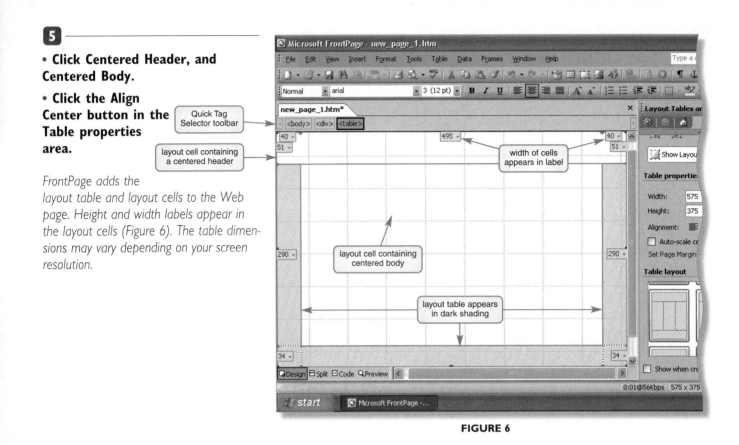

FIGURE 6

In Figure 6, the Design view indicates the areas, or layout cells, that should contain the content of the Web page. The centered header layout cell provides an area for a Web page header. The centered body layout cell provides an area for the rest of the content of the Web page. The remainder of the layout table appears as gray cells, indicating that content should not be added to these areas of the Web page. Each layout cell includes labels that indicate the height and width of the layout cell. Clicking the label displays a shortcut menu that allows you to modify the dimensions and behavior of the layout cell. The layout table's Alignment property is changed to center so that the entire layout table appears centered in the Web page visitor's browser no matter what the screen resolution or browser window size.

Formatting Layout Cells with Rounded Corners, Borders, and Shadows

Once a layout table is added to a page, you can customize the size and position of the layout cells. As you have learned, graphics and images provide a method for drawing a Web page user's attention to content and serve to provide a unified look and feel to the pages within a Web site. FrontPage also allows you to add graphic effects to layout cells. Layout cells may include a background color, rounded corners, a header, a footer, margins, borders, and shadows.

More About

Drawing Layout Tables and Cells

If you wish to embed a layout table within another layout table, you can click the Draw Layout Table button in the Layout Tables and Cells task pane and then draw the table within a layout cell. You also can draw a new layout table on any Web page, even those not created with a layout table template. Similarly, you can draw additional layout cells by clicking the Draw Layout Cell button in the Layout Tables and Cells task pane.

Resizing Layout Cells

In order to give the President's Responsibilities Web page a more balanced appearance, the centered header layout cell should be resized to match the width of the centered body layout cell. The following steps resize the centered header layout cell to match the width of the centered body layout cell.

To Resize a Layout Cell

1

• **In Design view, use the scroll bar to scroll the Web page to the top of the Web page.**

• **Click the centered header layout cell.**

• **Click the <td> tag selector in the Quick Tag Selector toolbar.**

FrontPage displays a bold border around the centered header layout cell. The <td> quick tag is selected in the Quick Tag Selector toolbar (Figure 7).

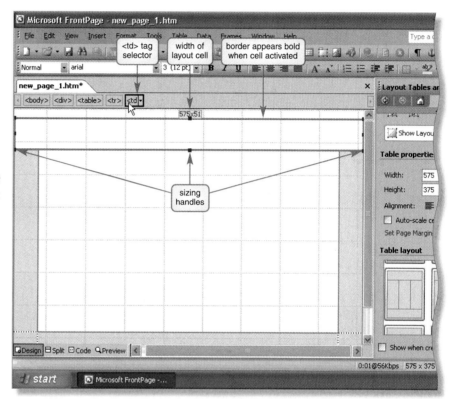

FIGURE 7

2

• **Position the mouse pointer over the left border of the centered header layout cell until the mouse pointer appears as the table repositioning pointer.**

The mouse pointer changes to a table repositioning pointer to indicate that the layout cell now can be modified by dragging the mouse pointer (Figure 8).

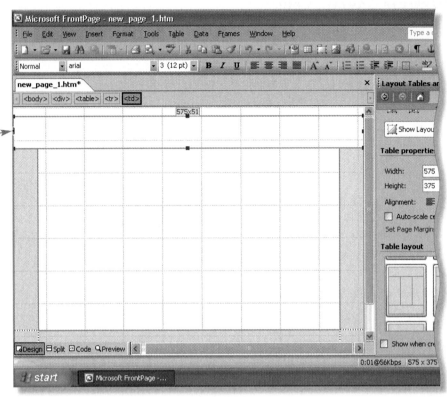

FIGURE 8

3

• **Click and drag the left border of the centered header layout cell until it snaps into position in alignment with the left border of the centered body layout cell, and then release the mouse button.**

The left border of the centered header layout cell appears aligned with the left border of the centered body layout cell (Figure 9).

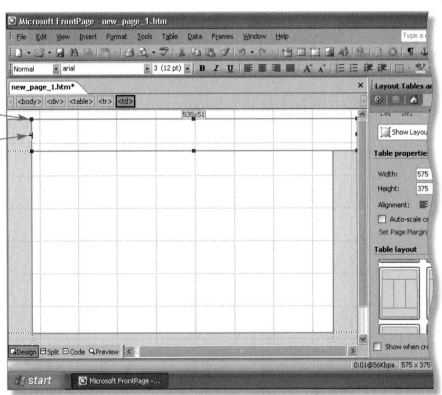

FIGURE 9

4

• **Repeat Step 3 for the right border of the centered header layout cell.**

• **If necessary, use the task pane up scroll arrow to scroll to the top of the task pane.**

The centered header layout cell appears as shown in Figure 10.

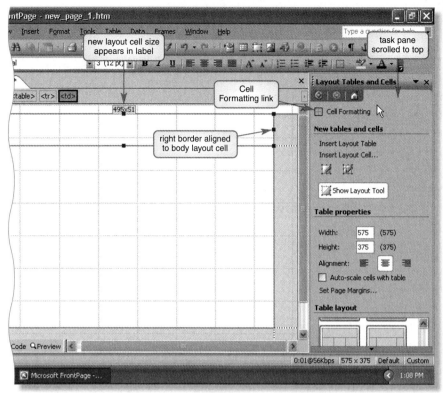

FIGURE 10

Other Ways

1. Click the layout cell border

As shown in Step 3 of the previous set of steps, the layout cell border can be resized to an exact pixel position, or it can snap to the size of an adjacent layout cell. As the size of the layout cell changes, FrontPage updates the label on the layout cell that indicates the size in pixels of the layout cell.

Changing the Background Color of a Layout Cell

Both layout cells in the Web page require a new background color, rounded corners, a border, and a shadow. When working with layout cells, the best practice is to format one cell at a time until you achieve the desired effect for that cell. The first step in applying the custom formatting to the Web page is to apply a background color to the centered header layout cell. The steps on the next page change the alignment for the text that will be added to the layout cell and then apply a yellow background to the layout cell.

More About

Formatting Multiple Layout Cells

FrontPage allows you to select multiple layout cells. You cannot, however, format the selected cells at the same time. You must select each cell individually to format it. If you want to copy and paste layout cell formatting, you can switch to Code view and carefully copy and paste the HTML code for the layout cells.

To Change the Background Color of a Layout Cell

1

• **Click the Cell Formatting link in the Layout Tables and Cells task pane.**

• **When FrontPage displays the Cell Formatting task pane, click the VAlign box arrow and select Middle in the VAlign list.**

• **Click the BgColor box arrow.**

FrontPage displays the Cell Formatting task pane. The VAlign property of the centered header layout cell appears as Middle. FrontPage displays a color palette from which a background color can be selected (Figure 11).

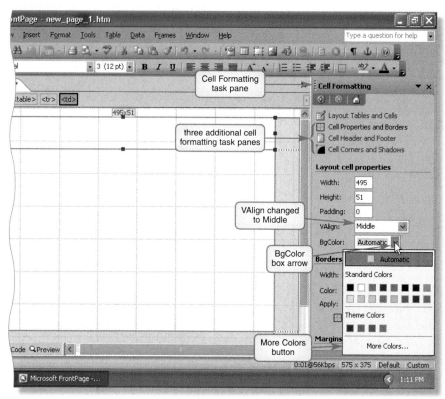

FIGURE 11

2

• **Click More Colors.**

• **When FrontPage displays the More Colors dialog box, select the yellow color with the hex value of {FF,FF,CC} and then click the OK button.**

The centered header layout cell appears with a yellow background (Figure 12).

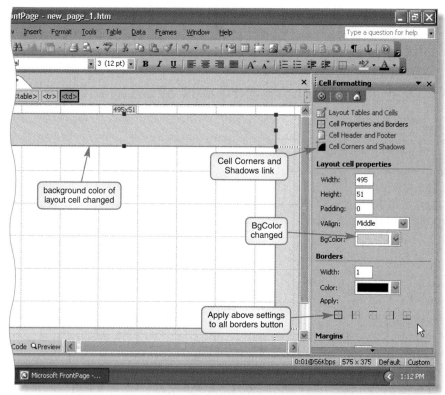

FIGURE 12

The centered header layout cell now includes a yellow background color. As shown in Figure 12, the Cell Formatting task pane also allows you to modify the width and height of the layout cell by specifying the number of pixels in the Width and Height text boxes. You can apply **padding** to the cell, which specifies the number of pixels between the content in the layout cell and the layout cell's border. The next step is to apply the remaining formatting to the layout cell, including rounded corners, a border, and shadows.

Adding Corners, Borders, and Shadows to a Layout Cell

Layout cells allow you to add enhanced formatting that cells in a standard table do not allow. In Project 2, a table was added to a Web page to contain images and other content. The cells in the table provided very little flexibility in the formatting as compared with layout cells. When you select a layout cell, all of the options on the Cell Formatting task pane become available to you, including cell headers and footers, borders, rounded corners, and shadows. The following steps add single-pixel, black borders to all four sides, ten-pixel rounded corners to all four corners, and a ten-pixel shadow to the bottom and right of the centered header layout cell.

> **More About**
>
> ### Layout Cell Padding
>
> If you attempt to add too many elements to a layout cell, such as padding, headers, footers, shading, and rounded corners, the cell may not be large enough to accommodate all of the elements. FrontPage displays an error message when it cannot fit an element that you are attempting to add. If you receive such an error, resize or reformat your layout cells or table.

To Add Corners, Borders, and Shadows to a Layout Cell

1

• **Click the Apply above settings to all borders button in the Borders area.**

• **Click the Cell Corners and Shadows link at the top of the task pane.**

The Cell Corners and Shadows options are displayed in the Cell Formatting task pane (Figure 13).

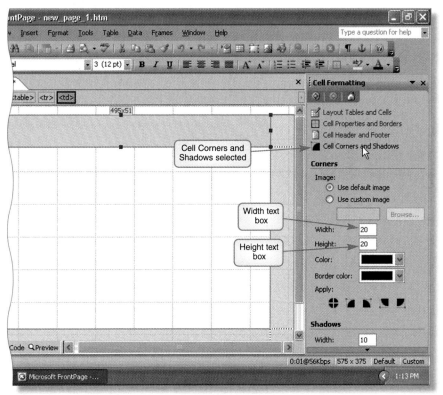

FIGURE 13

2

• **Type** 10 **in the Width text box in the Corners area.**

• **Type** 10 **in the Height text box in the Corners area.**

• **Click the Color box arrow.**

The Height and Width for the corners appear as 10. FrontPage displays the color palette for selecting the color of the corners that will be added to the layout cell (Figure 14).

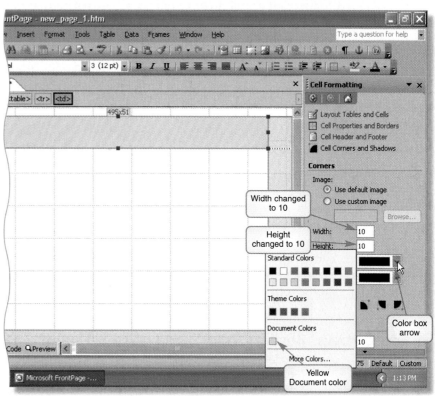

FIGURE 14

3

• **Click the yellow color in the Document Colors area.**

• **Click the Apply above settings to all corners button in the Corners area of the task pane.**

FrontPage adds corners to the centered header layout cell as shown in Figure 15.

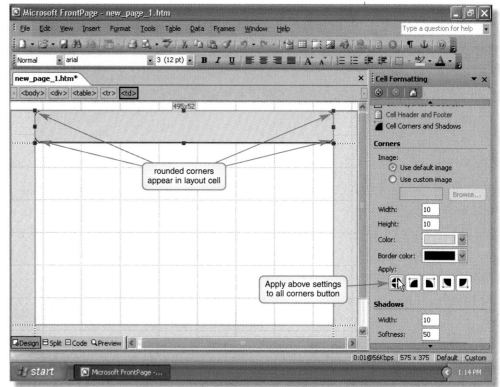

FIGURE 15

4

- **Click the task pane down scroll arrow so that the bottom of the task pane appears.**
- **Click the Apply above settings to bottom and right shadows button in the Shadows area.**

FrontPage adds a shadow to the bottom and right sides of the centered header layout cell (Figure 16).

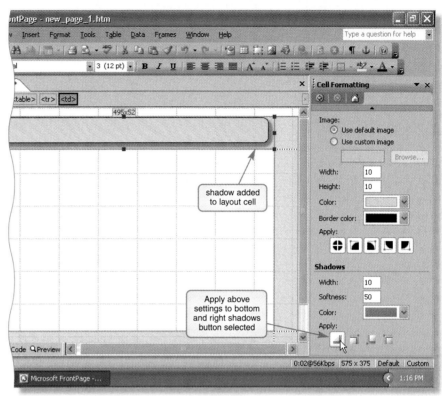

FIGURE 16

5

- **Click anywhere in the centered header layout cell and type** Responsibilities of the President of the **and then press** SHIFT+ENTER.
- **Type** Future Entrepreneurs Honor Society.
- **Select Heading 2 in the Style box on the Formatting toolbar.**
- **Click the Center button on the Formatting toolbar.**
- **Click the Apply above settings to bottom and right shadows button twice in the Shadows area in the Cell Formatting task pane.**

The text appears in the centered header layout cell as shown in Figure 17. FrontPage extends the shadow to the portion of the cell that was extended by the newly added text.

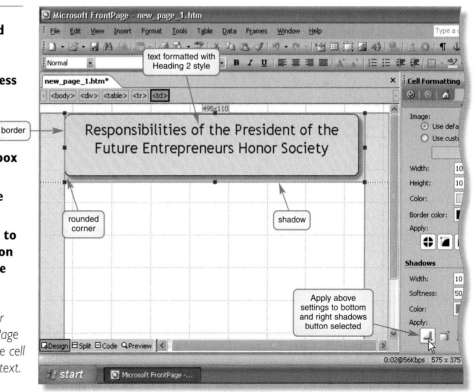

FIGURE 17

Figure 13 on page FP 243 shows that the Cell Formatting task pane includes three different views. The first view is the Cell Properties and Borders view. This view allows modification of the overall layout cell, including width, height, padding, alignment, and background color. Additionally, you can add borders and margins to the cell. A **border** appears on one or more sides of the cell as a line of the chosen color. A **margin** appears as an area outside of the border. By adding a margin, the border moves closer to the inside of the layout cell by the size in pixels of the margin. FrontPage displays margins using the background color of the Web page, rather than the background color of the layout cell.

The second view of the Cell Formatting task pane is the Cell Header and Footer view. A layout cell header appears at the top of the layout cell, but below any top margin. A layout cell footer appears at the bottom of the layout cell, but above any bottom margin. A cell header or footer can be assigned a color and a border and may include cell padding.

The third view of the Cell Formatting task pane is the Cell Corners and Shadows view. The corners of a layout cell appear in the header or footer of a layout cell if a header or footer is selected for the layout cell. Otherwise, the corners appear in the layout cell's content area, which is not in the margin area. By default, FrontPage displays a rounded, colored area for the corner that is the height and width specified in the Height and Width text boxes. FrontPage also allows you to specify an image to use for the corners. You can specify only one image, meaning that if you select several corners, they all will appear with the same image. FrontPage rotates the image in the appropriate manner to display the image properly for each corner. The Apply area allows you to specify which corners of the layout cell should display the corner image.

The Shadows area allows you to place a colored shadow around the layout cell. Like the corners, the shadow appears on the content area of the layout cell and not the margin. By adding a shadow, therefore, FrontPage makes the content area of the layout cell smaller to accommodate the shadow. You adjust the intensity of the shadow by changing the Softness text box. FrontPage also allows you to specify which sides of the layout cell display the shadow, the color of the shadow, and the width of the shadow.

The next step is to format the centered body layout cell and copy and paste the content for the cell from a Word document. The second layout cell is formatted using the same steps used to format the centered header layout cell.

To Format and Add Content to the Second Layout Cell

- Click anywhere in the centered body layout cell.
- Use the up scroll arrow of the task pane to scroll to the top of the task pane.
- Click the Cell Properties and Borders link.
- Click the BgColor box arrow to display the BgColor list, and then click the yellow color in the Document Colors area.

- Click the Apply above settings to all borders button in the Borders area.
- Click the Cell Corners and Shadows link at the top of the task pane.
- If necessary, click the Color box arrow and then click the yellow color in the Document Colors area.

3

- Click the Apply above settings to all corners button in the Corners area of the task pane.
- Click the task pane down scroll arrow so that the bottom of the task pane appears.
- Click the Apply above settings to bottom and right shadows button in the Shadows area.

The centered body layout cell appears with a background color, a border, rounded corners, and a shadow (Figure 18).

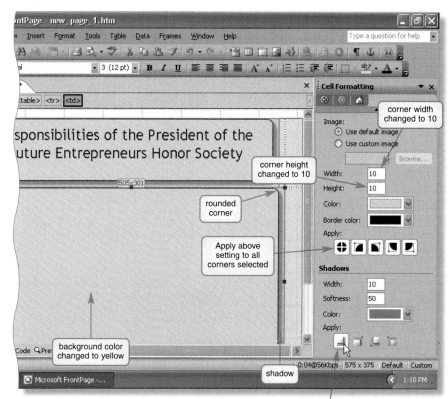

FIGURE 18

4

• Click the Start button on the taskbar.

• Point to All Programs on the Start menu.

• Click Microsoft Office on the All Programs menu and then click Microsoft Office Word 2003 on the Microsoft Office submenu.

• Click the Open button on the Standard toolbar.

• When the Open dialog box is displayed, select the file, FEHSPresidentResponsibilities.doc, from the Feature1 folder on the Data Disk.

5

• Click the Open button.

• If necessary, close the New Document task pane.

• Drag through all of the text after the first line in the document to select it and then press CTRL+C to copy it to the Office Clipboard.

• Click the Close button on the Microsoft Word title bar.

6

• If necessary, click the Microsoft FrontPage button on the taskbar to switch to FrontPage.

• If necessary, click the centered body layout cell to position the insertion point.

• Press CTRL+V to paste the copied text from Word into the Web page.

FrontPage pastes the contents of the Word document into the centered body layout cell. FrontPage formats the text and bullets according to the settings for the Global Marketing theme (Figure 19).

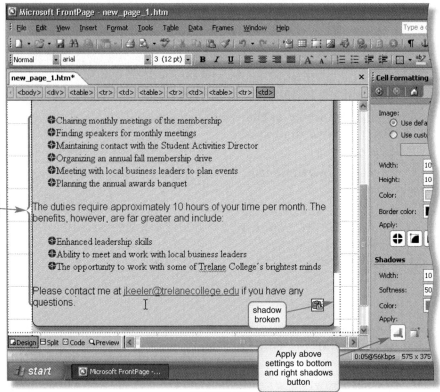

FIGURE 19

7

• **Click the Apply above settings to bottom and right shadows button twice in the Shadows area.**

FrontPage extends the shadow to the portion of the cell that was extended by the newly added text (Figure 20).

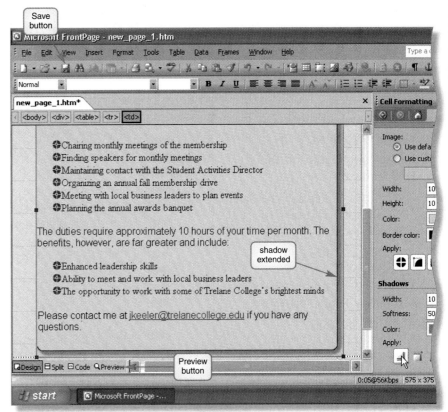

FIGURE 20

As shown in Figure 19, as the added content changes the layout cell's size, the shadow size does not change. By reapplying the shadow in the last step, the shadow is extended across the full height of the layout cell. Because a theme is applied to the Web page, FrontPage automatically formats the newly added text so that it requires no additional formatting.

Previewing and Saving the Web Page

After you have finished the steps in this feature and developed the Web page, you can preview the Web page in Preview view and quit FrontPage. The steps on the next page save the Web page, preview the Web page, and quit FrontPage.

More About

The Quick Reference

For more information, see the Quick Reference Summary at the back of this book, or visit the FrontPage 2003 Quick Reference Web page (scsite.com/fp2003/qr).

To Save the Web Page, Preview the Web Page, and Quit FrontPage

1

• **Click the Close button on the Cell Formatting task pane.**

• **Click the Save button on the Standard toolbar.**

• **When FrontPage displays the Save As dialog box, select Local Disk (C:) in the Save in box.**

• **Click the Create New Folder button and type** jkeelerHonorSociety **in the Name box in the New Folder dialog box.**

• **Click the OK button.**

• **Type** PresidentsResponsibilities **in the File name text box and then click the Save button.**

• **When the Save Embedded Files dialog box appears, click the Change Folder button and select C:\jkeelerHonorSociety\images as the folder for the embedded images by clicking the Create New Folder button in the Change Folder dialog box.**

• **Click the OK button in the Save Embedded Files dialog box.**

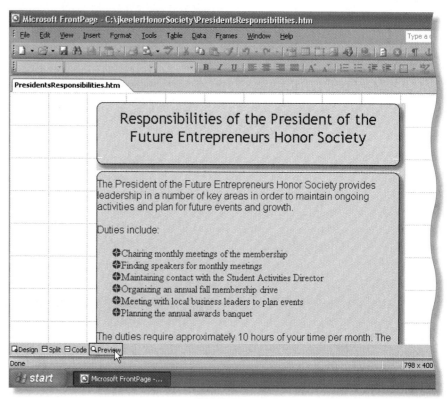

FIGURE 21

2

• **After FrontPage saves the files, click the Preview button.**

• **When the Web page appears in Preview view, use the scroll bar to view the entire page.**

FrontPage displays the completed Web page in Preview view (Figure 21).

3

• **Click the Design button to return to Design view.**

• **Click File on the menu bar and then click Close.**

FrontPage closes the Web page.

4

• **Click the Close button on the right side of the FrontPage title bar.**

The FrontPage window closes.

After saving the Web page, the files and folder created with the Web page can be added to a Web site or distributed to another Web site developer so that he or she can include the Web page in another site. FrontPage does not provide the capability to publish an individual Web page to a server.

Feature Summary

This Table feature introduced you to using layout tables and layout cells to position content on a Web page. Layout tables allow you to position content precisely in columns and rows. Layout cells include enhanced design elements such as rounded corners, shadows, borders, and background colors. By combining the functionality of layout tables and layout cells, you learned how to create sophisticated layouts for Web page content.

What You Should Know

Having completed this feature, you should be able to perform the tasks below. The tasks are listed in the same order they were presented in this feature. For a list of the buttons, menus, toolbars, and commands introduced in this feature, see the Quick Reference Summary at the back of this book and refer to the Page Number column.

1. Start FrontPage and Create a New Web Page (FP 235)
2. Add a Layout Table to a Web Page (FP 236)
3. Resize a Layout Cell (FP 239)
4. Change the Background Color of a Layout Cell (FP 242)
5. Add Corners, Borders, and Shadows to a Layout Cell (FP 243)
6. Format and Add Content to the Second Layout Cell (FP 247)
7. Save the Web Page, Preview the Web Page, and Quit FrontPage (FP 250)

1 Creating a Web Page with a Centered Header, and Centered Body Layout Table

Problem: Fairway Lawn Care runs a summer special each year during slow work periods. Create a Web page advertisement that promotes the summer special.

Instructions: Perform the following tasks.

1. Create a new Web page and apply the Compass theme to the page.
2. Open the Layout Tables and Cells task pane and apply the Centered Header, and Centered Body layout table to the Web page. Center the layout table.
3. Select the centered header layout cell. Add a 1-pixel border to the layout cell. Change the background color of the layout cell to Fuchsia. Add rounded corners and a shadow to the layout cell. Type the text in the layout cell as shown in Figure 22. Center the text and apply the Heading 1 style. Make sure the shadow on the cell extends through the entire length and width of the cell.
4. Select the centered body layout cell. Add a 1-pixel border to the layout cell and add rounded corners and a border to the layout cell. Add 10 pixels of padding to the cell. Type the text in the layout cell as shown in Figure 22. The text at the top of the cell has a style of Heading 3. Resize the centered body layout cell so that the text fits the cell appropriately.
5. Preview the Web page in your browser. Save the Web page as SummerSpecial.htm in the Feature1\ LabSF1-1FairwayLawnCare folder on the Data Disk or your hard drive. Save the embedded images in a new images subfolder.

In the Lab

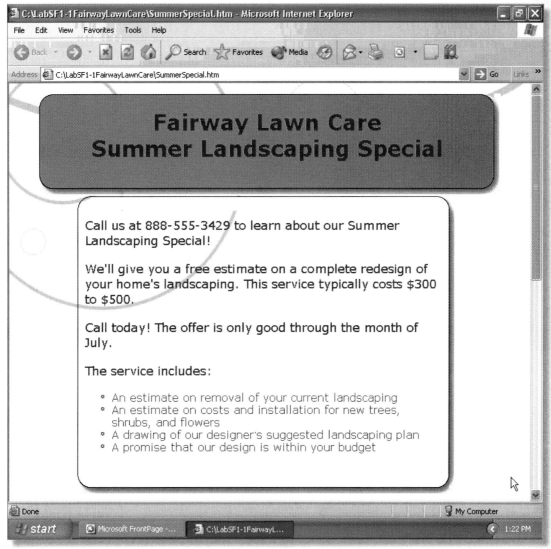

FIGURE 22

In the Lab

2 Creating a Web Page with a Header, Footer, and 3 Columns Layout Table

Problem: You are hosting a running seminar and need to provide details about the event to prospective attendees. Create a Web page that lists the details about the three sessions of the seminar.

Instructions: Perform the following tasks.

1. Create a new Web page and apply the Echo theme to the page.
2. Open the Layout Tables and Cells task pane and apply the Header, Footer, and 3 Columns layout table to the Web page. Center the layout table.
3. Add the content to the five layout cells as shown in Figure 23. Format the header layout cell with the Heading 2 style for line 1 and the Heading 3 style for line 2. Set the VAlign property of the header layout cell to Bottom. Center the text in the cell.
4. Center the content in the footer layout cell. Provide a link for your e-mail address using the word, me. Set the VAlign property for the footer cell to Middle.
5. For each of the three column layout cells, format the background to a gray color. Set the Padding to 5. Set the first line of each layout cell to the style of Heading 3. Add a 1-pixel black border to each layout cell.
6. Preview the Web page in your browser. Save the Web page as MarathonTraining.htm in the Feature1\LabSF1-2RunningMyWaySeminar folder on the Data Disk or your hard drive.

In the Lab

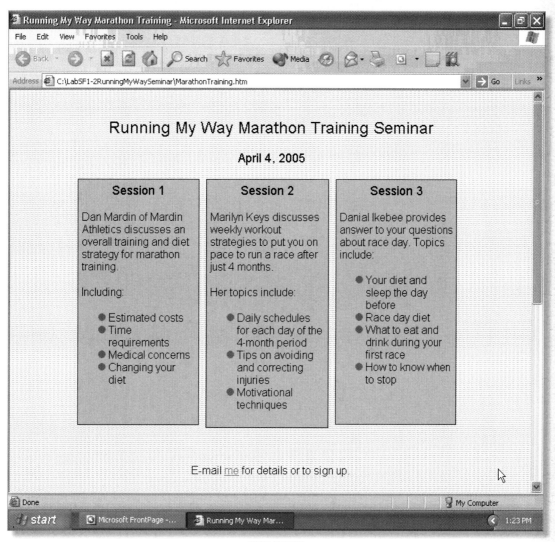

FIGURE 23

Appendix A

Microsoft Office FrontPage Help System

Using the FrontPage Help System

This appendix shows you how to use the FrontPage Help system. At anytime while you are using FrontPage, you can interact with its Help system and display information on any FrontPage topic. It is a complete reference manual at your fingertips.

As shown in Figure A-1, five methods for accessing the FrontPage Help system are available:

1. Microsoft Office FrontPage Help button on the Standard toolbar
2. Microsoft Office FrontPage Help command on the Help menu
3. Function key F1 on the keyboard
4. Type a question for help box on the menu bar
5. Office Assistant

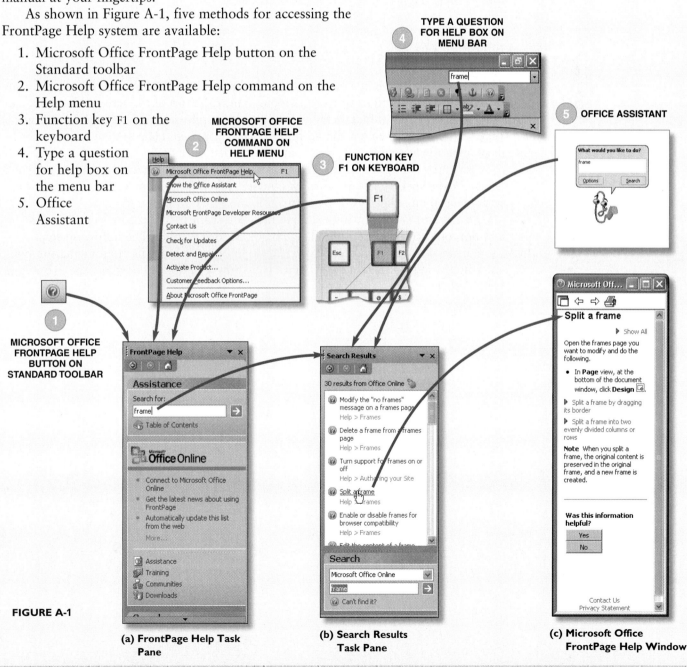

FIGURE A-1

(a) FrontPage Help Task Pane

(b) Search Results Task Pane

(c) Microsoft Office FrontPage Help Window

All five methods result in the FrontPage Help system displaying a task pane on the right side of the FrontPage window. The first three methods cause the **FrontPage Help task pane** to appear (Figure A-1a on the previous page). This task pane includes a Search for text box in which you can enter a word or phrase on which you want help. Once you enter the word or phrase, the FrontPage Help system displays the Search Results task pane (Figure A-1b on the previous page). With the Search Results task pane displayed, you can select specific Help topics.

As shown in Figure A-1, methods 4 and 5 bypass the FrontPage Help task pane and immediately display the **Search Results task pane** (Figure A-1b) with a list of links that pertain to the selected topic. Thus, the result of any of the five methods for accessing the FrontPage Help system is the Search Results task pane. Once the FrontPage Help system displays this task pane, you can choose links that relate to the word or phrase on which you searched. In Figure A-1, for example, frame was the searched topic (Split a frame), which resulted in the FrontPage Help system displaying the Microsoft Office FrontPage Help window with information about splitting a frame (Figure A-1c on the previous page).

Navigating the FrontPage Help System

The quickest way to enter the FrontPage Help system is through the Type a question for help box on the right side of the menu bar at the top of the screen. Here you can type words, such as table, theme, or stylesheet, or phrases, such as preview a Web page, or how do I create a shared border. The FrontPage Help system responds by displaying the Search Results task pane with a list of links.

Here are two tips regarding the words or phrases you enter to initiate a search: (1) check the spelling of the word or phrase; and (2) keep your search very specific, with fewer than seven words, to return the most accurate results.

Assume for the following example that you want to add a row to a table, and you do not know how to do it. The likely keyword is table. The following steps show how to use the Type a question for help box to obtain useful information by entering the keyword, table. The steps also show you how to navigate the FrontPage Help system.

To Obtain Help Using the Type a Question for Help Box

1

• **Click the Type a question for help box on the right side of the menu bar, type** table, **and then press the ENTER key.**

The FrontPage Help system displays the Search Results task pane on the right side of the window. The Search Results task pane includes 30 resulting links (Figure A-2). If you do not find what you are looking for, you can modify or refine the search in the Search area at the bottom of the Search Results task pane. The results returned in your Search Results task pane may be different.

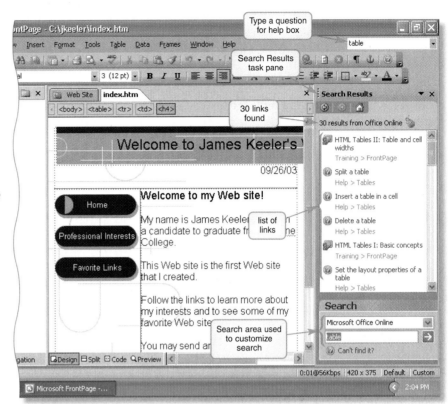

FIGURE A-2

2

• **Scroll down to the bottom of the list of links in the Search Results task pane and then click the Add a cell, row, or column to a table link.**

• **If necessary, when FrontPage displays the Microsoft Office FrontPage Help window, click its Auto Tile button in the upper-right corner of the window (Figure A-4 on the next page) to tile the windows.**

FrontPage displays the Microsoft Office FrontPage Help window with the desired information (Figure A-3). With the Microsoft Office FrontPage Help window and Microsoft FrontPage window tiled, you can read the information in one window and complete the task in the other window.

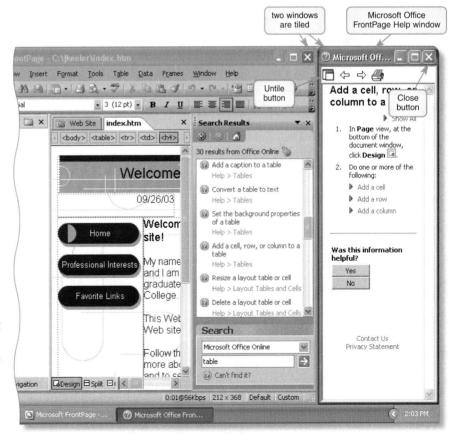

FIGURE A-3

3

• **Double-click the Microsoft Office FrontPage Help window title bar.**

• **Click the Show All link in the upper-right corner of the window.**

• **After reviewing the information, click the Hide All link that replaced the Show All link.**

The Microsoft Office FrontPage Help window is maximized so it fills the entire screen (Figure A-4). If you are connected to the Internet, you can give Microsoft your opinion as to whether the information was helpful by clicking the Yes or No button at the bottom of the page. The Show All link expands the coverage of information and the Hide All link condenses the information displayed on the topic in the Microsoft Office FrontPage Help window.

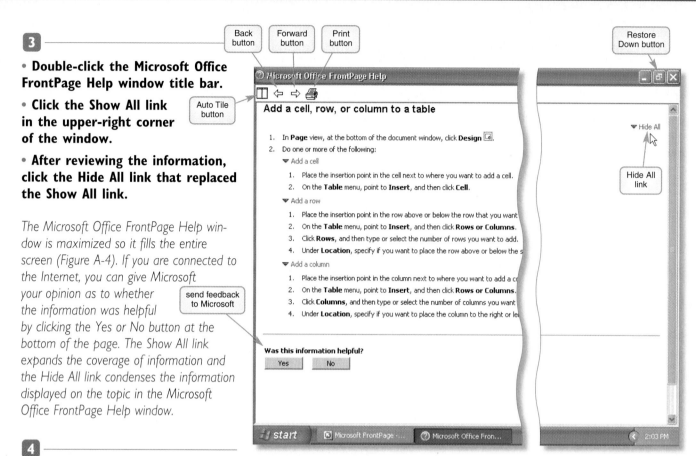

FIGURE A-4

4

• **Click the Restore Down button on the right side of the Microsoft Office FrontPage Help window title bar to return to the tiled state shown in Figure A-3 on the previous page.**

• **Click the Close button on the Microsoft Office FrontPage Help window title bar.**

The Microsoft Office FrontPage Help window is closed and the Web page is active.

Use the four buttons in the upper-left corner of the Microsoft Office FrontPage Help window (Figure A-4) to tile or untile windows, navigate through the Help system, or print the contents of the window. As you click links in the Search Results task pane, the FrontPage Help system displays new pages of information. The FrontPage Help system remembers the links you visited and allows you to redisplay the pages visited during a session by clicking the Back and Forward buttons (Figure A-4).

If none of the links presents the information you want, you can refine the search by entering another word or phrase in the Search text box in the Search Results task pane (Figure A-2 on the previous page). If you have access to the Web, then the scope is global for the initial search. **Global** means all the categories listed in the Search box of the Search area in Figure A-5 are searched. For example, you can restrict the scope to **Offline Help**, which results in a search of related links only on your hard disk.

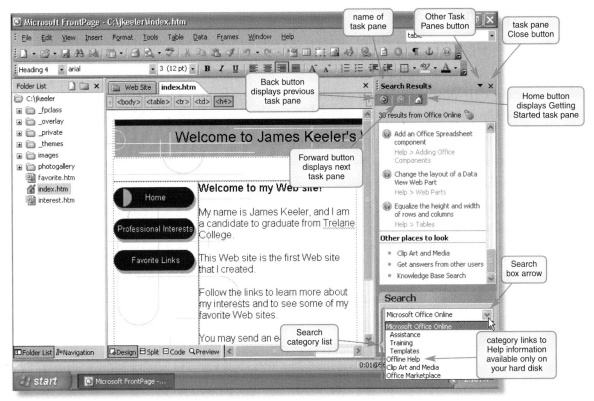

FIGURE A-5

Figure A-5 shows several additional features of the Search Results task pane with which you should be familiar. The buttons immediately below the name of the task pane allow you to navigate between task panes. The Other Task Panes button and the Close button on the Search Results task pane title bar let you change task panes and close the active task pane.

As you enter questions and terms in the Type a question for help box, the FrontPage Help system adds them to its list. Thus, if you click the Type a question for help box arrow, a list of previously used words and phrases is displayed (Figure A-6).

FIGURE A-6

The Office Assistant

The **Office Assistant** is an icon (middle of Figure A-7) that FrontPage displays in the FrontPage window while you work. For the Office Assistant to appear on the screen, it must be activated by invoking the Show the Office Assistant command on the Help menu. This Help tool has multiple functions. First, it will respond in the same way as the Type a question for help box with a list of topics that relate to the entry you make in the text box in the Office Assistant balloon. The entry can be in the form of a word or phrase as if you were talking to a person. For example, if you want to learn more about creating a custom theme, in the balloon text box, you can type any of the following words or phrases: theme, custom theme, how do I create a custom theme, or anything similar.

In the example in Figure A-7, the phrase, custom theme, is entered into the Office Assistant balloon. After you click the Search button, the Office Assistant responds by displaying the Search Results task pane with a list of links from which you can choose. Once you click a link in the Search Results task pane, the FrontPage Help system displays the information in the Microsoft Office FrontPage Help window (Figure A-7).

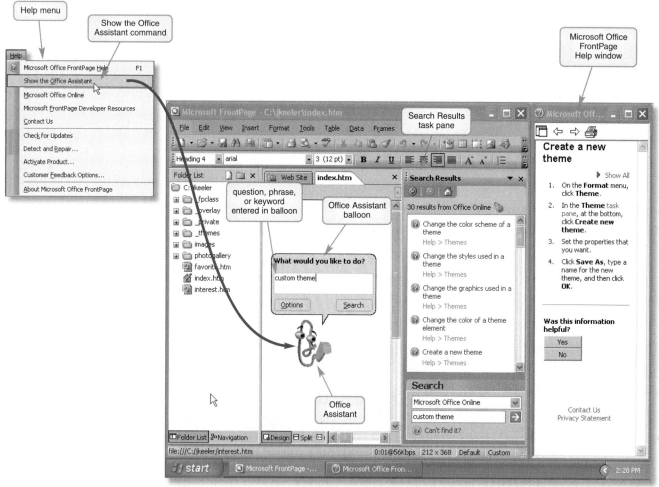

FIGURE A-7

In addition, the Office Assistant monitors your work and accumulates tips during a session on how you might increase your productivity and efficiency. The accumulation of tips must be enabled. You enable the accumulation of tips by right-clicking the Office Assistant, clicking Options on the shortcut menu, and then selecting the types of tips you want accumulated. You can view the tips at anytime. The accumulated tips appear when you activate the Office Assistant balloon. Also, if at anytime you see a light bulb above the Office Assistant, click it to display the most recent tip. If the Office Assistant is hidden, then the light bulb shows on the Microsoft Office FrontPage Help button on the Standard toolbar.

You hide the Office Assistant by invoking the Hide the Office Assistant command on the Help menu or by right-clicking the Office Assistant and then clicking Hide on the shortcut menu. The Hide the Office Assistant command shows on the Help menu only when the Office Assistant is active in the FrontPage window. If the Office Assistant begins showing up on your screen without you instructing it to show, then right-click the Office Assistant, click Options on the shortcut menu, click the Use the Office Assistant check box to remove the check mark, and then click the OK button.

If the Office Assistant is active in the FrontPage window, then FrontPage displays all program and system messages in the Office Assistant balloon.

You may or may not want the Office Assistant to display on the screen at all times. As indicated earlier, you can hide it and then show it later through the Help menu. For more information about the Office Assistant, type `office assistant` in the Type a question for help box and then click the links in the Search Results task pane.

Help Buttons in Dialog Boxes and Subsystem Windows

As you invoke commands that display dialog boxes or other windows, such as the Print Preview window, you will see buttons and links that offer helpful information. Figure A-8 shows the types of Help buttons and links you will see as you work with FrontPage.

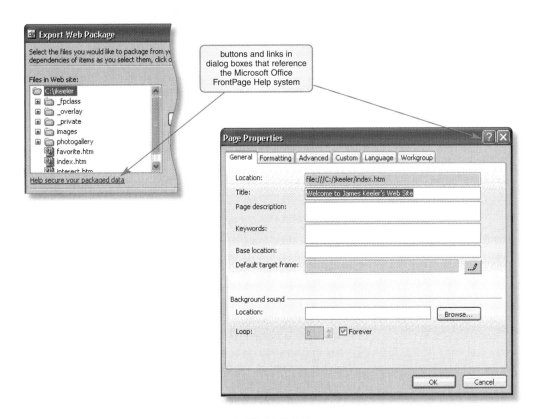

buttons and links in dialog boxes that reference the Microsoft Office FrontPage Help system

FIGURE A-8

Other Help Commands on the Help Menu

Thus far, this appendix has discussed the first two commands on the Help menu: (1) the Microsoft Office FrontPage Help command (Figure A-1 on page APP 1) and (2) the Show the Office Assistant command (Figure A-7 on page APP 6). Several additional commands are available on the Help menu, as shown in Figure A-9. Table A-1 summarizes these commands.

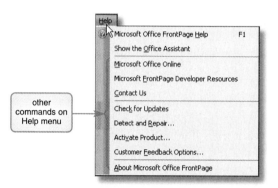

other
commands on
Help menu

FIGURE A-9

Table A-1 Summary of Other Help Commands on the Help Menu	
COMMAND ON HELP MENU	**FUNCTION**
Microsoft Office Online	Activates your browser, which displays the Microsoft Office Online Home page. The Microsoft Office Online Home page contains links that can improve your Office productivity.
Contact Us	Activates your browser, which displays Microsoft contact information and a list of useful links.
Check for Updates	Activates your browser, which displays a list of updates to Office. These updates can be downloaded and installed to improve the efficiency of Office or to fix an error in one or more of the Office applications.
Detect and Repair	Detects and repairs errors in the FrontPage program.
Activate Product	Activates FrontPage if it has not been activated already.
Customer Feedback Options	Gives or denies Microsoft permission to collect anonymous information about your hardware.
About Microsoft Office FrontPage	Displays the About Microsoft Office FrontPage dialog box. The dialog box lists the owner of the software and the product identification. You need to know the product identification if you call Microsoft for assistance. The three buttons below the OK button are the System Info button, the Tech Support button, and the Disabled Items button. The System Info button displays system information, including hardware resources, components, software environment, and applications. The Tech Support button displays technical assistance information. The Disabled Items button displays a list of disabled items that prevent FrontPage from functioning properly.

1 Using the Type a Question for Help Box

Instructions: Perform the following tasks using the FrontPage Help system.

1. Use the Type a question for help box on the menu bar to get help on inserting pictures.
2. Click About WordArt in the list of links in the Search Results task pane. Tile the windows. Double-click the Microsoft Office FrontPage Help window title bar to maximize it. Click the Show All button. Read and print the information. At the top of the printout, write down the number of links the FrontPage Help system found.
3. One at a time, click two additional links in the Search Results task pane and print the information. Hand in the printouts to your instructor. Use the Back and Forward buttons to return to the original page.
4. Use the Type a question for help box to search for information on stylesheets. Click the Apply a style link in the Search Results task pane. When the Microsoft Office FrontPage Help window is displayed, maximize the window. Read and print the information. One at a time, click the links on the page and print the information for any new page that is displayed. Close the Microsoft Office FrontPage Help window.
5. For each of the following words and phrases, click one link in the Search Results task pane, click the Show All link, and then print the page: text; layer; background; borders and shading; reveal tags; task pane; and bookmarks.

2 Expanding on the FrontPage Help System Basics

Instructions: Use the FrontPage Help system to understand the topics better and answer the questions listed below. Answer the questions on your own paper, or hand in the printed Help information to your instructor.

1. Show the Office Assistant. Right-click the Office Assistant and then click Animate! on the shortcut menu. Repeat invoking the Animate command to see various animations. Right-click the Office Assistant, click Options on the shortcut menu, click the Reset my tips button, and then click the OK button. Click the light bulb above the Office Assistant if it appears. When you see the light bulb, it indicates that the Office Assistant has a tip to share with you.
2. Use the Office Assistant to find help on undoing tasks. Print the Help information for three links in the Search Results task pane. Close the Microsoft Office FrontPage Help window. Hand in the printouts to your instructor. Hide the Office Assistant.
3. Press the F1 key. Search for information on Help. Click the first two links in the Search Results task pane. Read and print the information for both.
4. One at a time, invoke the first three commands in Table A-1. Print each page. Click two links on one of the pages and print the information. Hand in the printouts to your instructor.
5. Click About Microsoft Office FrontPage on the Help menu. Click the Tech Support button and print the resulting page. Click the System Info button. Below the Components category, print the CD-ROM and Display information. Hand in the printouts to your instructor.

Appendix B

Speech and Handwriting Recognition

Introduction

This appendix discusses the Office capability that allows users to create and modify worksheets using its alternative input technologies available through **text services**. Office provides a variety of text services, which enable you to speak commands and enter text in an application. The most common text service is the keyboard. Other text services include speech recognition and handwriting recognition.

The Language Bar

The **Language bar** allows you to use text services in the Office applications. You can utilize the Language bar in one of three states: (1) in a restored state as a floating toolbar in the FrontPage window (Figure B-1a or Figure B-1b if Text Labels are enabled); (2) in a minimized state docked next to the notification area on the Windows taskbar (Figure B-1c); or (3) hidden (temporarily closed and out of the way). If the Language bar is hidden, you can activate it by right-clicking the Windows taskbar, pointing to Toolbars on the shortcut menu (Figure B-1d), and clicking Language bar on the Toolbars submenu. If you want to close the Language bar, right-click the Language bar and then click Close the Language bar on the shortcut menu (Figure B-1e).

(b) **Language Bar with Text Labels Enabled**

(c) **Minimized Language Bar Docked on Windows Taskbar next to Notification Area**

FIGURE B-1

(a) **Language Bar with Text Labels Disabled**

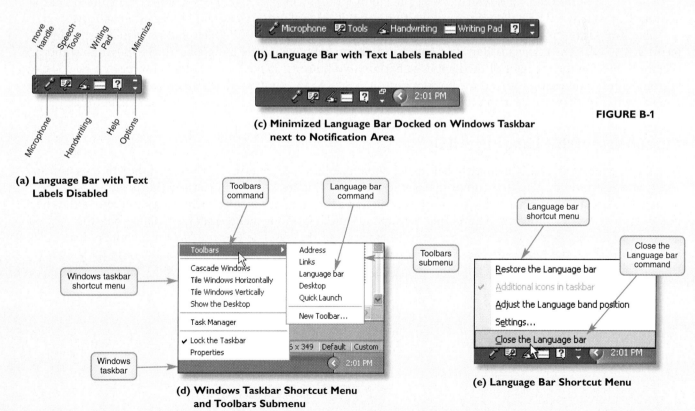

(d) **Windows Taskbar Shortcut Menu and Toolbars Submenu**

(e) **Language Bar Shortcut Menu**

When Windows was installed on your computer, the installer specified a default language. For example, most users in the United States select English (United States) as the default language. You can add more than 90 additional languages and varying dialects such as Basque, English (Zimbabwe), French (France), French (Canada), German (Germany), German (Austria), and Swahili. With multiple languages available, you can switch from one language to another while working in FrontPage. If you change the language or dialect, then text services may change the functions of the keys on the keyboard, adjust speech recognition, and alter handwriting recognition. If a second language is activated, then a Language icon appears immediately to the right of the move handle on the Language bar. This appendix assumes that English (United States) is the only language installed. Thus, the Language icon does not appear in the examples in Figure B-1 on the previous page.

Buttons on the Language Bar

The Language bar shown in Figure B-2a contains seven buttons. The number of buttons on your Language bar may be different. These buttons are used to select the language, customize the Language bar, control the microphone, control handwriting, and obtain help.

The first button on the left is the Microphone button, which enables and disables the microphone. When the microphone is enabled, text services adds two buttons and a balloon to the Language bar (Figure B-2b). These additional buttons and the balloon will be discussed shortly.

The second button from the left is the Speech Tools button. The Speech Tools button displays a menu of commands (Figure B-2c) that allow you to hide or show the balloon on the Language bar; train the Speech Recognition service so that it can interpret your voice better; add and delete words from its dictionary, such as names and other words not understood easily; and change the user profile so more than one person can use the microphone on the same computer.

The third button from the left on the Language bar is the Handwriting button. The Handwriting button displays the Handwriting menu (Figure B-2d), which lets you choose the Writing Pad (Figure B-2e), Write Anywhere (Figure B-2f), or the on-screen keyboard (Figure B-2g). The On-Screen Symbol Keyboard command on the Handwriting menu displays an on-screen keyboard that allows you to enter special symbols that are not available on a standard keyboard. You can choose only one form of handwriting at a time.

The fourth button indicates which one of the handwriting forms is active. For example, in Figure B-2a, the Writing Pad is active. The handwriting recognition capabilities of text services will be discussed shortly.

The fifth button from the left on the Language bar is the Help button. The Help button displays the Help menu. If you click the Language Bar Help command on the Help menu, the Language Bar Help window appears (Figure B-2h). On the far right of the Language bar are two buttons stacked above and below each other. The top button is the Minimize button and the bottom button is the Options button. The Minimize button minimizes the Language bar so that it appears on the Windows taskbar. The next section discusses the Options button.

Customizing the Language Bar

The down arrow icon immediately below the Minimize button in Figure B-2a is called the Options button. The Options button displays a menu of text services options (Figure B-2i). You can use this menu to hide the Speech Tools, Handwriting, and Help buttons on the Language bar by clicking their names to remove the check mark to the left of each button. The Settings command on the Options menu displays a dialog box that lets you customize the Language bar. This command will be discussed shortly. The Restore Defaults command redisplays hidden buttons on the Language bar.

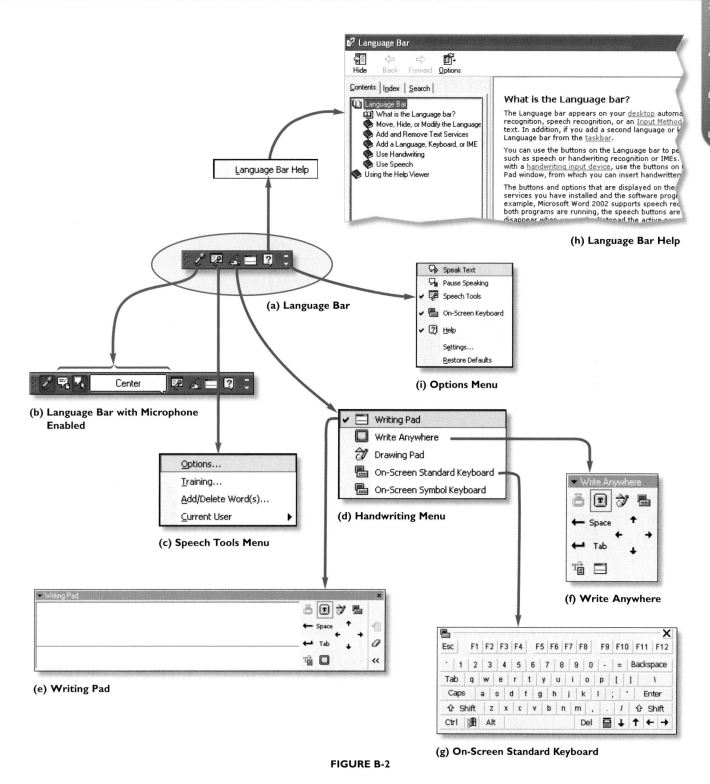

(h) Language Bar Help

(a) Language Bar

(i) Options Menu

(b) Language Bar with Microphone Enabled

(c) Speech Tools Menu

(d) Handwriting Menu

(f) Write Anywhere

(e) Writing Pad

(g) On-Screen Standard Keyboard

FIGURE B-2

If you right-click the Language bar, a shortcut menu appears (Figure B-3a on the next page). This shortcut menu lets you further customize the Language bar. The Minimize command on the shortcut menu docks the Language bar on the Windows taskbar. The Transparency command in Figure B-3a toggles the Language bar between being solid and transparent. You can see through a transparent Language bar (Figure B-3b). The Text Labels command toggles on text labels on the Language bar (Figure B-3c) and off (Figure B-3b).

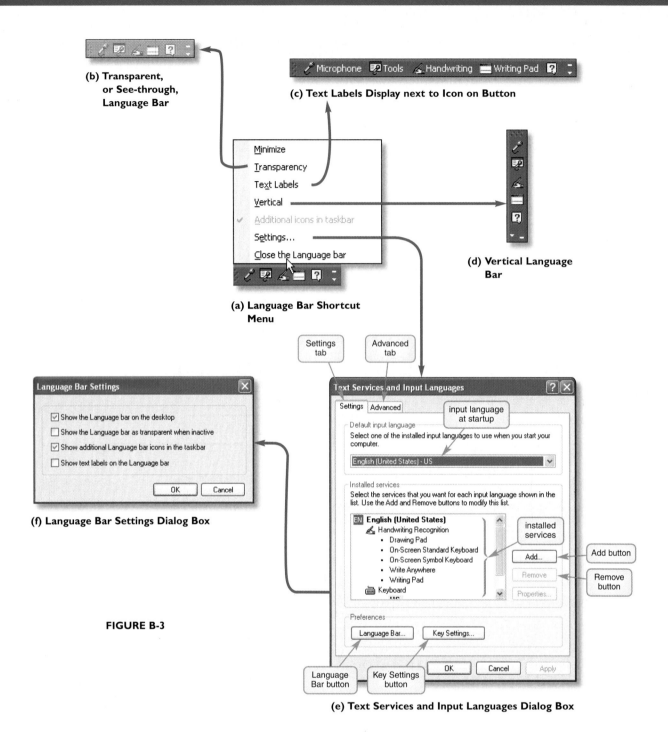

(b) Transparent,
or See-through,
Language Bar

(c) Text Labels Display next to Icon on Button

(d) Vertical Language Bar

(a) Language Bar Shortcut Menu

(f) Language Bar Settings Dialog Box

FIGURE B-3

(e) Text Services and Input Languages Dialog Box

The Settings command in Figure B-3a displays the Text Services and Input Languages dialog box (Figure B-3e). The Text Services and Input Languages dialog box allows you to add additional languages, add and remove text services, modify keys on the keyboard, modify the Language bar, and extend support of advanced text services to all programs, including Notepad and other programs that normally do not support text services (through the Advanced tab). If you want to remove any one of the services in the Installed services list, select the service, and then click the Remove button. If you want to add a service, click the Add button. The Key Settings button allows you to modify the keyboard. If you click the Language Bar button in the Text Services and Input Languages dialog box, the Language Bar Settings dialog box appears (Figure B-3f). This dialog box contains Language bar options, some of which are the same as the commands on the Language bar shortcut menu shown in Figure B-3a.

The Close the Language bar command on the shortcut menu shown in Figure B-3a closes or hides the Language bar. If you close the Language bar and want to redisplay it, see Figure B-1d on page APP 11.

Speech Recognition

The **Speech Recognition service** available with Office enables your computer to recognize human speech through a microphone. The microphone has two modes: Dictation and Voice Command (Figure B-4). You switch between the two modes by clicking the Dictation button and the Voice Command button on the Language bar. These buttons appear only when you turn on Speech Recognition by clicking the Microphone button on the Language bar (Figure B-5a on the next page). If you are using the Microphone button for the very first time in FrontPage, it will require that you check your microphone settings and step through voice training before activating the Speech Recognition service.

The Dictation button places the microphone in Dictation mode. In **Dictation mode**, whatever you speak is entered as text. The Voice Command button places the microphone in Voice Command mode. In **Voice Command mode**, whatever you speak is interpreted as a command. If you want to turn off the microphone, click Microphone button on the Language bar or in Voice Command mode, say "Mic off" (pronounced mike off). It is important to remember that minimizing the Language bar does not turn off the microphone.

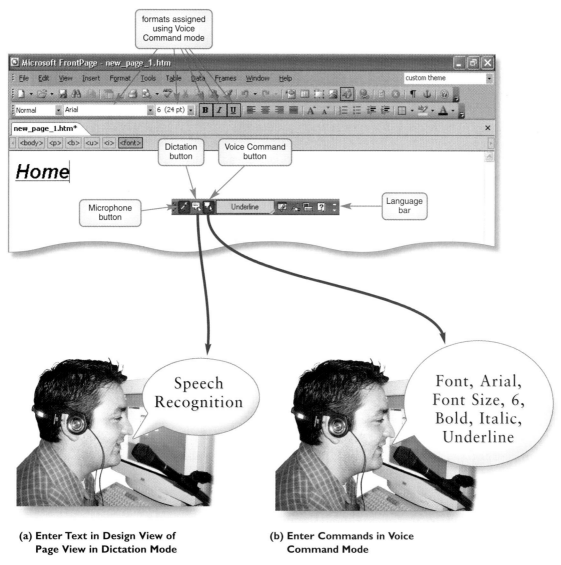

(a) Enter Text in Design View of
Page View in Dictation Mode

(b) Enter Commands in Voice
Command Mode

FIGURE B-4

The Language bar speech message balloon shown in Figure B-5b displays messages that may offer help or hints. In Voice Command mode, the name of the last recognized command you said appears. If you use the mouse or keyboard instead of the microphone, a message will appear in the Language bar speech message balloon indicating the word you could say. In Dictation mode, the message, Dictating, usually appears. The Speech Recognition service, however, will display messages to inform you that you are talking too soft, too loud, too fast, or to ask you to repeat what you said by displaying, What was that?

Getting Started with Speech Recognition

For the microphone to function properly, you should follow these steps:

1. Make sure your computer meets the minimum requirements.
2. Start FrontPage. Activate Speech Recognition by clicking Tools on the menu bar, pointing to Speech, and then clicking Speech Recognition on the Speech submenu.
3. Set up and position your microphone, preferably a close-talk headset with gain adjustment support.
4. Train Speech Recognition.

The following sections describe these steps in more detail.

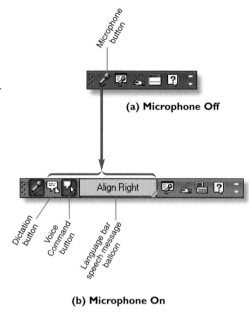

(a) Microphone Off

(b) Microphone On

FIGURE B-5

SPEECH RECOGNITION SYSTEM REQUIREMENTS   For Speech Recognition to work on your computer, it needs the following:

1. Microsoft Windows 98 or later or Microsoft Windows NT 4.0 or later
2. At least 128 MB RAM
3. 400 MHz or faster processor
4. Microphone and sound card

SET UP AND POSITION YOUR MICROPHONE   Set up your microphone as follows:

1. Connect your microphone to the sound card in the back of the computer.
2. Position the microphone approximately one inch out from and to the side of your mouth. Position it so you are not breathing into it.
3. On the Language bar, click the Speech Tools button, and then click Options on the Speech Tools menu (Figure B-6a).
4. When text services displays the Speech input settings dialog box (Figure B-6b), click the Advanced Speech button. When text services displays the Speech Properties dialog box (Figure B-6c), click the Speech Recognition tab.
5. Click the Configure Microphone button. Follow the Microphone Wizard directions as shown in Figures B-6d, B-6e, and B-6f. The Next button will remain dimmed in Figure B-6e until the volume meter consistently stays in the green area.
6. If someone else installed Speech Recognition, click the New button in the Speech Properties dialog box and enter your name. Click the Train Profile button and step through the Voice Training dialog boxes. The Voice Training dialog boxes will require that you enter your gender and age group. It then will step you through voice training.

You can adjust the microphone further by clicking the Settings button in the Speech Properties dialog box (Figure B-6c). The Settings button displays the Recognition Profile Settings dialog box that allows you to adjust the pronunciation sensitivity and accuracy versus recognition response time.

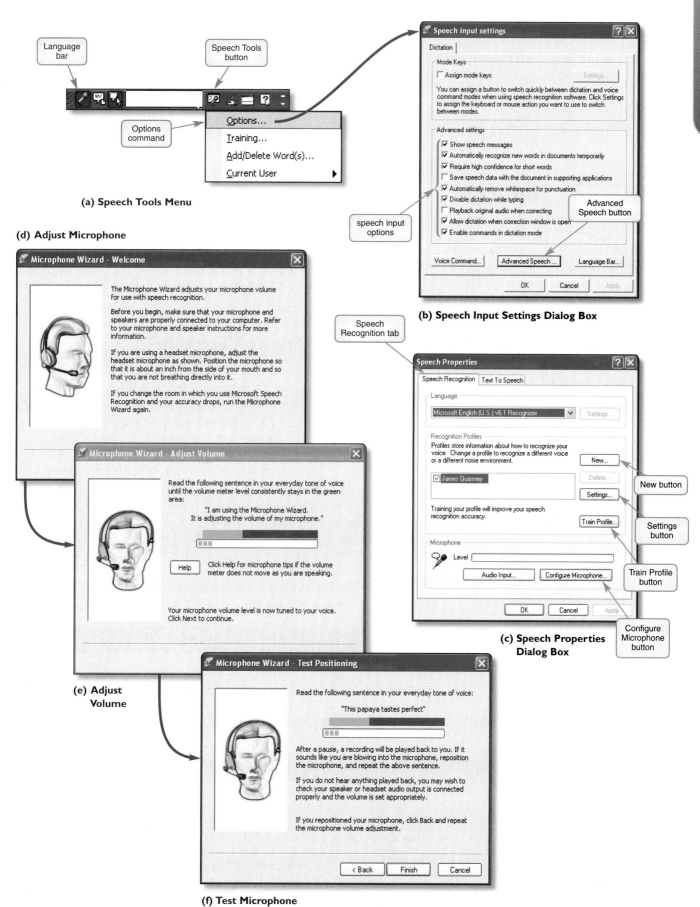

(a) Speech Tools Menu

(b) Speech Input Settings Dialog Box

(c) Speech Properties Dialog Box

(d) Adjust Microphone

(e) Adjust Volume

(f) Test Microphone

FIGURE B-6

TRAIN THE SPEECH RECOGNITION SERVICE   The Speech Recognition service will understand most commands and some dictation without any training at all. It will recognize much more of what you speak, however, if you take the time to train it. After one training session, it will recognize 85 to 90 percent of your words. As you do more training, accuracy will rise to 95 percent. If you feel that too many mistakes are being made, then continue to train the service. The more training you do, the more accurately it will work for you. Follow these steps to train the Speech Recognition service:

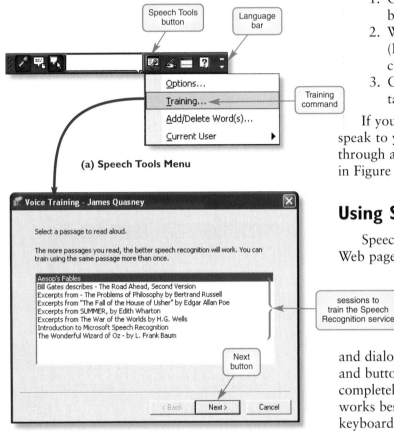

(a) **Speech Tools Menu**

(b) **Voice Training Dialog Box**

FIGURE B-7

1. Click the Speech Tools button on the Language bar and then click Training (Figure B-7a).
2. When the Voice Training dialog box appears (Figure B-7b), click one of the sessions and then click the Next button.
3. Complete the training session, which should take less than 15 minutes.

If you are serious about using a microphone to speak to your computer, you need to take the time to go through at least three of the eight training sessions listed in Figure B-7b.

Using Speech Recognition

Speech recognition lets you enter text into a Web page similarly to speaking into a tape recorder. Instead of typing, you can dictate text that you want to add to a page, and you can issue voice commands. In Voice Command mode, you can speak menu names, commands on menus, toolbar button names, and dialog box option buttons, check boxes, list boxes, and button names. Speech recognition, however, is not a completely hands-free form of input. Speech recognition works best if you use a combination of your voice, the keyboard, and the mouse. You soon will discover that Dictation mode is far less accurate than Voice Command mode. Table B-1 lists some tips that will improve the Speech Recognition service's accuracy considerably.

Table B-1	Tips to Improve Speech Recognition
NUMBER	**TIP**
1	The microphone hears everything. Though the Speech Recognition service filters out background noise, it is recommended that you work in a quiet environment.
2	Try not to move the microphone around once it is adjusted.
3	Speak in a steady tone and speak clearly.
4	In Dictation mode, do not pause between words. A phrase is easier to interpret than a word. Sounding out syllables in a word will make it more difficult for the Speech Recognition service to interpret what you are saying.
5	If you speak too loudly or too softly, it makes it difficult for the Speech Recognition service to interpret what you said. Check the Language bar speech message balloon for an indication that you may be speaking too loudly or too softly.
6	If you experience problems after training, adjust the recognition options that control accuracy and rejection by clicking the Settings button shown in Figure B-6c on the previous page.
7	When you are finished using the microphone, turn it off by clicking the Microphone button on the Language bar or in Voice Command mode, say "Mic off." Leaving the microphone on is the same as leaning on the keyboard.
8	If the Speech Recognition service is having difficulty with unusual words, then add the words to its dictionary by using the Add/Delete Word(s) command on the Speech Tools menu (Figure B-8a). The last names of individuals and the names of companies are good examples of the types of words you should add to the dictionary.
9	Training will improve accuracy; practice will improve confidence.

The last command on the Speech Tools menu is the Current User command (Figure B-8a). The Current User command is useful for multiple users who share a computer. It allows them to configure their own individual profiles, and then switch between users as they use the computer.

For additional information on the Speech Recognition service, enter `speech recognition` in the Type a question for help box on the menu bar.

Handwriting Recognition

Using the Office **Handwriting Recognition service**, you can enter text and numbers into FrontPage by writing instead of typing. You can write using a special handwriting device that connects to your computer or you can write on the screen using your mouse. Four basic methods of handwriting are available by clicking the Handwriting button on the Language bar: Writing Pad; Write Anywhere; Drawing Pad; and On-Screen Keyboard. The Drawing Pad button is not available in FrontPage. Although the on-screen keyboard does not involve handwriting recognition, it is part of the Handwriting menu and, therefore, will be discussed in this section.

If your Language bar does not include the Handwriting button, then, for installation instructions, enter `install handwriting recognition` in the Type a question for help box on the menu bar.

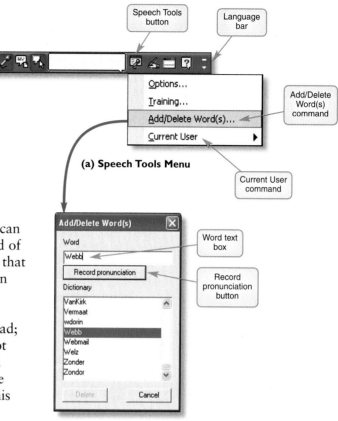

(a) **Speech Tools Menu**

(b) **Add/Delete Word(s) Dialog Box**

FIGURE B-8

Writing Pad

To display the Writing Pad, click the Handwriting button on the Language bar and then click Writing Pad (Figure B-9). The **Writing Pad** resembles a notepad with one or more lines on which you can use freehand to print or write in cursive. With the Text button enabled, you can form letters on the line by moving the mouse while holding down the mouse button. To the right of the notepad is a rectangular toolbar. Use the buttons on this toolbar to adjust the Writing Pad, make selections, and activate other handwriting applications.

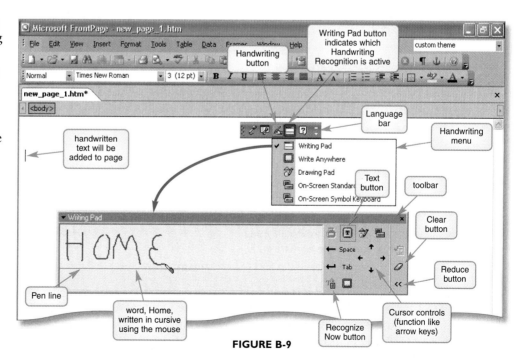

FIGURE B-9

Consider the example in Figure B-9 on the previous page. Home is written in cursive on the **Pen line** in the Writing Pad. As soon as the word is complete, the Handwriting Recognition service automatically places the word on the page.

You can customize the Writing Pad by clicking the Options button on the left side of the title bar and then clicking the Options command (Figure B-10a). Invoking the Options command causes the Handwriting Options dialog box to display. The Handwriting Options dialog box contains two sheets: Common and Writing Pad. The Common sheet lets you change the pen color and pen width, adjust recognition, and customize the toolbar area of the Writing Pad. The Writing Pad sheet allows you to change the background color and the number of lines that are displayed in the Writing Pad. Both sheets contain a Restore Default button to restore the settings to what they were when the software was installed initially.

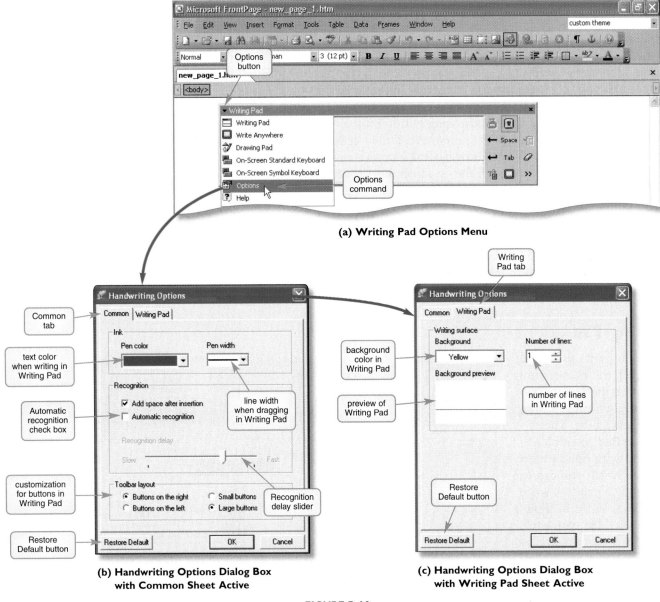

(a) **Writing Pad Options Menu**

(b) **Handwriting Options Dialog Box with Common Sheet Active**

(c) **Handwriting Options Dialog Box with Writing Pad Sheet Active**

FIGURE B-10

When you first start using the Writing Pad, you may want to remove the check mark from the Automatic recognition check box in the Common sheet in the Handwriting Options dialog box (Figure B-10b). With the check mark removed, the Handwriting Recognition service will not interpret what you write in the Writing Pad until you click the Recognize Now button on the toolbar (Figure B-9 on the previous page). This allows you to pause and adjust your writing.

The best way to learn how to use the Writing Pad is to practice with it. Also, for more information, enter handwriting recognition in the Type a question for help box on the menu bar.

Write Anywhere

Rather than use Writing Pad, you can write anywhere on the screen by invoking the Write Anywhere command on the Handwriting menu (Figure B-11) that appears when you click the Handwriting button on the Language bar. In this case, the entire window is your writing pad.

In Figure B-11, the word, Home, is written in cursive using the mouse button. Shortly after the word is written, the Handwriting Recognition service interprets it, adds it to the Web page, and erases what was written.

It is recommended that when you first start using the Writing Anywhere service that you remove the check mark from the Automatic recognition check box in the Common sheet in the Handwriting Options dialog box (Figure B-10b). With the check mark removed, the Handwriting Recognition service will not interpret what you write on the screen until you click the Recognize Now button on the toolbar (Figure B-11).

Write Anywhere is more difficult to use than the Writing Pad, because when you click the mouse button, FrontPage may interpret the action as selecting a table cell rather than starting to write. For this reason, it is recommended that you use the Writing Pad.

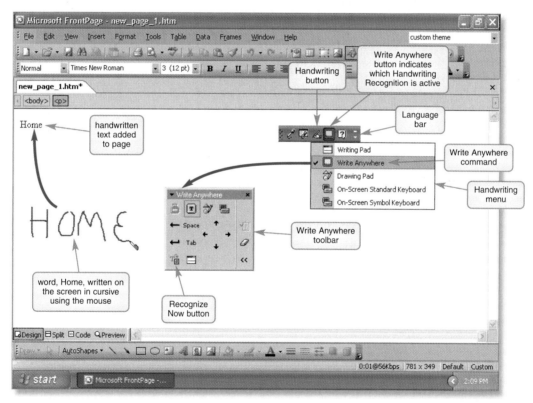

FIGURE B-11

On-Screen Keyboard

The On-Screen Standard Keyboard command on the Handwriting menu (Figure B-12) displays an on-screen keyboard. The **on-screen keyboard** lets you enter data into a cell by using your mouse to click the keys. The on-screen keyboard is similar to the type found on handheld computers.

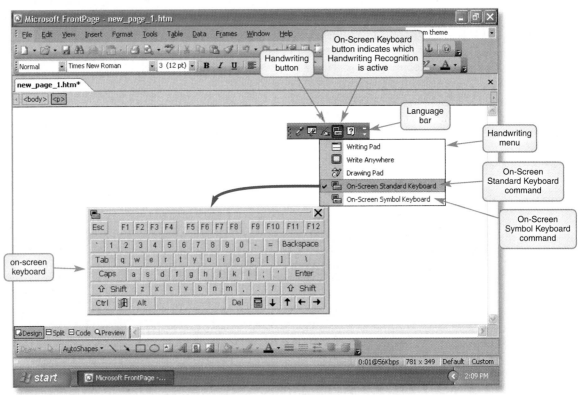

FIGURE B-12

The On-Screen Symbol Keyboard command on the Handwriting menu (Figure B-12) displays a special on-screen keyboard that allows you to enter symbols that are not on your keyboard, as well as Unicode characters. **Unicode characters** use a coding scheme capable of representing all the world's current languages.

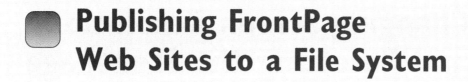

Appendix C

Publishing FrontPage Web Sites to a File System

If you do not have access to a Web server for publishing the Web sites developed in this book, you can publish the sites to a file system. A **file system** is a folder on a hard drive or a network drive. This appendix lists the steps necessary to publish a Web site to a file system. When a Web site is published to a file system, the site does not have access to FrontPage Server Extensions. Some functionality of the Web sites developed in this book do not work without FrontPage Server Extensions. For example, Web components, such as counters, cannot work when a Web site is published to a file system. By publishing to a file system, however, you will be able to use a browser to navigate to the Web site.

The Remote Web Site view allows you to select an existing folder or create a new folder to which to publish a site. You must have access rights to the folder that allow you to write files to the folder. Table C-1 explains how to publish a Web site to a folder on drive C. After publishing the site to a folder, you can click the View your Remote Web site link in Remote Web Site view to view the site. Table C-2 explains how to use your browser to navigate to a Web site that has been published to a file system.

Table C-1 Publishing to a File System
1. Click View on the menu bar. When the View menu is displayed, click Remote Web Site. When the Remote Web Site view appears, click the Remote Web Site Properties button.
2. Click the File System button and then click the Browse button.
3. When the New Publish Location dialog box is displayed, use the Look in box to select the location to which to publish the site. If necessary, use the Create New Folder button to create a new folder.
4. Click the Open button on the New Publish Location dialog box and then click the OK button on the Remote Web Site Properties dialog box. When the Microsoft Office FrontPage dialog box appears, click the Yes button.
5. Click the Publish Web site button in the Publish all changed pages area.

Table C-2 Navigating to a Web Site on a File System
1. Open Microsoft Internet Explorer.
2. Click File on the menu bar and then click Open. When the Open dialog box is displayed, click the Browse button.
3. When the Microsoft Internet Explorer dialog box is displayed, use the Look in box to navigate to the folder to which you published the Web site. Select the index.htm file in the folder.
4. Click the Open button. Click the OK button in the Open dialog box.

Appendix D

Changing Screen Resolution and Resetting the FrontPage Toolbars and Menus

This appendix explains how to change your screen resolution in Windows to the resolution used in this book. It also describes how to reset the FrontPage toolbars and menus to their installation settings.

Changing Screen Resolution

The **screen resolution** indicates the number of pixels (dots) that your system uses to display the letters, numbers, graphics, and background you see on your screen. The screen resolution usually is stated as the product of two numbers, such as 800 × 600. An 800 × 600 screen resolution results in a display of 800 distinct pixels on each of 600 lines, or about 480,000 pixels. The figures in this book were created using a screen resolution of 800 × 600.

The screen resolutions most commonly used today are 800 × 600 and 1024 × 768, although some Office specialists operate their computers at a much higher screen resolution, such as 2048 × 1536. The following steps show how to change the screen resolution from 1024 × 768 to 800 × 600.

To Change the Screen Resolution

1

• **If necessary, minimize all applications so that the Windows desktop appears.**

• **Right-click the Windows desktop.**

Windows displays the Windows desktop shortcut menu (Figure D-1).

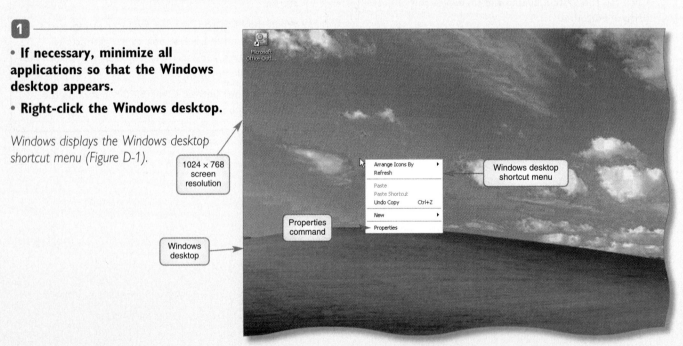

FIGURE D-1

2

• **Click Properties on the shortcut menu.**

• **When Windows displays the Display Properties dialog box, click the Settings tab.**

Windows displays the Settings sheet in the Display Properties dialog box (Figure D-2). The Settings sheet shows a preview of the Windows desktop using the current screen resolution (1024 × 768). The Settings sheet also shows the screen resolution and the color quality settings.

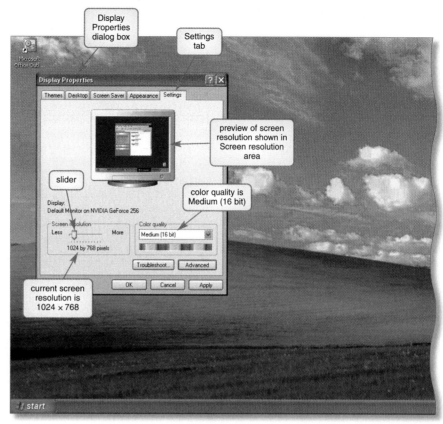

FIGURE D-2

3

• **Drag the slider in the Screen resolution area to the left so that the screen resolution changes to 800 × 600.**

The screen resolution in the Screen resolution area changes to 800 × 600 (Figure D-3). The Settings sheet shows a preview of the Windows desktop using the new screen resolution (800 × 600).

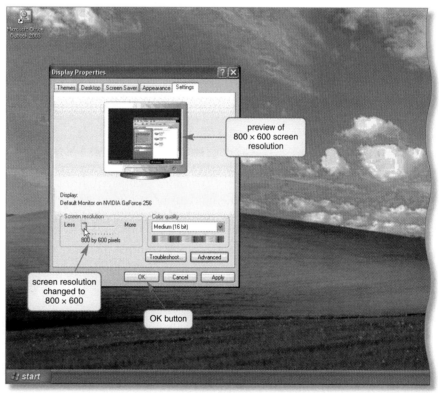

FIGURE D-3

4

• **Click the OK button.**

• **If Windows displays the Monitor Settings dialog box, click the Yes button.**

Windows changes the screen resolution from 1024 × 768 to 800 × 600 (Figure D-4).

800 × 600 screen resolution

FIGURE D-4

As shown in the previous steps, as you decrease the screen resolution, Windows displays less information on your screen, but the information increases in size. The reverse also is true: as you increase the screen resolution, Windows displays more information on your screen, but the information decreases in size.

Resetting the FrontPage Toolbars and Menus

FrontPage customization capabilities allow you to create custom toolbars by adding and deleting buttons and personalize menus based on their usage. Each time you start FrontPage, the toolbars and menus are displayed using the same settings as the last time you used FrontPage. The figures in this book were created with the FrontPage toolbars and menus set to the original, or installation, settings.

Resetting the Standard and Formatting Toolbars

The following steps show how to reset the Standard and Formatting toolbars.

To Reset the Standard and Formatting Toolbars

1

• **Start FrontPage following the steps outlined at the beginning of Project 1 on page FP 14.**

• **Click the Toolbar Options button on the Standard toolbar and then point to Add or Remove Buttons on the Toolbar Options menu.**

FrontPage displays the Toolbar Options menu and the Add or Remove Buttons submenu (Figure D-5).

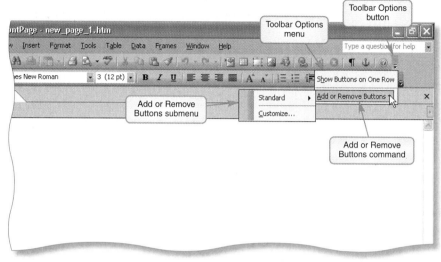

FIGURE D-5

2

• **Point to Standard on the Add or Remove Buttons submenu.**

• **Scroll down and then point to Reset Toolbar on the Standard submenu.**

FrontPage displays the Standard submenu indicating the buttons and boxes that appear on the Standard toolbar (Figure D-6). To remove a button from the Standard toolbar, click a button name with a check mark to the left of the name to remove the check mark.

3

• **Click Reset Toolbar.**

• **If FrontPage displays the Microsoft Office FrontPage dialog box, click the Yes button.**

FrontPage resets the Standard toolbar to its original settings.

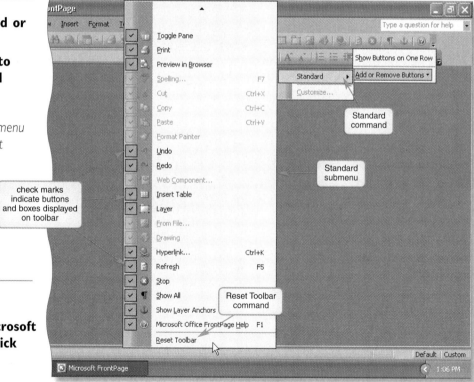

FIGURE D-6

4

• **Reset the Formatting toolbar by following Steps 1 through 3 and replacing any reference to the Standard toolbar with the Formatting toolbar.**

Not only can you use the Standard submenu shown in Figure D-6 on the previous page to reset the Standard toolbar to its original settings, but you also can use it to customize the Standard toolbar by adding and deleting buttons. To add or delete buttons, click the button name on the Standard submenu to add or remove the check mark. Buttons with a check mark to the left currently are displayed on the Standard toolbar; buttons without a check mark are not displayed on the Standard toolbar. You can complete the same tasks for the Formatting toolbar, using the Formatting submenu to add to and delete buttons from the Formatting toolbar.

Resetting the FrontPage Menus

The following steps show how to reset the FrontPage menus to their original settings.

To Reset the FrontPage Menus

1

- **Click the Toolbar Options button on the Standard toolbar and then point to Add or Remove Buttons on the Toolbar Options menu.**

FrontPage displays the Toolbar Options menu and the Add or Remove Buttons submenu (Figure D-7).

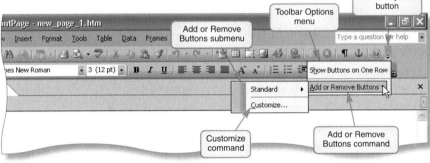

FIGURE D-7

2

- **Click Customize on the Add or Remove Buttons submenu.**
- **When FrontPage displays the Customize dialog box, click the Options tab.**

FrontPage displays the Customize dialog box (Figure D-8). The Customize dialog box contains three sheets used for customizing the FrontPage toolbars and menus.

3

- **Click the Reset menu and toolbar usage data button. When FrontPage displays the Microsoft Office FrontPage dialog box, click the Yes button. Click the Close button in the Customize dialog box.**

FrontPage resets the menus to the original settings.

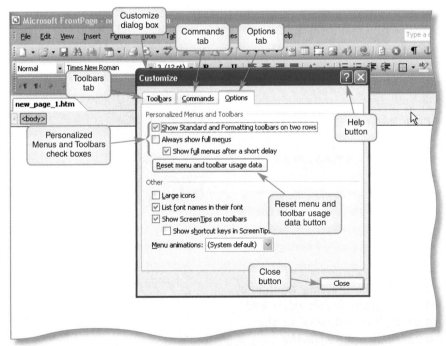

FIGURE D-8

Using the Options sheet in the Customize dialog box, as shown in Figure D-8, you can select options to personalize menus and toolbars. For example, you can select or deselect a check mark that instructs FrontPage to display the Standard and Formatting toolbars on two rows. You also can select whether FrontPage always displays full menus or displays short menus followed by full menus, after a short delay. Other options available in the Options sheet include settings to instruct FrontPage to display toolbars with large icons; to use the appropriate font to display font names in the Font list; and to display a ScreenTip when a user points to a toolbar button. Clicking the Help button immediately to the left of the Close button on the Customize dialog box's title bar (Figure D-8) instructs FrontPage to display topics that will assist you in customizing toolbars and menus.

Using the Commands sheet in the Customize dialog box, you can add buttons to toolbars and commands to menus. Recall that the menu bar at the top of the FrontPage window is a special toolbar. To add buttons to a toolbar, click a category name in the Categories list and then drag the command name in the Commands list to a toolbar. To add commands to a menu, click a category name in the Categories list, drag the command name in the Commands list to a menu name on the menu bar, and then, when the menu appears, drag the command to the desired location in the list of menu commands.

Using the Toolbars sheet in the Customize dialog box, you can add new toolbars and reset existing toolbars and the menus. To add a new toolbar, click the New button, enter a toolbar name in the New Toolbar dialog box, and then click the OK button. After you create the new toolbar, you can use the Commands sheet to add or remove buttons, as you would with any other toolbar. If you add one or more buttons to an existing toolbar and want to reset the toolbar to its original settings, click the toolbar name in the Toolbars list so a check mark displays to the left of the name and then click the Reset button. If you add commands to one or more menus and want to reset the menus to their default settings, click Menu Bar in the Toolbars list on the Toolbars sheet so a check mark displays to the left of the name and then click the Reset button. When you have finished, click the Close button to close the Customize dialog box.

Other Ways

1. On View menu point to Toolbars, click Customize on Toolbars submenu, click Options tab, click Reset menu and toolbar usage data button, click Yes button, click Close button

2. Right-click toolbar, click Customize on shortcut menu, click Options tab, click Reset menu and toolbar usage data button, click Yes button, click Close button

3. In Voice Command mode, say "View, Toolbars, Customize, Options, Reset menu and toolbar usage data, Yes, Close"

Appendix E

FrontPage Web Design Tips

This appendix lists in project sequence the Design Tips boxed throughout this book. The first column contains the page number on which the corresponding Design Tip in the second column is presented. Use this page number to focus on the circumstances surrounding the development of the Design Tip. Use the second column as a quick overview of the Design Tips and as preparation for examinations.

Project 1 Design Tips	
PAGE NUMBER	**DESIGN TIP**
FP 9	As you develop a Web site, test the Web pages in as many browsers as your audience might use.
FP 11	Many Web pages use common elements to which users are accustomed. When designing your page, consider using standard design elements such as a title, page banners, and link bars.
FP 13	Plan to publish your Web site on a regular basis to keep content up to date after your Web site is up and running. Do not allow your content to become stale, or out of date.
FP 19	Before creating a Web site from scratch, lay out the navigation structure of your Web site and consider a template to alleviate a great deal of manual work when creating the Web site.
FP 23	If your Web site's navigation structure is both well-designed and focused on your users, your visitors will be able to move to different locations on a page or to other pages in your Web site to find usable information quickly and easily.
FP 25	Generate a sense of unity or familiarity within your Web site by utilizing a common graphic theme and a common color theme.
FP 31	If the main content for your Web page is not already in a word-processing document, consider first placing all of your content in one. You and other contributors can manage the content much easier in a common file format. When the content is ready to be made available on the Web, simply copy and paste the content from the document into the Web page in FrontPage.
FP 47	Consider adding hyperlinks from key terms or phrases in the content on your page to other Web pages or external Web sites that include more information about the topic than you are willing to provide on your Web page.
FP 48	If your Web page contains a link to external Web sites, periodically check the link to be sure that the external Web site still exists or has not changed location. One of the more important elements of the World Wide Web is the ease of navigation to other sites through the use of hyperlinks.
FP 52	Build into your Web pages simple and convenient ways for Web site visitors to interact with you or your organization.

Project 2 Design Tips

PAGE NUMBER	DESIGN TIP
FP 85	Each individual Web page should have one purpose or present one concept. Avoid splitting one concept into two parts simply to reduce the size of a page. Likewise, refrain from combining two unrelated ideas just to make a Web page larger. If information is designed to be read online, limit the pages to two screens, and provide links to additional information.
FP 85	Use the criteria outlined in Table 2-1 on page FP 84 as a guide for designing Web pages.
FP 86	Begin your Web page design with a single purpose in mind. If something appears on the Web page, then it should serve some purpose. If something serves no purpose, then it should not be on the Web page. Choose content that adds value, that is, content that is relative, informative, timely, accurate, and usable.
FP 92	Use descriptive names for file names and maintain a standard for naming files. Over time and as your site includes more pages, a well-maintained organizational structure for the files in the Web site can decrease the amount of time spent on maintenance.
FP 95	Browser title bars display approximately 80 to 90 characters, so keep this limitation in mind when designing Web page titles.
FP 98	Generate a sense of oneness within your Web site by utilizing consistent alignment, a common graphic theme, and a common color theme. Be judicious about whether a page properly fits within the chosen scheme.
FP 103	Before you create any table, sketch it on paper. Determine the number of rows and columns and the content that you will place in the cells. Calculate the overall width of the table and necessary width for each column.
FP 107	When you design a Web page, do not limit your creativity to the print environment. Where appropriate, include color, photographs, animation, video, and sound clips.
FP 109	Before downloading photos or other media from the Web, ensure that they have no copyright restrictions or royalty charges that you cannot or will not pay. Royalty charges are fees to be paid to the creator/owner of the art for its use.
FP 110	Using images with a transparent background allows the color or image used in a Web page background to show through the background of the inserted image, thus hiding the rectangular shape of the image. Cropping an image can eliminate distracting background elements and establish the focal point of the image. Discarding unwanted portions of an image also reduces its file size.
FP 120	Use common fonts in your Web pages to increase the chances of overriding default font settings and allowing the visitor to view the page in the manner in which it was designed. Type that is 10 points or smaller may not be readable to many Web page visitors.
FP 122	It is customary to separate logical sections of Web pages, such as the header and body, using dividing elements called horizontal lines, or horizontal rules. Use headers and footers on pages that comprise the main navigational structure of your site. Secondary pages need not fit a rigid design structure.

Project 3 Design Tips

PAGE NUMBER	DESIGN TIP
FP 157	GIF files are best suited for solid-colored images such as logos and illustrations. The 256-color limitation of GIF files makes them inappropriate for displaying photographs.
FP 157	Each time a JPEG image is edited and saved, the image is compressed and decompressed, which degrades the image quality. You should make a copy of the original source image file and never alter the original image.
FP 170	Use shared borders when multiple pages in a Web site contain identical information in the same location on the page.
FP 181	Copy and paste text from other documents into your Web page when the source application of the document cannot save the document in a suitable Web page format. Be sure to keep the Web page updated with any changes to the original document.
FP 191	If there are a number of links to relatively short pieces of information, and the user is likely to go back and forth from one page to another visiting these links, it may be better to place all of the information on a single Web page and use bookmarks to navigate to the short pieces of information.
FP 199	To hide the rectangular shape common to all images, use images that have the same background color as the Web page, or use images that have a transparent background. Using images with a transparent background allows the color or graphic used in a Web page background to show through the background of the image, thus hiding the rectangular shape of the image.
FP 201	To make an image transparent, select one of the colors in the image to be the transparent color. The transparent color is replaced by the background color, background design, or image of the page. An image can have only one transparent color.
FP 203	When working with large image files, resample the images after adding the image to the page if the image is resized on the page. The resulting smaller file size allows the page to download faster.
FP 205	When designing a Web page that contains elements that are positioned absolutely, be sure to test the page with all browsers that Web page visitors use.
FP 213	When creating an image map, the use of a motif, or metaphor, for the images helps to guide the user. Consider image maps as a replacement for related text hyperlinks.
FP 216	Avoid broken hyperlinks by testing the Web site before publishing the Web site, after publishing the Web site, and on a regular basis once the Web site is published.

Index

Office FrontPage 2003

 # Quick Reference Summary

In Microsoft FrontPage 2003, you can accomplish a task in a number of ways. The following table provides a quick reference to each task presented in this textbook. The first column identifies the task. The second column indicates the page number on which the task is discussed in the book. The subsequent four columns list the different ways the task in column one can be carried out. You can invoke the commands listed in the MOUSE, MENU BAR, and SHORTCUT MENU columns using Voice commands.

Microsoft Office FrontPage 2003 Quick Reference Summary

TASK	PAGE NUMBER	MOUSE	MENU BAR	SHORTCUT MENU	KEYBOARD SHORTCUT
Align Left	FP 114	Align Left button on Formatting toolbar	Format | Paragraph | Indents and Spacing tab	Paragraph | Indents and Spacing tab	CTRL+L
Align Right	FP 114	Align Right button on Formatting toolbar	Format | Paragraph | Indents and Spacing tab	Paragraph | Indents and Spacing tab	CTRL+R
AutoShape, Add	FP 206	AutoShapes button on Drawing toolbar	Insert | Picture | AutoShapes		ALT+U
Background Color, Modify	FP 99		Format | Background | Background tab	Page Properties | Background tab	ALT+O | K
Bold	FP 120	Bold button on Formatting toolbar	Format | Font | Font tab	Font | Font tab	CTRL+B or ALT+ENTER
Bookmark, Create	FP 190	Insert Hyperlink button on Standard toolbar	Insert | Bookmark	Hyperlink	CTRL+G
Center	FP 114	Center button on Formatting toolbar	Format | Paragraph | Indents and Spacing tab	Paragraph | Indents and Spacing tab	CTRL+E
Clip Art, Insert	FP 107	Insert Picture From File button on Standard toolbar	Insert | Picture | Clip Art; Insert | Picture | From File		
Clip Art, Replace	FP 110	Insert Picture From File button on Pictures toolbar	Insert | Picture | Clip Art; Insert | Picture | From File	Picture Properties | General tab | Browse	
Color Characters	FP 122	Font Color button arrow on Formatting toolbar	Format | Font | Font tab	Font | Font tab	ALT+ENTER
Copy	FP 112	Copy button on Standard toolbar	Edit | Copy	Copy	CTRL+C
Create Web Site, Template or Wizard	FP 20	New Page button arrow on Standard toolbar, Web Site	File | New		
Delete Page	FP 44		Edit | Delete	Right-click file name in Folder List pane, Delete	DELETE
Delete Text	FP 31	Cut button on Standard toolbar	Edit | Cut or Edit | Delete	Cut	DELETE or BACKSPACE
Design View	FP 24	Design button			
File, Rename	FP 92			Right-click file name in Folder List, click Rename	
Font	FP 120	Font button on Formatting toolbar	Format | Font | Font tab	Font | Font tab	ALT+ENTER

Microsoft Office FrontPage 2003 Quick Reference Summary *(continued)*

TASK	PAGE NUMBER	MOUSE	MENU BAR	SHORTCUT MENU	KEYBOARD SHORTCUT
Font Size	FP 126	Font Size box arrow on Formatting toolbar	Format | Font | Font tab	Font | Font tab	ALT+ENTER
Full Menu	FP 17	Double-click menu name or click menu name, wait a few seconds	Tools | Customize | Options tab		
Help	FP 63 and Appendix A	Microsoft Office FrontPage Help button on Standard toolbar	Help | Microsoft Office FrontPage Help		F1
Horizontal Rule, Insert	FP 123		Insert | Horizontal Line		ALT+I | L
Hotspot, Add Polygonal	FP 213	Polygonal Hotspot button on Pictures toolbar			
Hotspots, Highlight	FP 213	Highlight Hotspots button on Pictures toolbar			
Hyperlink, Create	FP 52	Hyperlink button on Standard toolbar	Insert | Hyperlink	Hyperlink	CTRL+K
Hyperlink, Edit	FP 52	Hyperlink button on Standard toolbar		Hyperlink Properties	CTRL+K
Hyperlinks, Display	FP 215	Hyperlinks icon on Views bar	View | Hyperlinks		ALT+V | H
Hyperlinks, Verify	FP 218	Verify Hyperlinks button on Reporting toolbar	View | Toolbars | Reporting, Verify Hyperlinks button	Reporting	
Image, Insert from File	FP 106	Insert Picture From File button on Standard toolbar	Insert | Picture | From File		
Image, Resample	FP 203	Resample button on Pictures toolbar			
Image, Resize	FP 203	Drag sizing handles	Format | Properties	Picture Properties | Appearance	
Image, Select	FP 112	Click graphic			position insertion point before image, CTRL+SHIFT+ RIGHT ARROW
Image, Transparent	FP 201	Set Transparent Color button on Pictures toolbar			
Italicize	FP 120	Italic button on Formatting toolbar	Format | Font | Font tab	Font | Font tab	CTRL+I or ALT+ENTER
Language Bar	FP 19 and Appendix B	Language indicator button in tray	Tools | Speech		ALT+T | H
Layout cell, Properties	FP 249			Cell Properties	
Layout cell, resize	FP 246	Drag sizing handles		Cell Properties	
Layout table, add	FP 243		Table | Layout Tables and Cells		ALT+T | B
Modify Component	FP 42	Double-click component		<component name> Properties	
Navigation View	FP 44	Navigation icon on Views bar	View | Navigation		
Page in Web Site, Open	FP 24	Double-click file name in Folder List pane	File | Open	Right-click Folder List pane, Open	CTRL+O
Page Label, Change	FP 96	Click page icon in Navigation view, click text box		Right-click page icon in Navigation view, click Rename	

Microsoft Office FrontPage 2003 Quick Reference Summary

TASK	PAGE NUMBER	MOUSE	MENU BAR	SHORTCUT MENU	KEYBOARD SHORTCUT
Page Title, Change	FP 94		File | Properties	Right-click page icon in Navigation view, click Properties, click General tab; right-click file name, click Properties, click General tab; right-click Page, click Page Properties, click General tab	
Page, Edit	FP 97	Double-click page icon in Navigation pane			
Page, New	FP 89	Create a new normal page button on Standard toolbar	File | New		CTRL+N
Page, View	FP 97		View | Page		
Paste	FP 112	Paste button on Standard toolbar	Edit | Paste	Paste	CTRL+V
Preview Page	FP 41	Preview tab			CTRL+PAGE UP, CTRL+PAGE DOWN
Preview Page in Browser	FP 41	Preview in Browser button on Standard toolbar	File | Preview in Browser		
Print Page	FP 54	Print button on Standard toolbar	File | Print		CTRL+P
Print Preview	FP 137		File | Print Preview		ALT+F | V
Publish Web Site	FP 56	Publish Web button on Standard toolbar	File | Publish Web		
Quit FrontPage	FP 65	Close button on title bar	File | Exit		ALT+F4
Redo	FP 106	Redo button on Standard toolbar	Edit | Redo		CTRL+Y
Reports, View Site Summary Report	FP 218	Report box arrow on Reporting toolbar, Site Summary	View | Reports | Site Summary		ALT+V | R | M
Save Page - Same Name	FP 39	Save button on Standard toolbar	File | Save		CTRL+S
Save Web - Embedded Files	FP 139	Save button on Standard toolbar	File | Save		CTRL+S
Shared Border, Add	FP 169		Format | Shared Borders		ALT+O | D
Shortcut menu	FP 33	Right-click object			SHIFT+F10
Start FrontPage	FP 13	Start button on taskbar, All Programs, Microsoft Office, Microsoft Office FrontPage 2003			
Style, Modify Paragraph	FP 121	Style box arrow			
Table Cells, Align	FP 125		Table | Table Properties | Cell	Cell Properties	ALT+A | R | E
Table Cells, Delete	FP 33		Table | Delete Cells	Delete Cells	ALT+A | D
Table Cells, Merge	FP 105		Table | Merge Cells	Merge Cells	
Table Cells, Select	FP 32	Click first cell, hold SHIFT key, click last cell	Table | Select | Cell		ALT+A | C | E
Table, Adjust Cell Borders	FP 115	Drag cell border	Table | Table Properties | Cell	Cell Properties	ALT+A | R | E

Microsoft Office FrontPage 2003 Quick Reference Summary *(continued)*

TASK	PAGE NUMBER	MOUSE	MENU BAR	SHORTCUT MENU	KEYBOARD SHORTCUT
Table, Create	FP 103	Insert Table button on Standard toolbar	Table | Insert | Table		ALT+A | I | T
Table, Hide Borders	FP 119		Table | Table Properties | Table	Table Properties	
Table, Insert Column	FP 165		Table | Insert | Rows or Columns	Insert Columns	ALT+A | I | N
Table, Insert Row	FP 165		Table | Insert | Rows or Columns	Insert Rows	ALT+A | I | N
Table, Modify Properties	FP 117		Table | Table Properties | Table	Table Properties	
Table, Select	FP 32	Drag through table	Table | Select | Table		
Task Pane	FP 15		View | Task Pane		ALT+V | K
Text, Add to Image	FP 207	Text button on Pictures toolbar		Add text	
Text, Select	FP 29	Drag through text			
Theme, Apply	FP 25		Format | Theme		ALT+O | H
Toolbar, Customize	FP 18	Toolbar Options button on toolbar, Add or Remove Buttons, click Customize		Customize	
Toolbar, Dock	FP 18	Drag toolbar to dock			
Toolbar, Reset	FP 18 and Appendix D	Toolbar Options, Add or Remove Buttons, Customize, Toolbars tab		Customize | Toolbars tab	ALT+V | T | C | T
Underline	FP 120	Underline button on Formatting toolbar	Format | Font | Font tab	Font | Font tab	CTRL+U or ALT+ENTER
Undo	FP 106	Undo button on Standard toolbar	Edit | Undo		CTRL+Z
Web Component, Insert Link bar	FP 133	Web component button arrow on Standard toolbar, Link Bars	Insert | Web Component | Link Bars		ALT+I | W
Web Component, Insert Photo Gallery	FP 128	Web component button arrow on Standard toolbar, Photo Gallery	Insert | Web Component | Photo Gallery		ALT+I | W
Web Component, Insert Hit Counter	FP 167	Web component button arrow on Standard toolbar, Hit Counter	Insert | Web Component | Hit Counter		ALT+I | W
Web Site, Open Site	FP 88	Open Site button arrow on Standard toolbar, Open Site	File | Open Site		ALT+F | I